WILDLIFE

AND

LANDSCAPES

IN MALAWI

SELECTED ESSAYS ON NATURAL HISTORY

—————————— BY BRIAN MORRIS —

Order this book online at www.trafford.com
or email orders@trafford.com

Most Trafford titles are also available at major online book retailers.

Print information available on the last page.

ISBN: 978-1-4251-7183-4 (sc)

Trafford rev. 10/30/2020

 www.trafford.com
North America & international
toll-free: 844-688-6899 (USA & Canada)
fax: 812 355 4082

CONTENTS

INTRODUCTION

I first came to Malawi in 1958, sitting with my rucksack on the back of a pick-up truck as it passed through Fort Manning (Mchinji) customs post. I had spent the previous four months hitch-hiking around South and Central Africa, mostly sleeping rough. During that time I encountered no other hitch-hiker, and very few tarred roads, and the only place I met tourist was at the Victoria Falls. I was, however, so attracted to Malawi and its people that I decided to give up my nomadic existence. I was fortunate to find a job working as a tea planter for Blantyre and East Africa LTD, an old Scottish company. I spent over seven years as a tea planter working in the Thyolo (Zoa) and Mulanje (Limbuli) districts, spending much of my spare-time engaged in natural history pursuits – my primary interests being small mammals (especially mice), the flora of Mulanje Mountain and Epiphytic Orchids.

Since those days I have regularly returned to Malawi to undertake ethnobiological studies – in relation to medicinal plants, fungi and animal life, specifically mammals and insects. I thus have a life-long interest in Malawi – in its history, in the culture of its people, and in its flora and fauna. Some of my most memorable life experiences have been in Malawi, and many of my closest and cherished friendships have been with Malawians, or with "expatriates" who have spent their lives in Malawi.

For over forty years I have been giving talks, seminar papers and lectures on the wildlife of Malawi, always being especially concerned to explore the relationships between the matrilineal peoples of Malawi and their natural environment . This present book consists of selection of my various writings on the wildlife of Malawi, which formed the basis of my oral presentations. Aiming to bridge the divide between academic scholarship and a wider audience, they combine the perspectives of ethnobiology, environmental history and cultural anthropology.

The collection is dedicated to the people of Malawi.

Brian Morris
February 15, 2008

ACKNOWLEDGEMENTS

I am appreciative of the wildlife magazines and academic journals which have published my various writings over the years and would like to convey my warm thanks to the editors of the Society of Malawi Journal, Nyala, Food and Foodways, Journal of the Royal Anthropological Institute, Anthropology and Medicine, Antenna, Environment and History, Herbal Review, The Commonwealth Forestry Review and The Linnean Society.

"FOLK CLASSIFICATIONS"(1980)

I want this evening to talk about 'folk classifications' - the way ordinary people conceptualize and classify the natural world.[1] It may come as a surprise to some people that I'm going to talk specifically on this topic; partly because I'm billed to give you insights into the "traditional uses, superstitions and medicines" related to animals and plants, and partly because 'classification1 is often seen as something only taxonomic biologists do. We tend to forget that human beings are by nature 'classifying' animals and that human life as we understand it would not be possible without classification.

Folk Versus Scientific Classifications

Now for many ordinary naturalists there is a wide, almost unbridgeable gulf between the classifications of science on the one hand, embodied as these are in Latin nomenclature, and the names and natural classifications of ordinary people. Towards the first we show amazing respect, even reverence. No priest of old was treated with as much awe as that accorded to contemporary systematic botanists. I mean, if you showed somebody a plant and he or she told you it was *Brassica oleracea* var *bullata* of the family Cruciferae you'd be impressed; you wouldn't be impressed if he told you it was a cabbage. This respect towards scientific classifications is often deserved - but it is unnecessary, and it is exaggerated. There's nothing esoteric or unfathomable about the activities of systematic biologists or the Latin they espouse, so there's no need for any of us to have an inferiority complex. On the other hand naturalists have an unnecessarily negative even derogatory attitude towards the names and classifications of ordinary people. I'll give you an example. It comes from a man

---

[1] /, This article is from a lecture given to the Society of Malawi in March 1980.

7

I knew quite well. I met him when I was still a *mnyamata* and he was in his seventies. He was a good naturalist, and did a lot of good work with respect to the conservation of wild life in Malawi. I have a high opinion of Rodney Wood; yet this is what he wrote in one of his articles devoted to small mammals - of which he made an important collection. He wrote:

"I have added a list of 'native' names referable to certain species, but would caution any future workers to pay little attention to them. My experience over many years has been that they are almost always unreliable. Having no knowledge whatsoever of systematic natural history, the African has nearly always applied a local vernacular name to 'groups' of animals that may have a superficial similarity of appearance, but not actually be clearly allied."

And he goes on to suggest that the sooner all vernacular terms are forgotten the better (Wood, 1949).

You see, he was a good enough naturalist to realise the need to record common names, but his attitude towards them is essentially a negative one. And he's not alone in this.

Now what I want to try and do this evening is two things. Firstly, I want to suggest to you that the names and classifications of ordinary people *ape* worth something, reiterating what the worthy John Buchanan (1895) wrote about nearly a hundred years ago, when he briefly looked at the semantics of some local plant names. Secondly, and linked to this, I want to suggest to you that there is not an unbridgeable gulf between folk and scientific classifications, and that they are related in rather interesting ways.

The Universality of Terms

Let me start first with a criticism that is always levelled at folk classifications, namely that they do not provide standardized or universal terms for animals and plants. This is one of the things that Rodney Wood bewailed when he noted that certain vernacular terms covered more than one scientific species. Given the fact that there *is* no universal common language, that there is no one-to-one correspondence between folk and scientific taxonomies, and that synonyms are widely used in folk taxonomies, this must be the case. But the criticism is rather overstated. Firstly, synonyms are not "rampant" in folk taxonomies, as many have implied; in fact within a given locality or culture there is very wide agreement regarding plant and animal names. The names of the more common plants and animals are by no means ambiguous or cluttered with synonyms. Take, for example, the names of trees here. Trees like *Uapaca kirkiana (Msuku), Adansonia digitata* - the Baobab *(Mlambe), Pseudo lachnostylis maprouneifolia* - Kudu berry *(Msolo)* - all widespread - have vernacular terms that are pretty standard, common to both Yao and Chewa languages, Synonyms only become conspicuously evident with trees that are uncommon, like *Canthium geuinzii,* a shrub found in evergreen forests which has two Yao and two Chewa names - and probably only known to a few herbalists. Secondly, scientific classifications themselves are by no means standard. It is interesting to read Charles Jeffrey's useful introduction to 'Biological Nomenclaturel (1973), On page 5 he insists that a fundamental principle of nomenclature is that "names must be unambiguous and universal", and so common names are dismissed as unsatisfactory. Yet given the fact that scientific classifications must inevitably change with our increasing knowledge of the natural world and that such classifications attempt to reflect phylogenetic relationships, a few pages later he notes that scientific classifications are subject to "continuous change", and that scientific terms, like common names, are by no means either unambiguous or universal. There is, as he notes, an "inherent conflict" between the stability of nomenclature and the need to have a system of classification that best reflects our present knowledge. That shrub you find on the rocky outcrops of Zomba and Mulanje is still called *Cheyo* here, but at Kew they no longer call it *Vellozia*. And, you only have to read John Alder's review (1978) of the new Bird Checklist to realise the considerable changes and revisions in nomenclature that have taken place during only two decades.

The Cultural Importance of Latin

Scientific nomenclature, as you well know, is based on Latin -not the classical Latin of the Ancients, but a rather technical, refined Latin derived from the medieval herbalists. Some two hundred years ago one of these herbalists wrote: "Those who wish to remain ignorant of the Latin language, have no business with the study of botany" (John Berkenhout). Now if you're not a biological taxonomist, and I'm not, the tendency is to think that Latin belongs to a past world, that it has no relevance at all in understanding the present one. I want to try and indicate to you that it has, and in particular that study-ing Latin is helpful - and I shall come to this presently - in understanding the nature of English *folk* taxonomies. I'm not a Latin scholar either: my second language was standard English, my first being a Black Country dialect. So I'll have to approach these issues by way of anthropology.

One thing that is universal in almost all human cultures is the belief in an immaterial essence that survives the body - *Mzimu* is the Chewa term. In the English language there are two basic terms for this - soul, and spirit. Now if you look at the present connotations of these two terms you will see that they are quite different, though neither has entirely lost its religious tinge. Soul is connected with music, emotions, sadness; spirit is connected with vitality and uplift. If you are spiritual or spirited we can admire you; if you are soulful we can only sympathize. So although their original meanings were very similar, the shifts in meaning of the two terms have gone in quite different directions; spirit, as it were, has moved in an upward, soul in a downward direction. And of interest of course is that spirit is a word of Latin origin, soul is Teutonic, derived from the early tribal communities of Western Europe. And if you know your English history, you will know that for several hundred years Latin was the language of the aristocracy and the literate, which may indeed be one reason why taxonomic biologists are still accorded such esteem.

But you'll realise of course that this division permeates English language and culture. And that there are real social implications in our use of words. If you use in your everyday speech words like make, want, get, sweat (my home language) instead of words like construct, require, acquire and perspiration, nobody will think that you are a person of any standing! And note too how we use such terms. Terms like 'get' can be used to convey a variety of different meanings with only a slight addition - get up, get off, get over, get to, get on ... get away.1 Whereas 'acquire' only leads you on to bigger words. But the im-portant point, need I tell you, is that the low-status words are of Anglo-Saxon origin, while the others are of Latin derivation. I will not embarrass you by reciting the terms for the genitals, but you will note that I could if I wanted) indicate those of Latin origin without too much embarrassment!

Where does all this lead? Well, to our understanding of English folk classifications. Take first a typical botanical description. I will give you one, although there will be no prizes for guessing the plant species.

    " Tree: 4-6 m in height, occurring in deciduous woodland

Bark: Light green, fissured and cracked

Leaves: Alternate, ovate - elliptic, apex rounded, margin entire, rarely serrate

Flowers: Small, in axillary clusters or cymes

Fruit: Spherical with persistent style, indehiscent

Well, it's a description of *Msolo*, adapted from Palgrave's (1977) book. And you will note that while all the basic terms here -tree, bark, leaf, fruit - are of Teutonic origin, the descriptive terms are all derived and adapted from Latin terms (Stearn, 1966). But note also that the botanic Latin is not pure Latin but is derived from Latin and Greek words that have been modified and refined for scientific purposes. "Serrate" is from *serra,* Latin for "saw"; "pubescent" from *pubes,* meaning pubic hairs. The early botanists virtually created a new language.

I shall return to Latin shortly. But let me first indicate to you just what is the nature of a folk classification system, and then I will try to say something about the way in which English folk taxonomies have developed, and been modified over the centuries.

The Nature of Folk Classifications

All folk taxonomic systems are essentially comprised of a large number of primary terms which represent the most commonly designated concepts of the animal and plant world. They stand for groupings of organisms that have a certain "natural" or objective standing in the world. In English we have terms like elephant, gull, blackbird, viper, buttercup, badger, perch, cowslip; in Chichewa we have terms like *nyalugwe, chambo, msuku, kanyimbi, njiwa, nyani, chinomba, tsabola.* Ethno-biologists refer to these terms as 'generic names'. They are usually single terms, and there are lots of them in every language. Such categories are normally incorporated into a higher-level taxa referred to as a 'life-form' category (Berlin, *et al.,* 1974). In English we have snake, beast, fowl, (you'll note I'm using biblical terms), tree, fish, bush and the like, while in Chichewa we have *nyama, mbalame, mtengo, njoka, bowa, nsomba.* These terms - or those rough equivalents - are found in many different languages. Besides these two primary levels there is a third important taxonomic rank, namely, that often the generic categories are subdivided into two or more specific categories. In English we have two sorts of celendine, three or four doves and woodpeckers, several kinds of mice, horse and sweet chestnuts, while in Chichewa we have two kinds of forest mice *(Granmomys) sonto wankulu* and *sonto wang'ono,* and several allied trees; *mpoloni* and *mpoloni wamuna. (Steganotaenia araliacec* and *Heteromorpha arborescens* - both Umbelliforae shrubs) and *thombozi* and *thombozi chipeta (Diplorhynchus condylocarpon* and *Holarrhena pubescens)* being typical examples. In folk taxonomic systems generally the number of genera that are subdivided in this manner are relatively few - and Chewa is no exception here.

Now there are a number of interesting features to be noted about such classifications. Firstly, it is very rare to find any taxa which are equivalent to the English terms 'plant' and 'animal' -these terms are absent from almost all folk classifications on which we have details. This is not to say that people do not conceptualize the distinction between the two main types of living organisms, but these are not named categories. It is interesting to note, however, that in Chichewa the noun classes to some extent reflect this distinction, for whereas many animals beling to the munthu class *a/fisi, a/nyalugwe, a/mende* (or the plural is the same) most members of the *mtengo* category - which includes the majority of plants known to the Chewa - belong to the noun class typically referred to by that same term - *mtengo*. Thus we have *mkuvu, mkundi,nsopa mlombwa* (taking the plural prefix *mi-).* Chichewa grammatical rules are complex and variable, but this does seem to indicate a differential treatment, in ordinary language, of animals and plants. But importantly, there are no folk terms in Chewa that are equivalent to these.

Secondly, folk taxonomies have not only a shallow hierarchy, essentially of three levels, but it is also a discrepant one. There are for instance few intermediate categories between generic and life-form terms, and many generic categories are unaffiliated to any of the main life-forms. In a study of the plant classifications of one Mayan-speaking community in Mexico, for example, one anthropologist (Berlin, *et al,* 1974) found that they had four basic life-forms which can be broadly translated as 'trees', 'herbs', 'grasses', and 'vines'. Out of a total of 471 generic categories approximately 75 per cent were incorporated into one or other of these four basic categories, leaving about 100 generic forms unaffiliated. In many folk classifications there is often a residual category - somewhat equivalent to *chircmbo* (or *chikoko* in Yao) that incorporates some of these discrepant generics. The taxonomic hierarchy of folk classifications is therefore not a systematic one.

Thirdly, many of the terms in folk classifications are polysemous, their meaning varying according to context. Quite generally a generic is a single term that applies both to a group of plants or animals, and to a specific species. In some Amerindian languages the term for a life-form category is often also a generic term. Amongst the Shoshoni, for example, the word for 'eagle' also means 'bird'. And there is some evidence that the English word 'tree in its original meaning not only stood for trees universally but for a specific kind of habitat and the generic "oak".

Fourthly, and as one would expect, many classes of organisms of interest to the biologists are given very scant treatment in folk taxonomies. The English generics toadstool, fern, worm, beetle cover a multitude of species known to present biologists, and their Chichewa equivalents are the same, although it is worth noting that the Chichewa have a detailed classification of edible fungi and rodents.

Fifthly, in case one should get the idea that folk taxonomies are all ad hoc and highly unsystematic, I should note that the classificatory proclivities of pre-industrial people typically do not end with the ordering of a specific domain, like that of animals or plants. People classify all aspects of life: there is a colour classification; people are divided up into various social categories; there is a recognition of different kinds of planets or minerals; space is divided up and given values; individuals are classified according to their temperament, and time, too, has its categories. To people like us Europeans all these aspects of human experience are distinct and unrelated. Given industrial production, and the high degree of economic and intellectual specialization that modern society involves we do not look upon the world as a 'totality' of interrelated things. For us, there are no real connections between colours, or people's temperaments and animals and plants, though we may link them descriptively or metaphorically. But with the culture of more pre-industrial people classification does not stop with the ordering of specific domains like colour or plants; there is often a more complex and systematized mode of classification that unites into a symbolic totality almost all aspects of human experience. As an example I will mention the symbolic classifications of one American Indian community, the Navaho, who have a complex symbolic classification organized around spatial categories (Levi Strauss, 1966). When we talk about totemism, or geomancy or astrology, we are simply (and somewhat misleadingly) looking at classificatory symbolism from one particular aspect.

Anyone who looks at Culpeper's Herbal will see the influence of the medieval conceptions of the world on this study. What's important about this is that it indicates that many pre-industrial people do not see our opposition between man and nature; what happens in the social world affects 'nature', and vice versa. Thus there is often an ecological perspective in the culture of pre-literate people even though mediated through religious symbolism.

Chewa Classification of Plants

But let me return to the classification of plants and the Chewa. As *I* said, there's no term for 'plant' here, but the plant kingdom itself is ordered through four basic categories:

Mtengo which is a general category for trees and woody plants.

Chitsamba which can be roughly translated as 'shrubs'- although often associated with regenerating *Brachystegia* type trees.

Maudzu: grass-like plants, and including often small lilies.

Bowa: edible fungi.

Some plants fit very uneasily into these primary categories. If you ask a local person what sort of plant, say, a balsam is, or whether it is a 'tree1, *mtengo* - he or she is or will be hesitant, and probably conclude that it is a *Maluwa* (flower) - significantly tending to use the plural. So in a sense *duim* (or *Luwa*) can take on the role of a general plant category, although herbs with inconspicuous flowers remain essentially unaffiliated, Intermediate categories are relatively few in Chichewa, but the terms which are used to designate a group of plant generics are of interest because they mainly have a functional rather than a purely taxonomic significance, Two examples:

Telele: a term that specifically denotes the cultivated hibiscus but which is used generally as a category to cover all plants whose leaves are utilized in the preparation of a specific kind of relish, referred to by the same name,

Mwanaa wa mphepo: a term focussed on *Cyphostemma* plants, but one used to cover a variety of plants associated with a complaint of the same name, for which the plant provides a remedy.

This pragmatic bias is very evident in Chichewa classifications, as Bruce Hargreaves (1976) suggests in one of his articles, and again I give two examples. The first is the well-known term *Nyama*, which is applied both as a category to cover all mammals and larger reptiles, and as a term for 'meat'. It is a -highly complex teem, and in specific contexts some of the larger mammals - hyena, leopard for example - will be excluded from it, and described as *Chirombo* - another complex category which can be roughly glossed as a "useless living thing". The latter term, as such, covers a variety of organisms, The second example of this utilitarian emphasis in Chichewa classification is the term *Bowa* - which also has a double meaning. In some contexts it could be used as a generic term for the larger fungi, but essentially it means *"edible fungi"*, and a woman will explicitly describe an inedible *Russula* or *Amanita* as '*Sibowa chirambo*', It's not a *bowa* but a "useless thing". This is an important point because anthropologists generally have overlooked or even denied the functional significance of folk categories.

Changes in English Folk Classification

Now if you look historically at English folk classifications - and we're returning now to the Latin issue - you will see that originally they were very similar to contemporary Chichewa, The basic "animal" categories were "beast", "fowl" (a term that covered birds, bats and butterflies, i.e. it meant "flying things"}, "snake" (which comes from the Teutonic verb "to creep" - and was also a wide category) and "bug" (the original meaning of which had connotations with ghosts, apparitions, and objects of terror). The term "bird" did not become a general category until about 1600. Its original meaning was a 'young bird" or nestling, particularly the young eagles; but with time it replaced "fowl" and both took on different meanings. The basic "plant" categories were "tree", "bush" and "herb". There was no general category for "fungi", only the terms "mushroom" and "toadstool", applying to the edible and inedible varieties respectively. All these terms were essentially of Teutonic tribal origin.

Significantly there were no terms in the early period to signify the two main groups of organisms; both the terms "animal" and "plant" are latecomers to the English language - and both, of course, derived from Latin. The term "animal" comes from "anima" meaning "breath" or "life essence", and did not become evident in English till around 1600. At that time a writer had to point out to ordinary folk the distinction between animal and beast. He wrote (1594):

'Many men by reason of ignorance of the Latin tongue think that an animal is a beast, whereas it signifieth a living thing."

"Plant" comes essentially from the Latin term "planta", to sprout, and again did not become widely used in English until the 16th century when various herbalists like Turner began to use it *(plantes) as* a general category to cover herbs, shrubs and trees. Some general categories of the earlier period, like *gomme* (used by Chaucer as a term equivalent to herb and tree) we know little about; it survives today only in the word "gum", but it is probable that it was a term of the same taxonomic status as the Chichewa name *Mpira* (which applies to many latex-producing plants).

After 1600 many other taxonomic concepts derived from Latin entered into English folk classifications - "vegetable", "quadruped", "fungi", "reptile" (like the Teutonic word snake, this was derived from the verb "to creep"). The term "quadruped" (four-footed) had an interesting history. For a while it replaced "beast" as a life-form category in English - and there were several scientific texts entitled the "History of the Quadrupeds" - but when it became evident that the distinction between mammals and reptiles and amphibians was important, it was displaced by the term "mammal". This term, derived from the Latin *mammae* meaning "breasts" did not become a part of the common language until well into the 19th century.

Now in all these changing developments in English folk classifications there are *three* kinds of processes going on which are important to distinguish. The *first* I have already tried to indicate, namely, the important influence that Latin has had on English culture generally and implicitly on folk classifications. The *second* is related to a general theory put forward by the American anthropologist Brent Berlin (Berlin, *et at*, 1972), that accompanying the more general development in the social and technical complexity of a society there has been an elaboration and growth of folk classifications. He has applied this theory both to the development of colour categories and to ethnobotanical nomenclature. With regard to the latter, his theory is briefly this. That in early human communities generic terms had primacy, and although one human community, the Tasmanians, appear to have lacked general life-form categories, in most small-scale societies three primary taxonomic levels (noted earlier) are developed. Over time, two other levels emerge: named intermediate categories begin to articulate concepts between the life forms and the generics (these, interestingly, may initially be covert), and specific categories may be subdivided giving rise to various taxa. He sees the latter as especially associated with the cultivation of crops. In the final stage of development in the classification, terms like "animal" and "plant" become named categories.

And *thirdly* there has been the important and quite fundamental influence of scientific taxonomy itself, which is primarily associated with the writings of the Swedish naturalist Carl Linnaeus, whose *Species Plantarum* (1753) is taken as the official starting point for plant nomenclature. Now when the name Linneaus is mentioned it is usually in connexion with naming, with the invention of the *binomial* system, the giving of plants (and animals) two terms, not one as in the generics of folk classifications. But this is only a reflection of a more fundamental shift of emphasis to the way of looking at plants that emerged in the 17th and 18th centuries, mainly through the work of herbalists. There was, as it were, a shift of focus. The major change was the realization that in "grouping" plants - and with increasing knowledge this is what the herbalists were systematically trying to do - the important criteria was not the general morphology of plants, whether they were shrubs or vines, or their use, but the structure of the flowering parts. Linnaeus in fact called his own classificatory method the "sexual system" (and for his explicit discussion of sex his books were banned in many places), and he classified plants simply on the number of stamens and styles a particular plant possessed. But even more important, he took and refined the concept of genus, which as one botanist has noted is "as old as folk science itself". When a friend of mine tells me that there are two kinds of *Mpoloni* - both good medicines - *Mpoloni* and *Mpoloni wamuna,* I doubt if he realises that he is articulating the generic concept or using the binomial system. There was no radical break, then, as Brent Berlin suggests, between folk and scientific classifications. But by combining a refined generic concept with a focus on the flowering parts, and by adopting the Latin of contemporary herbalists as the language of scientific classification, Linnaeus wrought a near-revolution in taxonomy. But even so, it is well to remember that almost all the generic terms utilized by Linnaeus in compiling his *Species Plantarum* (which include description of some 7300 species) are drawn from the folk taxonomic systems of the ancient Greeks and Romans, as codified by such herbalists as Dioscurides and Theophrastus. One only has to look at a book of plants'names to realise the degree to which scientific nomenclature has relied on folk taxonomies for the coinage of generic terms. *Viola, Scilla, Orchis, Cassia, Lilium, Cycas* are all ancient Greek or Latin names of plants, while *Angraecum, Kalanchoe, Datura, Ailanthus, Aloe, Brassica* are generics from the folk taxonomies of other cultures, Of the remainder a surprising number are named after botanists.

This shift of forms I mentioned is concretely illustrated if one compares the perspectives of the two contemporary experts or specialists in the plant field - the botanist and the person who is usually the most knowledgeable about folk classifications - the *Ng'anga* or diviner-herbalist. If *I* should show some roots of *Disoma kirkii (palibe kanthu)* or *Cyphostemma zambense (mwana wa mphepo)* to a botanist and asked for an identification, I doubt if there would be one in a hundred who could tell me what it is. Yet I wouldn't trust any *Ng'anga* who couldn't give me a positive response immediately. But you can imagine what they would say at Kew if you sent them along a pile of roots and asked for identifications! Conversely, if you showed the flowers of these plants to a botanist you *ought* to get an identification - if he (or she) is a botanist worth his salt - but you would stump most *Sing'angas*. Yet a woman *Ng'anga I* know to whom *I* showed a specimen said to me: "Bring me more leaves and the *root* and I'll tell you what it is!"

Finally, what is the relationship between scientific and folk classifications with regard to their content? Well, inspite of Rodney Wood's pleading, there is a surprisingly high degree of correspondence between the two, but by no means the one-to-one correspondence as implied by some plant dictionaries. In a recent analysis (1979) I made of the way the Navaho Indians classify insects I found a very close relationship between their classification and that of entomologists. And Brent Berlin and his associates, in their study of a Mayan community in Mexico, found that there was in fact a one-to-one correspondence between folk generics and biological species in about 61 per cent of the generic plant taxa examined by them.

So I trust that what I have had to say this evening has convinced you that there is not a "great divide" between folk and scientific classifications, and that folk taxonomies and names have an intrinsic interest in their own right.

References

Alder, J. R. (1978) Book Review; The *Birds of Malawi, C. W. And F. M. Benson* (1977). *Nyala 4(l):* 37-38.

Berlin, B. (1972) Speculations on the growth ethnobotanical nomenclature. *Language in Society* 1:56-86.

Berlin, B., D. E. Breedlove and P. H. Raven (1974) Principles *of Tzeltol Plant Classification.* Academic Press, New York.

Buchanan, J.   (1885) *The Shire Highlands (East Central Africa) as Colony and Mission,* W. Blackwood & Sons, London.

Hargreaves, B. J.   (1976) Killing and Curing: Succulent Use in Chitipa *Cactus and Succulent J. (US) 48:* 190-196.

Jeffrey, C.   (1973) Biological *Nomenclature.*   Arnold, London

Levi-Strauss, C.   (1966) The *Savage Mind.*   Weidenfeld & Nicolson, London

Linnaei, C.   (1753) Species *Planatrum.*   Holmiae, Impensis Laurentii Salvii.

Morris, B.   (1979)   Symbolism and   idiology: Thoughts   on Navaho clas-sifications.   In: R.   Ellen   (Ed.) Folk *Classifications in their Social Context.* Academic Press, New York.

Palgraves, K. C.   (1977) Trees *of Southern Africa.*   C. Struik Publs, Cape Town.

Stearn, W. T.   (1966) Botanical *Latin.*   David & Charles, London.

Wood, R. C.   (1949) Small Mammals of   southern Nyasaland.   *Nyasaland Soc. J.* 2(1): 38-43.

THE EPIPHYTIC ORCHIDS OF THE SHIRE HIGHLANDS, MALAWI (1967)

A collection of epiphytic orchids was made during 1964/65 from the Shire Highlands, Malawi, an area hitherto only partially explored botanically. The survey revealed not only a wealth of interesting epiphytic species, but also showed a degree of correlation between the main vegetation types covering the Highlands, and the epiphytic orchid-flora to be found in each respective habitat. This aspect of orchid ecology is discussed on the basis of personal observation.

INTRODUCTION

The first botanical collections in Malawi were made by two members of the Livingstone Expedition, Sir John Kirk and Mr J. C. Meller who, while exploring the River Shire and wandering over the Shire Highlands during the years 1859-62 made important plant collections which were transmitted to Kew. In the 1890's, largely through the patronage of the Johnston Administration, further important collections were made by Alexander Whyte, J. McClounie, J. Buchanan and G. F. Scott-Elliott (of the 1893-4 Ruwenzori Expedition), and these inevitably included many hitherto undescribed species. At the turn of the century, R. A. Rolfe in the *Flora of Tropical Africa,* listed a total of 26 epiphytic orchid-species from Malawi. An invaluable collection of orchids (accompanied by excellent drawings) was made by A. G. McLoughlin, who camped on Zomba Plateau in 1919, and since then further important collections by Mrs F. M. Benson, G. Jackson, Mrs H. M. Richards and L. J. Brass (of the Vernay Expedition), to name but a few of the principal collectors, have added to the sum total. On the whole, however, these latter collections included only a small proportion of epiphytic orchids. The fine plant collection made by the Vernay Expedition in 1946 for instance—2004 numbers—included only fire epiphytic species.

Similarly, in his study of the vegetation of Mlanje Mountains, J. D. Chapman recorded only a single species, *Angraecopsis parviflora*. During 1964-5, in an effort to fill the gaps in our knowledge of the epiphytic orchid flora, an intensive survey was made of the southern regions. The present paper, part of a larger study to be published shortly, deals with one aspect of orchid ecology, namely the degree of correlation between the broad vegetation types covering the Highlands and the epiphytic orchids to be found in each respective habitat.

The survey brought to light a number of taxonomic problems, and several species remain undescribed. The description of a new species of *Bulbophyllum* is contained in the Appendix. The numbers refer to my own collections; all specimens are to be found in the Herbarium of the Royal Botanic Gardens, Kew.

The Shire Highlands—theManganja Hills of the early botanists—are roughly 2000 sq. miles in extent and lie at an altitude of between 2000 and 4000 feet. Geologically it consists of a complex of schists and gneisses with the intrusions of syenite, exemplified in the higher

Fig. 1. Map of the Shire Highlands.[Map drawn by B. Thompson]

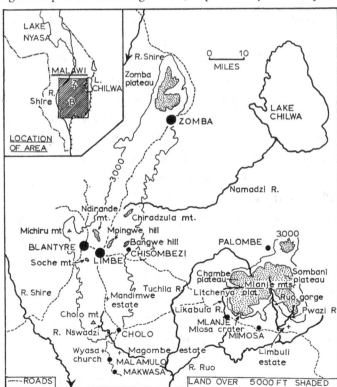

mountains, being a prominent feature of the landscape. The area is flanked on the west and south by the scarps of the Shire Valley, the eastern limits being marked by the Palombe-Chilwa depression.

The chief climatic characteristic of the region is an alternating wet and dry season, with abundant rainfall in summer and little or none during the colder months. The main rains occur from November to March but the higher altitudes and the escarpments facing the south-east receive considerable precipitation during the period May to July when the monsoon winds, locally termed 'chiperones', bring spells of cold mist and rain.

The vegetation of Malawi has been described by various authors, notably Jackson and Topham, and has been classified satisfactorily into broad physiognomic and floristic groups. These are discussed separately below.

SAVANNAH WOODLAND—BELOW 3500 FEET

Schimper (1903) suggested that savannah woodland came into existence under certain climatic conditions—namely a sharply defined wet and dry season, but modern ecologists refute this idea of climatic savannah and have tended to consider the vegetation type as a plagio-climax. Willan (1940) stated that *Brachystegia* woodland is 'definitely a secondary type of vegetation which has successfully asserted itself and assumed a degree of stability on degraded and impoverished soils'. This latter view is supported by the extreme sharpness of the present boundaries between savannah woodland and evergreen forest. On the majority of hills in the Blantyre District, particularly Soche Mt., this division is abrupt and clear-cut, there being no transition zone between the *Brachystegia spiciformis* on the piedmont slopes and the montane evergreen forest which covers the summit.

Brachystegia woodland covers a greater part of the Highlands and in appearance is remarkably uniform. Floristically, however, it is complex and the characteristic of this type of forest is its diversity; it varies from one acre to another, both in composition and condition. Each 'plot' has its own individual history which profoundly affects, and is reflected in, the epiphytic flora.

Thus we find in certain areas of woodland, untouched or protected over a number of years, trees—some of immense proportions—which are festooned with orchids. Such trees are noticeable in fire-free glades, but elsewhere past cultivation or severe annual burning has degenerated the forest-type to such an extent that orchids are either scarce or absent. Degenerate woodland in low rainfall zones, such as the northern slopes of Michiru Mt. are normally lacking in epiphytic species. It is noticeable that savannah woodland needs to have reached a definite climax, albeit a pseudo one, before epiphytic colonization takes place.

The dominant trees of this woodland are *Brachystegia* species (especially *B. spiciformis*), *Pterocarpus angolensis, Julbernardia globiflora, Cussonia kirkii, Afrormosia angolensis, Uapaca kirkiana* and *Parinari mobola*. In the Likabula valley, which lies in an evident rain shadow, *Monotes africana* and *Brachystegia longifolia* are more conspicuous, while the ground flora includes such elements as *Striga gesnerioides, Borreria dibrachiata, Kalanchoe lateritia* and *Hypericophyllum compositarum*, herbs unrecorded on the southern slopes of Mlanje. In the teabelt, sited in the latter region, which enjoys an annual rainfall of over 60 inches, the woodland is of unusual luxuriance. *Brachystegia spiciformis* here attains a height of 60 feet and *Parinari mobola* forms, on lateritic pans, stands of closed forest which have a rich herbaceous undergrowth. *Vitex doniana, Bridelia micrantha* and *Khaya nyasica* are also common, often far from riparian growth. Among the attractive herbs *Leucas milanjiana, Murdannia simplex,* the lily *Anthericum subpetiolatum, Dissotis debilis,* and the gingers *Afromomum zambesiacum* and *Kaempferia decora* are conspicuous and indicative of the higher rainfall.

The remainder of the Highlands, especially the Blantyre and Cholo districts, show a similar pattern, the vegetation type tending to deteriorate with the declining rainfall.

Four epiphytic orchids can be considered characteristic of savannah woodland— *Cyrtorchis praetermissa, C. crassifolia, C. arcuata variabilis,* and *Tridactyle teretifolia.* Associated with these in certain localities are *Bulbophyllum oreonastes, B. platyrhachis, Bulbophyllum* sp. *(Morris 27),* and *B. malawiense.* All show adaptation to the xerophytic

Fig. 2. Illustration of Bulbophyllum malawiense Morris, (a) Flowering plant x }; (b) anterior petal X 8; (c) lateral sepal x 8; (d) petal x 8; (e) individual flower x 8; (f) column and labellum; side view x 12; (g) column x 20; (h) labellum: end view x 12.

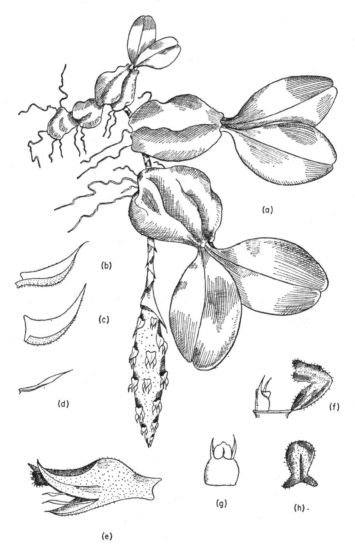

conditions they encounter, *T. teretifolia* and *C. crassifolia* in particular, having, as their Latin names suggest, succulent leaves. Only 13% of the epiphytic orchid-flora recorded in the area is known to occur in savannah woodland below 3500 feet. An analysis of the collections is contained in Table 1. The two ubiquitous orchids *Calyptrochilum christyanum*

Table 1. Distribution of orchids in savannah woodland below 3500 feet.
(In the following tables, x denotes occurrence)

Species	Blantyre District, 3500 feet	Nyasa Church, Cholo, 3000 feet	Limbuli Estate, Mlanje, 2400 feet	Makwasa, Cholo, 2800 feet	Magombe, Cholo, 3000 feet	Likabula valley, Mlanje, 3000 feet	Chisombezi, 3000 feet	Mimosa, Mlanje, 2100 feet	Pwazi R., Mlanje, 2600 feet
Ansellia gigantea nilotica	x								
Bulbophyllum platyrhachis	x	x	x					x	
B. malawiense		x	x			x			
B. sp. (Morris 27)			x					x	
B. oreonastes							x		
Cyrtorchis praetermissa	x	x	x	x	x		x	x	x
C. crassifolia						x			
C. arcuata variablis	x		x		x			x	x
Microcoelia exilis	x				x				
Polystachya tessellata		x	x			x			
Tridactyle teretifolia	x	x	x			x	x		

and *Cyrtorchis arcuata whytei* are included in another section, as although they may sometimes be abundant in sheltered areas of Brachystegia, they are essentially orchids of gallery forest. Surveys in typical Brachystegia have shown that from 3 to 6% of the total tree population normally held orchids.

SAVANNAH WOODLAND — ABOVE 3500 FEET

Above 4000 feet the tree *Brachystegia spiciformis* predominates, forming what Chapman terms 'a stunted, lichen-hung woodland'. On Mlanje it is 'the typical *Brachystegia* of the upper parts of the spurs, often festooned with lichen and *Orchidaceae* and in places extending to the plateau'. Zomba Plateau and the higher slopes of Soche, Bangwe and Ndirande Mountains — Chiradzula Mt. to a limited extent only — are characterized by this type of vegetation. The woodland consists of almost pure stands of *Brachystegia spiciformis,* with such associates as *Nuxia floribunda, Myrica pilulifera* and *Parinari mobola*. The ground flora is sparse, with the herbs *Gnidia glauca, Sopubia simplex, Hebenstretia dentata* and *Lotus mlanjeanus* in evidence.

Normally the trees are stunted owing to the exposed situation and the rocky shallow soil, but in certain localities near Cholo, such as Mandimwe Estate, patches of forest exist which have reached a high degree of development.

These sites are profoundly rich in species; the Mecca among them being Soche Mt.,2 where at an altitude of 4800 feet, a short distance below the montane forest, a wooded spur provided in an area of under half an acre, eighteen different species of epiphytic orchid. The trees are so heavily laden with epiphytic orchids, ferns and mosses, as to obscure the bark of the bole and main branches. There can be little doubt that epiphytic orchids reach their greatest concentration in the 'mist zone' of savannah woodland between 4500 and 5000 feet.

Increased light with increased altitude is an accepted fact, and as well as directing normal morphological and physiological variations, this would tend to influence the distribution of orchids. Coupled with high cloud precipitation, it is this which accounts for the fact that epiphytic orchids reach their maximum abundance at 5000 feet. Although in biology, as Moreau intimated, the term ' altitude ' has a rather loose meaning, it must, until we can find more precise labels to describe distribution, of necessity be employed. In this context I have used the term with caution, realizing that the factors which determine plant distribution are many and complex.

R. E. Moreau (1933), in his ecological studies of the montane forests of East Africa, concluded that continuous evergreen forest, stretching from the West African forest belt to the Usambara Mountains, may well have persisted until comparatively recent times — probably as late as 12, 000 years ago. Then, with the adverse dry conditions, came the retreat of the forest. The evergreen forests of East Africa declined in extent and at the present time they are but isolated patches of montane forest, 'like so many islands in a sea of savannah' Loveridge (1956). The presence of certain evergreen forest species in deciduous woodland tends to substantiate

---

[2] Overlooking the Blantyre-Limbe municipality the domed summit of Soche Mountain, 5030 feet is a prominent feature of the Shire Highlands. Capped with a remnant patch of montane rainforest, some 300 acres in extent, its rocky slopes are covered with degenerate savannah woodland, *Brachystegia spiciformis* being dominant. The rocks and trees near the summit are festooned with epiphytic orchids, and besides the species enumerated in the tables, *Stenoglottis fimbriata*, *Cynorkis leirkii* and *C. hanning-tonia* are common in humus-filled crevices.

this theory and the general conclusion therefore is that evergreen forest was once widespread or, alternatively, more extensive than it is at the present time.

If we accept this theory we may presume that much of the area now covered with *Brachystegia spiciformis* was once under evergreen forest, and that the epiphytic orchid flora represents a survival of the higher forest type. However, two confirmed facts contradict this theory: (a) the epiphytic orchid flora of montane forest is poor compared with that of the savannah woodland now under discussion; and (b) a comparison between the evergreen and savannah orchid lists shows clearly that they are entirely dissimilar. The conclusion one draws is that evergreen rain forest never covered, in even the Kamasian Epoch, the entire terrain of the Shire Highlands.

Fire is an important factor in the distribution of epiphytic orchids in savannah and severe fires over several years can deplete or completely destroy the orchids on all but the largest trees. Rocky outcrops serve to protect the *Brachystegia* from the devastating effects of annual fire, thereby saving the orchids, which have undoubtedly been considerably reduced in numbers during the last half-century. The sparsity of orchids on the northern slopes of Bangwe Hill is, I believe, primarily due to the lack of rock protection, for the terrain near the summit is regular, in contrast to the boulder-strewn spurs

Table 2. Distribution of orchids in savannah woodland 4-6000 feet

	Mandimwe Estate	Zomba Plateau	Chambe Plateau	Sombani Plateau	Soche Mt.	Mpingwe Hill
Angraecopsis amaniensis	×	×			×	×
Bulbophyllum oxypterum	×	×	×	×	×	×
B. mahonii		×			×	×
Cyrtorchis arcuata whytei	×	×	×	×	×	×
C. ringens	×				×	
Jumellea filicornoides	×		×	×	×	×
Microcoelia guyoniana					×	×
Polystachya villosa	×		×		×	×
P. vaginata		×			×	×
P. brassii		×	×		×	×
P. ruwenzoriensis					×	
Rangaeris muscicola					×	
Stolzia repens			×		×	
Tridactyle tricuspis	×	×		×	×	×
T. inaequilonga			×	×		
Ypsilopus longifolia			×	×		

of Soche Mt. The demarcation between the forest and the savannah on the former hill is also striking, being almost a straight line.

During the wet season the seepage slopes and rocky crevices of savannah woodland are dotted with attractive' Shade orchids', such as *Liparis neglecta, Cynorkis kirkii* etc.

Table 2 gives the distributional records of typical savannah orchids occurring over 4000 feet.

The division of savannah woodland into two distinct habitats, although arbitrary in many ways, is useful in outlining the distribution of orchids. The altitudinal range of the commoner species recorded in savannah woodland is given in Table 3.

Table 3. Altitudinal range of common savannah woodland orchids

Species	Altitude (thousand feet)				
	2	3	4	5	6
Angraecopsis amaniensis			xxxxxxxxxxxxx		
Bulbophyllum oxypterum		xxxxxxxxxxxxxxxxxxxxxxxxxx			
B. platyrhachis	xxxxxxxxxxxxxxxxx				
Cyrtorchis arcuata whytei		xxxxxxxxxxxxxxxxxxxxxx			
C. crassifolia			xxxxxxxx		
C. praetermissa	xxxxxxxx				
C. ringens				xxxxxxxxxxxxxxxxx	
C. teretifolia	xxxxxxxxxxxxxxxxx				
Jumellea filicornoides			xxxxxxxxx		
Polystachya brassii			xxxxxxxxxxx		
Stolzia repens				xxxxxxxxxxxxxxxxx	
Tridactyle ineaquilonga				xxxxxxxxxxxxxxx	
T. tricuspis			xxxxxxxxxxxxx		
Ypsilopus longifolia				xxxxxxxx	

EVERGREEN FOREST

Topham (1958) recognized two types of evergreen forest, the true montane closed forest and the Lower Mountain forest, the former characterized by such tree species as *Aphloia myrtifolia* and *Ekebergia meyeri*. However, the evergreen forests of Malawi have been so little studied that such a broad division can only be tentative.

My own records deal primarily with orchid collections made in the Ruo Gorge and the Mlosa Crater, with short notes from the montane forests of Soche and Bangwe. Botanical searches proved the forests of Cholo, Ndirande and

Mpingwe Hills to be singularly poor in orchids. When a large sector of the Mpingwe Forest near Limbe was wantonly burned I was able to examine the crowns of many timbered trees; giant figs, *Myrianthus arboreus* and *Khaya nyasica*. Surprisingly, the crowns of these immense evergreens held few orchids, an occasional *Tridactyle* sp. or a *Polystachya vaginata* perhaps, but little else.

Chapman's notes on the forests occurring in the gorges of Mlanje are concise. '*Newtonia buchananii* often of great size, is dominant along streams, and associated with it may be *Anthocleista zambesiaca, Khaya nyasica, Cola greenivayi, Trichoscypha ulugurensis* and others. Other common trees, not necessarily restricted to the vicinity of streams are *Albizia* sp., *Chrysophyllum gorungosanum, Conopharyngia* sp. and *Polyscias* sp. *Culcasia scandens* is a typical climber on the tree trunks and, like the massive epiphytic fern, *Polypodium polycarpon,* is found only on this side of the mountains'. To this may be added a note on the herbaceous flora. The flowering shrubs *Mostuea brunonis* and *Carvalhoa macrophylla* are abundant, and of the many attractive flowers *Brachystephanus africanus, Begonia nyassensis, Streptocarpus michelmorei, Dietes prolongata* and *Chlorophytum brevipes* may be mentioned here. The family *Acanthaceae* dominates the herb layer and epiphytic ferns are conspicuous, covering the rocks and trees. The feature which Schimper regarded as distinguishing true rainforest from other tropical forest formations—the presence of woody epiphytes — is lacking, and the forests come most easily under Phillip's definition of 'Broad- Leaved Evergreen Montane Forest'.

The moist ravines of Mlanje Mt. have a wealth of interesting epiphytic orchids (see Table 4). Four species are confined to this environment — *Polystachya fusiformis, Polystachya* sp. *(Morris 2), Bulbophyllum* nr *gravidum* and *Aerangis pachyura* — and it

Table 4. Distribution of orchids found in evergreen forest

	Soche Mt.	Mlosa Crater	Ruo Gorge	Limbuli Stream
Aerangis pachyura		×		
A. kotschyana			×	×
Angraecopsis parviflora	×	×	×	×
Angraecum sacciferum	×	×		
Bulbophyllum intertextum	×	×	×	
B. nr *gravidum*			×	
Diaphananthe stolzii	×	×	×	×
Liparis neglecta	×		×	
Mystacidium nr *tanganyikense*		×		
Polystachya fusiformis			×	
P. tessellata		×	×	×
P. sp. (*Morris* **2**)		×	×	
Rangaeris muscicola		×	×	
Stenoglottis fimbriata	×	×		
Tridactyle bicaudata		×	×	×
T. sp. (*Morris* **156**)	×		×	

is assumed that the humid micro-climactic conditions are the limiting factor. It is interesting to note that, with the sole exception *of Stenoglottis fimbriata* and perhaps *Liparis neglecta,* few orchids are found on rocks in the forest, ferns and mosses having the monopoly of such sites.

MONTANE CLOSED FOREST

In enumerating the orchid flora one is able to differentiate between the evergreen forest species listed in Table 4 and those found in the forests above 5500 feet. On Mlanje, of course, the latter community is the *Widdringtonia* Forest, the ecology of which has been fully discussed by Chapman (1962). It lies above the broad-leaved evergreen forest and fills the gulleys and ravines of the plateaux. It is associated with such trees as *Podocarpus milanjianus, Cussonia buchananii, Ochna longipes* and *Faurea forficuliflora.* The relic forest on Zomba Plateau although lacking the cedars, is a similar community, with *Craibia brevicaudata, Bersama abyssinica, Aphloia myrtiflora* and *Myrica* sp. among the commoner trees.

The Mlanje forest is aptly described by Brass: 'In an abundance of bryophytes, prominent throughout and normally saturated and cold from mist and rain, heavily padded on marginal trees, cushioned in tree-tops, and in moister ravines enveloping tree trunks and combining with matted surface roots to form springy and often treacherous ground cover, these were typical cloud forests. Associated with the mosses and hepatics as epiphytes were many orchids and ferns of rather few species.' Among the latter *Asplenium aethiopicum, Loxogramme lanceolata* and *Hymenophyllum* sp. are common. The forest borders are renowned for their floral excellence. 'Never before ', wrote John Buchanan, who made valuable botanical collections last century, 'have I met with more gorgeous displays of wild flowers than those to be seen in some favoured nooks of these Highlands'. Mention may be made of the commoner herbs found in the vicinity of the forest: *Plectranthus swynnertonii, Geranium mlanjense, Hypoestes triflora, Impatiens shirensis* and *Mimulopsis solmsii* are abundant, forming banks of colour, while in the depths of the forest *Isoglossa milanjiensis* and *Oldenlandia rupicola* brighten the damp, gloomy atmosphere.

The Widdringtonias harbour several epiphytic orchids, *Ypsilopus longifolia* and *Tridactyle inaequilonga* being the commonest, but they are inevitably obscured or partially hidden by the pale green lichen *Usnea monoliformis,* which attractively clothes the branches of the conifer. The sub-dominant trees are richer in epiphytes and such trees as *Podocarpus, Ilex mitis* and *Royena lucida* always hold several orchids. *Angraecum conchiferum* and *Polystachya transvaalensis* are abundant, together with tiny orchids like *Bolusiella* sp. *(Morris* 48), *Mystacidium* nr *tanganykense* and *Angraecum sacciferum,* many of the latter adhering to even the flimsiest branches and lianas. In the damper forests of Mlanje Mt. *Jumella* sp. *(Morris* 161) *and Stolzia* sp. *(Morris* 158) are common and conspicuous. A count of orchid plants on a small group of montane trees, filling a gulley near the Boma Cottage, Litchenya Plateau, 6500 feet, gave the following results:

Angraecum conchiferum	*70 plants*
Polystachya transvaalensis	*18 plants*
Bolusiella sp. (Morris 48)	*14 plants*
Jumellea sp. (Morris 161)	*11 plants*
Mystacidium nr tanganyikense	*4 plants*
Bulbophyllum oxypterum	*2 plants*
Stolzia sp. (Morris 158)	*2 plants*
Stolzia repens	*1 plant.*

It gives some indication of the relative abundance of orchids in the sub-dominant layer. Among the terrestrial shade orchids found in the forest *Disperis dicerochila,* the beautiful *Cynorkis kassnerana* and *Holoihrix johnstonii* may be mentioned here (see Table 5).

Table 5. Distribution of orchids found in montane closed forest

	Chiradzula Mountain	Zomba Plateau	Mlanje Mts.
Angraecum conchiferum	×	×	×
A. sacciferum		×	×
A. chamaeanthus		×	×
A. sp. (Morris 171)		×	
Bolusiella sp. (Morris 48)	×	×	×
Bulbophyllum stolzii	×	×	×
Cynorkis kassnerana		×	×
Disperis dicerochila		×	×
Jumellea sp. (Morris 161)		×	
Mystacidium nr tanganyikense		×	×
Polystachya transvaalensis	×	×	×
P. vaginata	×	×	
Stolzia sp. (Morris 158)			×
Tridactyle inaequilonga			×
T. sp. (Morris 157)			×
Ypsilopus longifolia			×

GALLERY FOREST

In reality, riparian forest is merely an extension of the broad-leaved evergreen forest, but as it extends into low rainfall regions and shows a distinctive orchid-flora it is, for convenience, considered here as a separate habitat. Riparian forest is an interesting and prominent feature of the Shire Highlands. Even in regions of intensive cultivation, i.e. the Chiromo-Cholo escarpment, where the population is over 200 people to the square mile, patches of excellent forest may still be found along the rivers and major streams and botanically they are of immense interest.

The dominant trees of these riparian tracts are *Pachystela brevipes, Bridelia micrantha, Syzygium cordatum, Adina microcephala, Macaranga* sp., *Trema guineense, Khaya nyasica, Erythophteum guineense,* with *Parkia filicoidea* prominent at the lower altitudes. The undergrowth consists of such shrubs as *Eryihroxylum emarginatum* and *Mussaemda arcuata,* while among the characteristic herbs the following may be noted: *Impatiens wallerana, Asystasia gangetica, Thunbergia alata,* the yellow day-flower *Aneilema aequinoctiale, Haemanthus zambesiacus* and *Lapeirousia grandiflora.*

With a fairly open canopy and abundant moisture throughout the year the gallery forests have a high density of orchids. On the tree *Syzygium cordatum,* for example, in five localities nearly a thousand orchids have been recorded, representing fifteen different species. I have published elsewhere the analysis of the gallery forest at Limbuli, Mlanje (1965). This is a typical site and clearly indicates the favourable microclimactic conditions which exist along forested streams. *Aerangis mystacidii, Tridactyle tridactylites, Angraecopsis parviflora,* and the two abundant indigenous orchids *Calyptrochilum christyanum* and *Cyrtorchis arcuata whytei* are the typical orchids found there. Table 6 gives the distribution pattern of the commoner plants.

Table 6. Distribution of orchids found in gallery forest

	Zomba Plateau	Limbuli Stream	Pwazi River	Nswadzi R., Cholo	Magombe Estate	Likabula River	Blantyre District
Aerangis mystacidii		×	×		×	×	×
Acampe pachyglossa		×					×
Angraecopsis parviflora	×	×	×		×	×	
Bolusiella maudae					×		
Bulbophyllum oxypterum	×			×		×	
B. encephalodes		×	×	×			
Calyptrochilum christyanum	×	×	×	×	×	×	×
Cirrhopetalum umbellatum		×	×	×	×		
Cyrtorchis arcuata whytei	×	×	×		×	×	×
Diaphananthe rutila	×			×			
D. stolzii	×	×					
Microcoelia exilis					×		×
Polystachya albescens	×	×	×		×	×	×
P. tessellata	×	×	×			×	
Tridactyle tridactylites	×		×	×		×	×

Mention must be made of the *Syzygium* forests. Consisting of pure stands *of Syzygium cordatum,* with an enclosed canopy, they are situated in the swampy areas and streamsides of the Highlands and are fruitful sites for epiphytic orchids. The vicinity of Hynde Dam, Limbe, is one typical site.

The ecological gradient which exists in many places between savannah and gallery forest should be mentioned. On Mandimwe Estate, Cholo, this is noticeable on many hillslopes, *Tridactyle tridactylites* and *Bulbophyllum oxypterum* being common in the riparian growth and on the lower slopes, *Jumellea filicornoides* and *Bulbophyllum platyrhachis* replacing them at the higher levels.

MOUNTAIN SPURS

The rocky ridges and spurs of the higher mountains are characterized by the shrub *Vellozia splendens,* renowned for its soft fibrous stem and attractive white flowers. Associated with it are such xeric rock-inhabiting plants as *Plectranthus crassus, Aloe mawii* and *Crassula globularioides*. The *Vellozia* is the prime host for several orchids (as well as the Everlasting flower *Helichrysum whyteanum* and the occasional epiphytic *Crassula)* and usually has a high quota of epiphytic plants. On a rock outcrop on Sombani Plateau, Mlanje 7000 feet, it was found that approximately 70% of the shrubs held epiphytic orchids, averaging about ten orchid plants per shrub. Orchids were especially plentiful on shrubs growing in sheltered coves. The list below details the number of specimens recorded on *Vellozia splendens*.

Polystachya zambesiaca	*24*
Polystachya johnstonii	*19*
Tridactyle tricuspis	*14*
Angraecum conchiferum	*4*
Ypsilopus longifolia	*2*
Polystachya ruwenzoriensis	*1*

On the rocky seepage slopes at the higher altitudes the following species were common, *Disa saxicola, Satyrium rhynchantoides, Cynorkis* sp., and *Holothrix johnstonii*.

MIXED SAVANNAH

The Shire valley and the drier parts of the Lake-shore have a varied vegetation which has been roughly grouped under this heading. Such vegetation-types as Mopane woodland (a closed forest of *Colophospermum mopane* on clay soils), alluvial parkland and *Acacia/Terminalia* are included. Many of the commonest and most familiar trees of Africa, such as the fever tree and the boabab, come from this region, but generally speaking it is a region poor in epiphytic orchids, although two species *Ansellia gigantea* and *Acampe pachyglossa* are widely distributed and in many places abundant. Leafless orchids *(Microcoelia* sp.) are also fairly common.

CONCLUSIONS

It has not been the purpose of this paper to discuss fully the ecology of epiphytic orchids, but rather to signify a correlation between a specific type of vegetation and its orchid flora. This is shown clearly in the tables. At the same time anomalies in the tables indicate the presence of other factors determining distribution. Why is *Polystachya vaginata,* one of the commonest orchids on Zomba Plateau and on the hills surrounding Blantyre, apparently absent from Mlanje? Conversely, why do present records of *Bulbophyllum encephalodes* come only from Cholo and Mlanje Districts? The mean annual rainfall may perhaps be a dominant factor, as it is in the distribution of small mammals. Almost all orchids have, within a specific forest-type, a limited distribution, bound by narrow micro-climactic requirements, and on all trees there appears to be a pronounced stratification of the epiphytic plants. A great deal of field-work has yet to be done on these wider aspects of orchid ecology.

In listing the orchids from any one locality, one is immediately struck by the wealth of orchid species to be found in the Shire Highlands. A total of 69 epiphytic orchids have been recorded from Mlanje Mt. alone, while the total number of species of epiphytic *Orchidaceae* listed from Malawi now stands at 104 and further intensive exploration will doubtlessly increase this figure. The Appendix contains a list of the orchids recorded by the present writer from the Shire Highlands and mentioned hi the paper.

ACKNOWLEDGEMENTS

I wish to thank Mr P. Francis Hunt of the Herbarium, Royal Botanic Gardens, Kew, for his guidance in the preparation of the paper, and for help in the identification of specimens. I am grateful also to Mr *G. H.* Welsh, Mrs Leslie Westrop, Mr B. L. Burtt, Mr and Mrs T. F. Shaxson and my wife Jacqueline, for assistance in various ways.

REFERENCES

Burtt-davy, J. & Hoyle, A. C., 1958. A Check List of the Forest Trees and Shrubs of the Nyasaland

Protectorate. Zomba Government Printer.

Brenan, J. P. M., 1953-54. Report on the Vernay Nyasaland Expedition 1946. *Mem. N.Y. bot. Gdn.,*8 (3); 9 (1). (This work contains an important introduction on the vegetation of Malawi by L. J.Brass.)

Chapman, J. D., 1962. The Vegetation of Mlanje Mountains. Zomba. Govn. Printer. Hirsh, C. R., 1960. *The dry woodlands of Nyasaland.* Salisbury, Rhodesia.: International Co-operation Administration.

Jackson, G., 1954. *Preliminary Ecological Survey of Nyasaland. Proceedings 2nd inter-African soilsconference,* p. 50.

Loveeidge, A., 1956. *Forest safari.* London.

Moreau, R. E., 1933. Pleistocene climactic changes and the distribution of life in East Africa. *J.Ecol.21:* 415-435

Moreau, R. E., 1935. Some eco-climactic data for closed evergreen forest in tropical Africa. *J. Linn.Soc.(Zool)39:285.*

Moreau, R. E., & Moreau, W. M., 1943. An introduction to the epiphytic orchids of East Africa. *Jl.E.Africanat.Hist.Soc.* **17:**1-32.

Morris, B., 1965. Epiphytic orchids of the Limbuli Stream, Mlanje. *Soc.Malawi J.* 18 (2): 59-70

Moeze, G., 1964, Personal communication.

Rolfe, R. A., 1898. Orchidaceae in *Theflora of tropicalAfrica(This the ton.-Dyer,ed.).* Volume7.London.

Schimper, A. F. W., 1903. Plant geography on a physiological basis. summerhayes, V. S., 1927-66. African orchids. In *Kew Bull,* and Botany Museum Leaflets Harvard University (1942-45).

Topham,p. 1958. In Burtt-Davy, J. & Hoyle A. C., 1958. A Check List of the Forest Trees and Shrubs of the Nyasaland Protectorate. Zomba Government Printer. willan, R. G. M., 1940. Notes on the vegetation of Northern Nyasaland. *Emp. For. J.* 19: 48-61.

"EPIPHYTIC ORCHIDS OF THE LIMBULI STREAM, MLANJE." (1965)

LIMBULI stream, a tributary of the Malosa River, has its source in the fringes of the Chisongeli rainforest which clothes the broken foothills below the south-eastern aspect of Manene Peak. The forest, one of the most extensive areas of closed montane forest on Mlanje Mountain, covers the upper reaches of the Chisongeli Stream, spreading over the I surrounding ridges with finger-like extensions reaching the [head-waters of the Kaombe, Muluzi and Swazi Streams,tributaries of the Ruo River. The Limbuli Stream emerges (abruptly from this forest as a crystal stream at about 4,500ft. The absence of an ecotone vegetation is striking. The evergreen forest, consisting of nearly pure stands of *Newtonia buchananii* with a sparse acanthaceous ground cover, gives way iddenly to open savannah grassland where *Braehystegia spiciformis* is dominant, and *Protea abyssinica* and *Heteromorpha trifoliata* common. The evergreen forest, which at the higher altitudes extends a considerable distance away from the stream, is now constricted to a narrow gallery forest of an entirely dissimilar floral composition. *Vitex doniana, Harungana madagascariensis, macaranga* sp., and *Brideria macrantha* are dominant trees in this riparian growth, *Newtonia* being scarce or, at the lower altitudes, entirely absent. The forest is bordered by a luxuriant undergrowth, rich in herbaceous species: *Landophia* sp,. *Aframomum zambesicam, Thunbegia alata* and *Dissotis phaestricha* are spicuous.

At 3,000ft. the stream reaches Limbuli Estate, 16°02' S, 35°44' E, and for the last four miles of its journey passes tea gardens and village cultivations where riparian forest has long been destroyed. The Limbuli valley, sited to receive the full precipitation of the summer monsoon rains, an annual rainfall of over 80 inches.

Contrary to what one would expect, montane rainforest is relatively poor in orchids, although such local terrestrial species as *Disperis rufina* and *Cynorchis* sp. are found there. The large, smoothbarked Nkwerenyani is invariably devoid of orchids. Only in ideal micro-climatic conditions, such as in the moist ravines of the Mlosa Crater and the Ruo Gorge, are epiphytic orchids found in any abundance, and even then the orchid population, both in numbers and species, is inferior to that of riparian forest or the *Brachystegia spiciformis* woodland such as to be found on the cloud-swept ridges of the plateau. This was certainly true of the rainforest at Limbuli which was extremely poor in epiphytic orchids. Above 3,500' *Tridactyle bicaudata* was the only common orchid recorded. *Andraecopsis, parviflora* was plentiful in parts of the forest but confined to stream edges, while *Cyrtorchis arcuata* I noted occasionally at the forest border. Two attractive orchids, *Aerangies kotschyam* and *Diaphananthe stolzii* were recorded in the montane forest and, from my limited observations, seem restricted to the midaltitudes between 4,000ft. and the plateau lip. The former, which was recorded by Meller (of the Livingstone expedition) from the "lower valley of the River Shire", is one of the few African orchids to have attracted the attention of horticulturists.

The gallery forest between 3,000 and 4,000ft. proved the most fruitful in epiphytic orchids: so fruitful as to persuade me to make a detailed survey of the stream, the results of which are tabled below. In certain sections, particularly where the Limbuli negotiates a steep rocky gully, V-shaped in cross-section, giving the enclosed vegetation full protection from the annual fires, epiphytic orchids festoon the trees. Here and there a rocky ravine, aside of the main stream and filled with fine specimens of *Brachystegia spiciformis* together with pioneer evergreen species like *Macaranga sp.* and *Trema guineensis,* also proved an attractive orchid habitat.

The savannah woodland itself which covered the valley slopes and surrounding foothills, and comprised of common tree species as *Parinari mobola, Pterocarpus angolensis* and *Uapaca kirkiana,* was relatively poor in epiphytes other than certain lichens. Only xerophilous orchid species such as *Cyrtorchis praetermissa, Tridactyle teretifotia* and several small species of the genus *Bulbophyllum* were recorded. Terrestrial orchids were commoner and in evidence during the early rains; the purple *Eulophia livingstonia;* the common Bee-orchis, *E. cuccullata; E. enantha;* the dambo orchids, *Playcoryne buchanana* and *Disa welwitchii;* were among the commoner ones noted.

The gallery forest, rarely more than 50 yards wide, provided, in the mile of stream studied, 9 species of epiphytic orchids. Belonging to 8 genera these are listed, with brief notes, below.

1. CYRTORCHIS ARC U AT A.

The sub species *C. arcuata* whytei is perhaps the most well known of Malawi tree orchids, and one frequently taken for garden cultivation, its long racemes of star like flowers being a familiar sight during the rains. A large orchid, its brittle strap-shaped leaves reaching a length of 12", it is abundant throughout the Shire Highlands. Mainly an orchid of Syzygium swamps it grows equally well in sheltered areas of savannah woodland. It is particularly noticeable at 4,500ft. in the Likabula valley growing near the river on rocks wherever sufficient debris and humus have gathered.

2. CALTPTROCHILUM CHRISTYANUM.

Although abundant, this orchid was overlooked by the early botanical collectors, neither Buchanan nor Whyte recording the species. With the preceding species it is perhaps the commonest epiphytic orchid and is widespread, especially on escarpment streams. The flowers are white, attractive but inconspicuous, being borne on a short raceme, on the underside and close to the stem. There are 8 to 12 pairs of elliptical-oblong leaves; roots are aerial, prolific and often pendant. It is rare to find this species associating with *C. arcuataa*. Although of similar habit, growing on the upper branches in the upper strata of trees, this species appears to fill an entirely different ecological niche, tending to prefer moister, less-illuminated conditions. In the shady gullies of the Limbuli Stream it reaches perhaps its optimum concentration. Mr. A. R. Westrop showed me specimens of this species which had germinated naturally and were flourishing on an exotic *Jacaranda mimosaefolia* at Magombe, Cholo.

3. DIAPHANANTHE STOLZII—

Only scattered records of this orchid from Mlanje and Zomba plateau, all over 3,700ft. There is a large *Acacia xiphocarpa* on the Zomba mountain road with its upper branches draped with this species. The leaves are short, ovate, 1-2" long and have a markedly bilobed apex. Aerial roots are pendant and delicate. The raceme is short, bearing 3 or 4 transparent flowers.

4. ANGRAECOPSIS PARVIFLORA.

Common and widespread but tending, due to its high moisture requirements, to be locally distributed. It is never found away from damp forests or the vicinity of streams, and appears to be little adapted to epiphytic conditions. It is an orchid of wet, mossy trees, often associating with *Stenoglottis fimbriata* near waterfalls. The leaves are narrow, flaccid, scytheshaped and of variable length, ranging from 3 to 12". Flimsily anchored by the roots which become swollen in a rich humus layer. I have records of this species from the southern slopes of Mlanje, Cholo and from Zomba plateau.

5. CIRRHOPETALUM AFRICANUM.

Orchid with typical sympodial growth. A single leaf, oblong, leathery, up to 8" long, emerges from the green, slightly conical pseudobulb. It resembles in general form, *Bulbophyllum encephalodes* but is largerand has a less complex inflorescence. It is of local occurence with few records.

6. POLYSTACHYA TESSELLATA.

A large *Polystachya* with large ovate leaves measuring up to 18" in length, this species is abundant in gallery forest throughout the Mlanje district, to which, according to present records, it seems confined. In February its long racemes of small lemon-yellow flowers are conspicuous. Unlike *P. albescens* which it resembles in its preference for shady environs, it has well developed pseudobulbs.

7. POLYSTACHYA ALBESCENS.

A smaller plant than *P. tessellata* with pale green linearoblong leaves, having an acute tip. A common forest species within the 3,000 to 5,000ft. limit, being replaced by the allied *P. transvaalensis* at the higher altitudes. Frequently found on moist rocks. The roots are fibrous forming a close mat on the rock or bark (a horizontal branch is the rule) and these collect adequate leaf humus.

8. AERANGIS MYSTACIDII.

An attractive orchid, smaller but otherwise identical to *Aerangis kotschyaum*. Common in shady situations along the rivers and larger streams of the Mlanje district, having a distintc preference (although this is not evident from the tables) for smooth-barked trees. Such trees as *Treculia africana. Parkia filicoidea* and *Bosqueia phoberos* invariably have, in suitable situations their quota of Aerangis. Like the leafless orchid of Blantyre *(Microcoelia exilis))* it commonly grows on the outer branches of the tree, amongst the foliage. Its pale olive-grey roots, though rarely aerial, extend for considerable distances along the branch. I have traced the roots of a small seedling specimen (with 3" leaves) for a distances of 6 feet.

9. *BULBOPHTLLUM PLATYRHACHIS.*

Growth sympodial. One of the larger species of the widespread genus *Bulbophyllum,* of which over 14 members have been recorded in Malawi. The pseudobulb is irregular, yellowish-green and 3" long. A pair of thick, fleshy, ovate leaves are borne at its apex. A striking feature is the distinctive inflorescence which has a broadly dilated rachis measuring 6" long by 1" broad, the inconspicuous greenish flowers being borne on both surfaces. The inflorescence resembles, to my imagination, a withered strap fern, yellow with a wavy margin. It is not a riparian species, being commoner in sheltered savannah woodland.

TABLE 1: ORCHIDS OCCURING ON THE LIMBULI STREAM LISTED IN ORDER OF ABUNDANCE.

	Number of tree-species on which present.	Total number of trees on which recorded	Total number of orchids.
CALYPTROCHILUM CHRISTYANUM	12	79	998
ANGRAECOPSIS PARVIFLORA	9	22	381
CYRTORCHIS ARCUATA	5	11	65
POLYSTACHYA TESSELLATA	6	19	19
CIRRHOPETALUM AFRICANUM	5	9	22
POLYSTACHYA ALBESCENS	5	6	17
AERANGIS MYSTACIDII	5	6	12
DIAPHANANTHE STOLZII	1	1	2

TABLE 2: ORCHID/HOST RELATIONSHIP

TREE	CYRTORCHIS ARCUATA	CALYPTROCHILUM CHRISTYANUM	CIRRHOPETALUM AFRICANUM	ANGRAECOPSIS PARVIFLORA	POLYSTACHYA TESSELLATA	AERANGIS MYSTACIDII	BULBOPHYLLUM PLATYRHACHIS	POLYSTACHYA ALBESCENS	DIAPHANANTHE STOLZII
HARUNGANA MADAGASCARIENSIS	x	x							
MACARANGA sp.		x	x	x	x	x	o	o	
BRIDELIA MACRANTHA	x	x	x	x	x	o		x	
BRACHYSTEGIA SPICIFORMIS		x		x					
DRYPETES? NATALENSIS	x	x	o	x	o				
CUSSONIA KIRKII		x			x	x			
SYZYGIUM CORDATUM	x	x	x	x	x			x	
ADINA MICROCEPHALA		x		x		o			
VITEX DONIANA	x	x	o	o	o			o	
CHRYSOPHYLLUM MAGALISMONTANUM		o							
FICUS CAPENSIS?		x		x				o	x
GARCINIA HUELLENSIS						x			
COLL. NO. 38		x		x					

o **Denotes Single Record only**

TABLE 3: ANALYSIS OF THE TREE CENSUS

Tree species	Total	No, with orchids	No. orchid species	Total No. orchi:s
HARUNGANA MADAGASCARIENSIS	21	5	2	27
MACARANGA SP.	92	15	7	69
BRIDELIA MACRANTHA	38	32	7	583
BRACHYSTEGIA SPICIFORMIS	3	3	2	13
DRYPETES NATALENSIS	6	5	5	378
CUSSONIA KIRKII	12	5	3	34
SYZYGIUM CORDATUM	22	15	6	274
ADINA MICROCEPHALA	8	6	3	49
VITEX DONIANA	21	9	6	61
FICUS CAPENSIS?	6	3	4	16
CHRYSOPHYLLUM MAGALISMONTANUM	1	1	1	1
GARCINIA HUELLENSIS	1	1	1	4
COLL. NO. 38	6	2	2	8
PTEROCARPUS ANGOLENSIS	5	0		
NEWTONIA BUCHANANII	23	0		
ERYTHRINA ABYSSINICA	2	0		
OLINIA USAMBARENSIS	7	0		
PAVETTA ABYSSINICA	1	0		
SECURIDACA LONGIPEDUNCULATA	1	0		
COMBRETUM SP.	1	0		
AFRORMOSIA ANGOLENSIS	2	0		
OTHER TREE SPECIES.	29	0		

TABLE 4: FLOWERING PERIOD

	OCTOBER	NOVEMBER	DECEMBER	JANUARY	FEBRUARY	MARCH	APRIL	MAY	JUNE	JULY	AUGUST	SEPTEMBER
CALYPTROCHILUM CHRISTYANUM	x	x										
CYRTORCHIS ARCUATA		x		x	x							
CIRRHOPETALUM AFRICANUM				x								
ANGRAECOPSIS PARVIFLORA					x	x						
POLYSTACHYA TESSELLATA					x	x						
AERANGIS MYSTACIDII						x						
BULBOPHYLLUM PLATYRHACHIS				x								
POLYSTACHYA ALBESCENS			x	x								
DIAPHANANTHE STOLZII						x						

W. M. and R. E. Moreau, in their excellent account of E. African epiphytic orchids,[3*] state, "there is little evidence of a specific relation between orchid and tree host," and that "in general, rough bark is naturally more favoured than smooth." The latter statement is vouched for by many authorities, for it is natural to assume that thick barked trees have a greater water holding capacity. My own observations tend to show that this assumption is erroneous. Two of the commonest 'rough-barked' trees, *Cussonia kirkii* and *Pterocarpus angolensis* are, in savannah woodland, completely lacking in orchids. The first assertion however is borne out by the tables. There appears to be no specific host/orchid relationship, but what is apparent is the tendency for certain trees to be, what I term, 'orchid prone'.

[3*] ."Introduction to the epiphytic orchids of E. Africa" Journal of the E. African Natural History Society. Vol. xvii. 1943

Thus three trees on the Limbuli stream, *Syzygium, Dypetes* and *Bridelia,* each held over 5 different orchid species and, although constituting only 21% of the total tree population, they held 81% of the orchids. Orchid counts in *Brachystegict:* woodland clearly demonstrate this tendency.

A walk through this type of forest will show how 'orchid prone' are such trees as *Parinari mobola* and *Uapaca kirkiana,* compared with other species. *Vellozia splendens,* common on rock outcrops, is famously 'orchid prone' and 6 orchid species have been recorded on this shrub, including the beautiful *Angraecum couchiferum.*

It is thought that this selective tendency by the orchid is not related directly to physical conditions, ie. the nature of the bark, but that chemical factors play a part. It is possible too that certain species of mycorrhizal fungi essential in the germination of many orchids and which form a symbiotic relationship with the mature plant, associate with specific trees. Thus orchid distribution could be controlled by the mycorrhiza. It is a common observation to see orchids withering after the host tree has been ring-barked, so the relationship between the two plants is more intricate and complex than has been realised. There is no evidence to show that the orchid is in any way parasitic. Yet, strangely, many orchids, *cyrtorchis* for instance, which succumb on the death of the host tree, thrive happily on dry rocks seemingly lacking in nutrients or moisture.

This short article barely touches an interesting facet of Malawi's flora, one, as yet hardly studied. To the present time over 50 species of epiphytic orchids have been recorded from the Shire Highlands. This gives some indication of the wealth of orchid species this country affords.

I may add that studying epiphytic orchids is a strenuous sport as well as an absorbing science.

THE WILD FLOWERS OF MLANJE MOUNTAIN (1967)

Situated 40 miles from Blantyre, the commercial capital of Malawi, the isolated massif of Mlanje mountain dominates the Shire Highlands landscape. An abrupt, syenite intrusion, its sleep, grey scarps rise precipitously from the surrounding undulating plain. This mountain has seen a continual stream of visiting botanists and naturalists ever since Alexander Whyte made his historic ascent to Litchcnya Plateau in October 1891. None have been disappointed. "Never before," wrote the pioneer plant-collector, John Buchanan, "have I met with more gorgeous displays of wild flowers than those to be seen in some favoured nooks of these highlands". Others have echoed these sentiments, marvelling at the profusion and variety of the flora to be found on the mountain, and regarding the arduous climb to the 6,000-ft. tableland as immensely rewarding.

Several shell-like plateaux, each a world of its own, are separated from each other either by wide valleys or high, distinctive ridges. They consist essentially of rolling grassland and forest-filled ravines — the latter dominated by the famous cedar, *Widdringtonia whytei*. No two are alike. Chambe Plateau, a crater-like basin set within an amphitheatre of hills, and the one most easily accessible — a three-hour climb from Likabula — has been largely reafforested with *Pinus patula* and other softwoods, whereas the Ruo Plateau still retains an atmosphere of wild, isolated grandeur.

The grassland community, considered by most authorities to be a secondary vegetation, having evolved after the destruction of the once-extensive cedar forests, has a rich herbaceous flora. Although dominated by such grasses as *Exotheca abyssinica* and *Loudetia simplex,* the montane meadows are by no means uninteresting to the wild flower enthusiast for the sward is scattered with attractive flowers. In an endeavour to control the annual fires that could sweep the mountain slopes and devastate the valuable cedar, the Forestry Department hoe firebreaks across the plateau and these account for the relative abundance of flowers and also provide a habitat for many of the more delicate herbs — Lobelias and the Iridaccae for example. At the break of the rains in early spring, conspicuous flowers on the bare firebreaks are the Fire Lily, *Cyrlanthus welwitschii* (the common name is rather a misnomer for it belongs to the Amaryllidaccac), the iris, *Moraea carsonii,* and the delightful blue orchid, *Disa hamapetala.* The latter, a common species, has a dorsal sepal conspicuously hooded and a labellum that is frilly and mauve-red. Described by J.D. Chapman, whose "Vegetation of the Mlanje Mountains" gives an admirable account of the ecology of the Widdringtonia forests, as "perhaps the most beautiful flower on the mountain", the Disa appears to be most plentiful at an altitude of 7,000 ft., in swampy ground immediately below the dill's of Manene Peak.

The predominant plants of the grassland are the everlasting flowers, *Helichrysum* spp., sixteen species having been recorded on the mountain. Helichrysum *kiikii* is plentiful, while H.nite*ns* with its rosette of glaucous leaves is widespread. The most attractive is the endemic H. *whyteamum,* locally common between 6,500 and 7,000 ft. (particularly on Linji Plateau), which has its silvery-white bracts delicately flushed with pink, making the plant an ideal component of dry flower arrangements.

A common herb found on the bauxite paths over a greater part of the mountain is the campanula, *Wahlenbergia virgata,* a small, wiry herb with reduced scale-like leaves. The white flowers, of live spreading lobes with a yellow clubbed stigma, bear a close resemblance to the English harebell. In September 1963 a note was made of its abundance in the pine forests of Chambe, where, with the sole exception of Asparagus spp. it seemed the only herbaceous plant not suppressed by the dense carpet of pine needles. Another characteristic element of the grassland flora is the Red Hot Poker, *Kiniphofia* sp., a delightful flower reaching its maximum concentration about 6,500 ft. — it serves as an ideal foreground in mountain photography.

There are many flowers which are common to both montane grassland and to the Protca woodland above 4,500 ft. Mention may be made *of Gnidia kraussiana,* belonging to the Thymclacaccae, which has its yellow flowers borne in a terminal capitulum, rather like the Compositae; *Gladiolus crassifolius,* with its pink-to-purple flowers, their colours suggesting that nature has painted the tints separately, and the rain has caused the colours to run; the white anemone *Knowltonia transvaalensis;* and the Michaelmas Daisy, *Athrixia rosmarinifolia.* Areas of burnt ground hold the Barberton Daisies, *Gerbera abyssinica* and the yellow *G. discolor.* Common also above 4,500 ft. are *Sopubia dregeana,* and members of the mint family, *Satureja* spp.; *Euphorbia depauperata, Cyphia nyassica* (a creeping campanula), *Silene burchelli,* and the orange-throated *Hebenstretia denlata.* Epiphytic orchids festoon the stunted Brachystegia spiciformis trees at the plateau lip (5,500 ft.). *Tridactyle* and *Bulbophyllun* are the principal genera present.

There is an interesting and marked similarity in the flora of the Protea region, 4,500-5,500 ft., and that of the lowland marshes or "dambos", as they are called locally. Thus we find in dambos at 2,000 ft. the orchid *Satyrium atherstonei,* a plant common also in montane grassland but entirely absent from the altitudes and woodlands in between. In the dambos grow also *Gladiolus permeabilis, Xyris capensis, Brachycorythis buchananii, Utricalaria odontosperma* and *Sopubia simplex,* all having their counterparts — allied species — in woodlands above 4,500 ft.

The swampy depressions and seepage slopes at altitudes above 6,00 ft., although supporting a rich variety of plants, have been little studied from the ecological standpoint; in fact no comprehensive list has been made of their flora. Marshes the world over are fascinating sites for the botanist and those of Mlunje are no exception. Orchidacae abound in the damp hollows — one species, the unusual *Holothrix longiflora* having the while petaloid segments so finely divided that the flowers have a "fuzzy" look. The allied species H.johnstonii, a smaller species with pinkish flowers and two basal, elliptical leaves, is abundant on damp, mossy rocks throughout the grassland. Other common species in these wetter areas are the purple iris, *Moraea schimperi,* the Rhodesian Tulp, *Xyris capensis,* a sedge-like plant with attractive yellow flowers, that forms dense, dark olive-green beds along streams, and the gay little blue flower *Utricularia odontosperma,* one of the bladderwort family. The last two species are often found together, especially near waterfalls, making an attractive show of colour. The sundew, *Drosera dielsiana,* flowering in July, is said by Francis Shaxson to be widespread on the mountain but it has been recorded by the present writer only from the banks of the Litchcnya River. On waterlogged ground the Gentian family is well represented, *Sebaea longicaulis* and *Swertia welwitschii* being the commonest, while *Lobelia blantyrensis,* a larger herb than the ubiquitous *L. filiformis,* with flowers of an intenser blue colour, is frequent everywhere.

It is significant to note the presence of families normally associated with the temperate zones — the Ericas, the Gentians and the Campanulas — and the comparative scarcity of the Malvaceae above 5,000 ft.

Above 7,000 ft. the grassland gives way to a broken, rugged terrain that rises for nearly 3,000 ft. to the summit of Sapitwa (in the Nyanja language meaning literally "don't go"), 9,843 ft., the highest point in Central Africa. Sapitwa and the neighbouring peak, Nakodwe, are part of the central massif — a mountain upon a mountain — but the Mlanje range has several other peaks and ridges which top the 8,000-fl. mark. Main Peak, a wild, windswept rock outcrop, set amid a labyrinth of granite boulders, is frequented only by Rock Hyraxes and White-Necked Ravens, with members of the Mlanje Mountain Club calling as occasional weekend visitors. But plant life is abundant; in fact pockets of lichen-hung forest persist to 8,000 ft. in protected gullies, and xerophytic rock-loving plants are to be found on exposed cliffs even at the highest altitudes.

On the summit itself the heath *Erica austronyasica,* the yellow daisy *Cineraria monticola* and the creeping Betony, *Stachys didymantha,* are common, with *Diclis tenella* frequent in wet rock crevices.

Typical rock-haunting plants to be found at the higher levels are *Chlorophytum nidulans,* a tiny white lily; *Aloe mawii* with its horizontal racemes of orange-red flowers; and the large aromatic labiate, *plectranthus crassus.* They are often found associating with one of the most characteristic plants on the mountain, *vellozia splendens,* a shrub growing to 20 ft. in height, that has a grey fibrous stem. Flowering in November, the attractive large white flowers arise singly from the leaf axils -— a feature distinguishing it from the Amaryllidaceae, a family in which the plant was first placed. Early botanists gave the shrub names that matched its uniqueness; Mellor termed it an "arborescent Hypoxis" ; McClounie, a "Yucca". Called by the local people "Ncheu", its soft stern, often covered with tiny epiphytic orchids, proves an excellent substitute for a toothbrush.

Two other wild flowers common over 7,000 ft. deserve mention. One is the yellow Mountain Daisy, *Senecio milanjianus.* An unusual member of the family

Compositae, its leaves being pale green (in the dry season turning a vivid red) and succulent, peltate — rather like a garden nasturtium — with a dentate margin and an amplexicaul base. Seen in rock clefts and other sheltered situations, it is a most striking plant. The other is the widespread succulent, *Crassula globularoides,* a small plant growing in close, compact tufts on lichen-covered rocks.

The cedar forests for which the mountain is rightly famous are found only over 5,000 ft., and at the present time probably do not exceed 10 square miles in extent (Chapman), having for centuries been subjected to fierce annual fires. As long ago as 1893 William Carruthers in his introduction to "The Plants of Milanji" (Trans. Linn. Soc.) remarked, "It is deplorable to witness the devastating effects of the annual bush fires, from which even this lofty and well-nigh inaccessible retreat is not exempt. During the months of August and September these fires, originating from the villages on the lower slopes of the mountain, gradually creep up the precipitous cliffs". Fortunately protective measures by the Department of Forestry have arrested the retreat of the forests in time and their future conservation seems assured.

These forests, though dominated by the conifer *Widdringtonia whytei,* hold, as one would expect, a unique flora . . . indeed the forests themselves are unique, having an atmosphere which is almost primeval. L. J. Brass in the "Report of the Vernay Expedition" gives a lucid description of the relic forests on Litchenya Plateau. "In an abundance of bryophytes prominent throughout, and normally saturated and cold from mist and rain, heavily padded on marginal trees, cushioned in tree tops, and in the moister ravines enveloping the tree trunks and combining with matted surface roots to form a springy and often treacherous ground cover, these were typical cloud forests."

The herb layer of the forest is dominated by the family Acanthaceae: attractive herbs that brighten an otherwise damp and gloomy scene; herbs such as Orange-throated Susan, *Mimulopsis solmsii,* a straggling, shrubby plant, in tangled masses 4-5 ft. high, having large, bluish-mauve flowers; *Hypoestes triflora* and H. *verticillaris,* both having two-lipped white flowers, marked on the upper lip with purple; and the endemic *Isoglossa milanjiensis.* Also common along forest paths is the White Star, *Oldenlandia rupicola* (Rubiaceae — known primarily for its woody plants, coffee and Gardenia), a small erect herb, rarely more than 12 in. high, with a red wiry stem.

Two balsams are frequent in the forests, forming splendid banks of colour near waterfalls, or in the deep shade of moist galleys: *Impatiens zombensis* with its mauve flowers, and the white I. *shirensis,* yet another plant known only from Mlanje. Like the English "Touch-me-not", and the lowland Balsam I. *wallerana,* the ripe capsules burst explosively, scattering the seeds. All the balsams have succulent, juicy stems, swollen at the nodes, and a spurred posterior sepal.

Epiphytic orchids and ferns abound in the sub-dominant layer of the forest, while the tree-fern *Cyathei dregei* and carpets *of Selaginnlla kraussiana* are noticeable in damp ravines. Near the 1,000 ft. Great Ruo Falls tree ferns are particularly abundant — so prolific that they give the impression that one is on another planet.

It is, however, the forest borders and the areas of open bracken-briar which give the finest displays of flowers. The Crane's Hill, *Geranium milanjense,* flowering throughout the rains, is to be found in such places. Although widespread on the plateaux, it was not described until 1961 — an indication of how little is known of the mountain's flora. In fringing forest, *Dissotis johnstoniana,* named after the famous naturalist and administrator, with its showy, deep purple flowers, and the "Pride of Manicaland", *Polygala virgata* are common. A member of the Milkwort family, Polygala grows to several feet and superficially resembles a legume, two of the five sepals being petaloid, and in the form of showy side-wings. On the mountain there are several other members of the genus, one, *Polygala stenopetala,* common about 4,500 ft., having delightful racemes of deep blue flowers, like a row of tiny bells. Flowering shrubs such as *Tecomaria nyassae,* a scarlet Bignonia, the legume *Tephrosia whyteana, Sparrmannia ricinocarpa* and the yellow St. John's Wort *Hypericum lanceolatum* border the forest.

Although Widdringtonia is found only at the higher altitudes, tropical rain forest extends down to as low as 2,'100 ft., in the gorges and moist ravines on the south-eastern side of the mountain. Sited to receive the full precipitation of the summer monsoon rains and enjoying an annual rainfall of over a hundred inches, the forests of the Ruo Gorge, above Lujeri Tea Estate, are the most extensive and perhaps the most interesting — certainly those most easily reached. The little-known Chisongeli forest, immediately below the dills of Manene, has hardly been penetrated let alone explored botanically. These primary forests, akin to the montane closed forests that clothe the summits of Soche, Chiradzulu and the other mountains of the Shire Highlands — "like so many islands in a sea of savannah" Arthur Loveridge called them — are dominated by huge evergreen trees such as *Newtonia buchananii* and the mahogany *Khaya nyasica.*

In Malawi an amusing rumour among naturalists has it that, when Sir John Kirk, the botanist, and a member of the Livingstone Expedition asked a local African the name of the tree, he received the reply "Kaya" — in Nyanja meaning "don't know" or "why ask me?" So he called the tree Khaya nyasica. Unfortunately the genus was described several years before Kirk reached Malawi (1859) and the story therefore — a pity — is apocryphal.

The wild flowers to be seen in the evergreen forest are distinctive although, as in the cedar forests higher up, the Acanthaceae tend to cover large areas of the forest floor, and epiphytic ferns and lianas are again common. *Mussaenda arcuata* with its attractive orange and yellow flowers, the epiphytic climbing arum, *Culcasia scandens,* and the giant lily, *Dracaena laxissima,* are characteristic of the forest, with such herbs as the Acanthus *Brachystephanus* sp., *Asystasia gangetica* and *Brilliantaisia subulugurlica;* the white lily, *Chloroptytum brevipes,* and the beautiful white *Begonia nyassensis* , adorning the forest glades.

There are two plants which, if not easily observed, make their presence felt — the stinging nettle, *Fleurya,* and a creeper, *Gynura* sp., a member of the Compositae which at night emits a distasteful, putrid smell, attractive to While Hawk Moths, but not to humans.

On damp, stony ground the sensitive plant, *Biophytum sensitivum* — allied to the *Oxalis* — and the white Iris, *Dites prolongata,* are conspicuous against the dark, mossy background. Also common, on mossy rocks and logs, is the widely known *Streptocarpus michelmoreii,* with its single, large, radical leaf and bluish-mauve flowers.

For some reason the Arums, and to some extent the Ceropegia creepers, are more noticeable in riparian forests — in reality gallery forest is merely an extension of the evergreen forest — than in the forests themselves. Of the former *Amorphophallus Fischeri* and *Gonatopus boivinii* have been recorded in early spring.

No account of the flowers of Mlanje would be complete without reference to the savannah woodlands that cover not only the slopes of the mountain from 2,000 ft. to 4,500 ft. but, to a large extent, the whole of the Shire Highlands — in fact most of the land not taken up with cultivations. For most of the year Brachystegia woodland has an air of stillness, of impending drought. It gives the impression of uniformity and, compared with the deciduous woodlands of temperate regions, an apparent scarcity of avian life. Although a study of its flora would fill many volumes, a walk through untouched Brachystegia woodland in search of wild flowers, though fruitful, is often frustrating — at least to the present writer — a frustration in no way lessened by the presence of the legume, *Mucana prariens,* the dreaded Buffalo Bean or Hell-fire Bean, the pods of which are covered in brown, extremely irritating hairs, and the equally distressing *Kakwaze* creeper, *Smilax kraussiana* - with its sharp, painful thorns.

Towards the end of the dry season the woodland scene in Mlanje becomes somewhat depressing. The lateritic soils bake and harden. The commoner herbaceous plants, *Dissolis* spp., *Hibiscus cannabinis, Clerodendron rotundifolium* and the Blue Salvia, *Pycnostachys urticifolia,* shed their seed and wither. By October the fires have reduced the undergrowth to ashes. But with the arrival of the rains a remarkable transformation occurs. The chaired embers are washed away: the earth cleansed. Almost overnight the foothills become a carpel of wild flowers.

Two families are prominent in this floral array — the Orchidaceae and the Zingiberaceae. Of the terrestrial orchids the *Eulophias* are by far the commonest, the Yellow Foxglove Orchid, *E. arenaria* and the Bee Orchid *K. cucullata* being the well-known species. Under bamboos, or on severely burnt ground one finds the strange *Nervilia purpurata,* leafless at the time of flowering, the single orbicular leaf appearing later. Several of the gingers, a purely tropical family, are common savannah flowers. The curious yellow trumpet, *Costus spectabilis* with its rosette of four radical leaves, pale green edged with red, is common and the genus *Kaempferia* well represented. The larger flowered *Kaempjferia decora,* the yellow Canna, is restricted to the high-rainfall areas, the Purple Canna, *Kaempferia carsonii* replacing it in the drier regions.

The northern aspects of the mountain, situated in an evident rain-shadow, have a very different flora from that of the tea belt, lying along the southern foothills. In the latter region *Leucas milanjiana, Murdannia simplex* and the ginger, *Afromomum zambesia-cum,* are pointers to the higher rainfall, being uncommon or entirely absent from the northern areas near Palombe. Here we find such flowers as the Orange Knapweed, *Hypericophyllum compositarum,*

Dychoriste verticillaris and the winged forget-me-not (a member of the Rnbiaccae), *Borreria dibrachiata.* The mean annual rainfall is an important factor in the distribution of savannah flowers.

The purple *Murdannia simplex* outwardly resembles an iris in having three showy petaloid segments, its straggling habit and the purple, swollen nodes however show at a glance its affinity to the Wandering Jews, to whose family, Commellinaceae, it belongs. The interesting feature about this flower is that it blooms, like the Rhodesian Pimpernel, *Wormskioldia longepedunculata,* only in the late afternoon; on the other hand, certain flowers, noticeably *Hypoxis nyasica,* the familiar Yellow Star, are closed by midday. One lily, the shade-loving *Anthericum subpteliolatum,* is actually at its best during a heavy shower — a curious feature which has been noted in some epiphytic orchids — its petals, glistening in the rain, make a gladdening sight.

During the rains, from January onwards, savannah woodland displays several wild flowers of sufficient interest to deserve comment. The Pineapple lily, *Eucomis zambesiaca,* is one; another *Lapeirousia grandiflora,* a beautiful red Iridaceae, illustrated in Johnston's "British Central Africa". Yet another is the parasitic *Orobanche minor,* the lesser Broomrape, which has a remarkable distribution extending across three continents, locally abundant in dry Brachystegia woodland. It is difficult to know where to stop.

THE NATURE AND ORIGIN OF BRACHYSTEGIA WOODLAND (1970)

Brachystegia woodland is a widespread forest formation covering a greater part of Eastern and Central Africa. With a range extending from the southern shores of Lake Victoria south to the Limpopo River it is the dominant vegetation-type of Tanzania, Malawi and Zambia. A single-storey woodland, often referred to as "Miombo," it is made up essentially of mixed stands of Brachystegia, Julbernardia, Uapaca and their associates, with a moderate ground cover of grass. As one would expect, it varies enormously throughout its wide range. In the Northern Province, of Zambia a mature stand of Brachystegia woodland forms a light canopy at a height of 40-50ft. and the dominant trees may attain girths of up to five feet,1 while at 4,500 ft. in Southern Malawi it forms what Chapman terms "a stunted,lichen-hung woodland," a formation —dominated by *Brachystegia spiciformis* — having a rich epiphytic flora.

When viewed superficially this type of forest appears to be remarkably uniform, and this has led to them being described by some authorities in very general terms i.e. "wooded savannah" (Phillips 2). This implies that they are natural forest formations as, for example, montane evergreen forest, but this is not so. Studies have shown that floristically they are complex ; not only do they vary according to local and specific factors such as altitudes, rainfall, drainage and soil-type, but they vary also from one acre to another, both in condition and composition. Each "plot" has its own individual history, and the principal characteristic of Brachystegia woodland is, in fact, its striking diversity. A transect through any section of woodland amply demonstrates this. As Hursh noted, in his invaluable study3:

"This paradox of inconsistency in composition, age and condition, from one stand to another, is the clue to the real nature of the Brachystegia woodlands."

The woodland is, as many have stressed, a plagio-climax — a community which has been formed and is maintained by continous human agency.

Schimper4 suggested that savannah woodland came into existence under certain climatic conditions, namely a sharply defined wet and dry season. Gillman5 also considered this type of woodland a function primarily of climate, a view endorsed by Brass6. Willan7, however, had earlier expressed the opinion, in referring to the vegetation of Malawi, that Brachystegia woodland "is definitely a secondary type of vegetation which has successfully asserted itself and assumed a degree of stability on degraded and impoverished soils." Modern ecologists have tended to this latter view.

Moreau in his studies of the montane forests of East Africa concluded that continuous evergreen forest, stretching from the West African forest belt to the Usambaras, may well have persisted until comparatively recent times — probably as late as 12 thousand years ago. Both Hursh and Lawton favoured a similar thesis, in regard to the Central African territories. Referring to the dry woodlands of Malawi Hursh wrote:

"Many scattered remnants of Lower Montane Evergreen Forest throughout Nyasaland do suggest the possibility that there was once a continuous Evergreen Forest throughout the country."

Lawton in a similar vein stated that in Zambia: "It is possible that the semi fire-tolerant Brachystegia and Julbernardia species replaced a moist closed tropical forest or a montane forest."

The extreme sharpness of the present boundaries between Brachystegia woodland and Evergreen forest, with little or no ecotone vegetation, supports this view.

It seems fairly certain that much of the area under discussion was once covered by a closed Evergreen Forest; or possibly, where climate and topography may have precluded this, by a Broad-leaved Deciduous Woodland. Even within the last hundred years there is recorded evidence of closed forest having persisted in many areas. Dr. Laws of Livingstonia testified before the Nyasaland Lands Commission in 1920 that he had personally witnessed during his missionary travels the extensive destruction of well-timbered hill-land in Northern Malawi.

What has led to the degeneration of this Broad-leaved Deciduous Woodland, and its replacement by a relatively poor Brachystegia Woodland?

Two factors are thought to have been primarily responsible for the present forest cover—fire and repeated clearing of the land under shifting cultivation.

Recent archaeological findings indicate that shifting agriculture has been continuous in Central Africa for a very long period. The excavations carried out by Dr. J. D. Clark8 near the Kalambo Falls in Zambia has revealed stone implements from the Upper Pleistocene, together with such wooden artifacts as digging-sticks. And, incorporating evidence from other sites the general conclusion is that man has been present in Central Africa for at least the last 50 thousand years. There is evidence too, to show that man even at this early period knew how to make and use fire.

The clearing of the original forest under a system of shifting cultivation led initially, it is inferred, to profound changes in the soil-type. The burning of debris on the site and the subsequent sterilisation of the soil, the depletion of nitrogen and bases by the growing crops, the exposure of the soil to erosion and leaching, and the oxidation promoted by changes in soil temperature all meant a marked deterioration of the site, with resulting physical changes in the soil. Accompanying this was the destruction of the original herbaceous ground cover, and its replacement by various grasses. Inevitably, fire then came to play an important role in determining the nature of the forest, and this resulted in fire-resistant tree species (that is, those trees now dominant in Brachystegia woodland) being favoured at the expense of the mesophytic types.

Thus it seems likely that Brachystegia woodland is an old-established vegetation-type having evolved many centuries ago. Large areas of Tanzania are said to have been without a settled human population for many centuries, and yet its terrain is dominated by a uniform "Miombo" woodland. The latter has, to some extent, attained a degree of stability, and can virtually be considered a recognisable vegetation-type. Where there has been recent interference by man, however, this is not the case. The observations of Hoyle on the hybridisation and distribution of the Brachystegia species are relevant here. It is suggested that areas where "pure" or distinct species of Brachystegia predominate are probably areas of woodland that have been untouched by man for a very long period, whereas areas in which hybrids predominate may indicate that related species have only recently come into contact through migration, that is of recent land clearance. Lawton suggests that a mapping of regions in which "pure" and "hybrid" species of Brachystegia predominate would perhaps throw some light on the past distribution of vegetation-types. The distribution pattern of the epiphytic orchidaceae in "Miombo" woodland may also contribute to this question.

The continued deterioration of Brachystegia woodland in recent centuries has been facilitated by the southerly migration of the Bantu. Coming into Central Africa from the Congo Basin about three hundred years ago they were largely a forest people, practising a form of shifting agriculture. But their numbers were both small and scattered, and consequently the woodland was given ample opportunity to regenerate itself. Nevertheless, the incidence of fire during the dry season continued as before, hampering any progressive trend towards the climatic climax. And. as Lawton asserted:

"It is almost impossible to over-emphasise the destructive effect that fire has on the vegetation in the seasonally dry tropics."

The retrogression of the woodland has, of course, accelerated considerably during the last 50 years. This has been partly due to the tremendous increase in the amount of reclearing for cultivation that has accompanied the rapid growth in population.* Such clearing has been mostly in long-established Brachystegia. But the population increase has modified the woodland in other ways.

The peasant farmer of Central Africa derives most of his cultural needs from "Miombo" woodland. Hoe-handles, hut poles, bee-hives, firewood, grain mortars, bark string, thatch—all these are imperative to traditional African culture, and all stem from the forest. The persistent culling of such products from an area of woodland has a marked effect on its growth and regeneration. Studies have shown that such practices as the stripping of bark for string can result in only stunted and badly crippled trees of the preferred species — often Miombo itself, Brachystegia longifolia — over a wide area. To recapitulate we may again quote Hursh. He writes that "the appearance of the Brachystegia woodlands today is the product of a series of retrogressive forces which have all expressed themselves in varying degrees in different places and at different times in the past. Such forces are still active today ; for example the desiccation of the land under shifting agriculture in a tropical climate, annual fires, livestock and the indiscriminate collection of small wood products by natives."

The Brachystegia woodland to be observed at the present time is, as we noted earlier, diverse in the extreme. Topham9, in outlining the vegetation of Malawi, recognised nine types of Brachystegia woodland, while Trapnell10 gave gradients with key species for the Zambia vegetation. Little ecological work, however, has been done on Brachystegia and the broad outline of its floristic composition given below—based on the classification of Hursh—can only be considered tentative and fragmentary.

DOMINANT TREE-SPECIES OF BRACHYSTEGIA IN MALAWI

	ON DEEP FERTILE WELL-DRAINED SOILS	ON SANDY, STONY, SHALLOW AND LESS FERTILE SOILS
BROAD-LEAVED WOODLAND occurring mainly as remnant patches	Bridelia micrantha Cordia abyssinica Vitex cuneata Erythrina abyssinica Combretum molle Burkea africana	Pterocarpus angolensis Parinari mobola Afrormosia angolensis Bauhinia petersiana Afzelia cuanzensis Dalbergia nitidula
	↓	↓
SECONDARY WOODLAND after cutting and clearing. Without fire regeneration includes many original species but with increase in these.	Piliostigma thonningii Acacia campylacantha Brachystegia boehmii Brachystegia appendiculata	Brachystegia floribunda Brachystegia spiciformis Terminalia sericea Faurea saligna Uapaca kirkiana Julbernardia globiflora
	↓	↓
SECONDARY WOODLAND with severe annual burning.	Brachystegia appendiculata Brachystegia bussei	Brachystegia boehmii Brachystegia spiciformis Brachystegia floribunda Brachystegia longifolia Julbernardia globiflora Uapaca kirkiana Cussonia kirkii Monotes africanas
	↘	↙

Leading to progressive stages of deterioration through annual fires, soil erosion, etc., in the following sequence:

• The population of Malawi, for instance, trebled in this period

1. Open Brachystegia/Uapaca woodland with conspicuous grass understory, and such elements as Protea, Cussonia and others.

2. Almost pure stands of Uapaca on eroding infertile soils.

3. Almost pure stands of Brachstegia spiciformis or B. taxifolia at high elevations and rocky spurs.

4. Open semi-scrub with Cussonia, Diplorrhynchus, etc., produced by over-grazing with spare grass and progressive exposure of soil.
5. Further deterioration of the scrub, with active sheet and gulley erosion.

At the present time Brachystegia woodland has largely disappeared in areas near the centres of population, and African agriculture is thus undergoing a transi-tion from a system of shifting agriculture to one akin to the European system of crop-rotation. The long-term effects of this are unforeseeable, but it is likely to lead to a marked change in the vegetation-types of Central and Eastern Africa. Some writers have conjectured that in the next two or three decades "Miombo" woodland will virtually disappear, to be replaced by open savannah and grassland.

Compared with evergreen forest, Brachystegia woodland has a poor herbaceous flora, and is noticeably lacking in both a scrubby understorey and a dense growth of scandent plants. The grass cover is usually sparse and poor in quality, with the genera *Hyprrhenia, Andropogan, Panicum* and *Digitaria* dominating. Despite the relative dominance of the *Gramineae,* herbaceous plants are abundant in Brachystegia woodland. The families *Compositae, Leguminosae* (the dominant tree-species are all legumes), *Malvaceae* and *Acanthaceae* are well-represented, and, as the majority are annuals, reach their optimum abundance at the end of the rains, which in Central Africa is about April or May. Most of the trees are deciduous for a short period during the dry season, and during this time the woodland scene becomes arid, and for the botanist, rather depressing. The commoner herbaceous plants of the genera *Dissotis, Vernonia, Dolichos, Hibiscus* and *Coreopsis* shed their seed and wither. By October the annual fires have reduced the undergrowth to ashes. But with the arrival of the first rains, or shortly before, a remarkable transformation occurs, and it is a phenomenon for which Brachystegia woodland is justly renowned. The trees break forth in a flush of new leaf growth, that has an impressive colour, and almost overnight the charred earth also becomes a carpet of wild flowers. Two families are prominent in this floral array—the *Orchidaceae* and the *Zingiberaceae,* many of the latter, a purely tropical family, having curious trumpet-like flowers.

Wildlife was once plentiful in Brachystegia woodland but their numbers have been drastically reduced during the last century, and, except for parts of Zambia and Rhodesia, it now holds little game. It is doubtful, however, if it is comparable with Acacia savannah of East Africa as a wildlife habitat, but such animals as Klipspringer, Sable, Common Duiker, Elephant, Warthog, Roan and Litchenstein's Hartebeest are typical of "miombo" woodland, particularly where grassy "dambos" are present.

The changing conditions of human life in Africa are reflected in environmental changes. Whether the degradation and destruction of Brachystegia woodland will lead to the eventual desiccation of the whole area, and thus make it uninhabitable to man, or whether we are observing at present merely the re-shaping of the habitat to meet new needs, history alone will tell.

REFERENCES

1. R. M. Lawton. Palaeoecological and Ecological studies in the Northern Province of Northern Rhodesia. KIRK'IA 3. Jan. 1963.

2. J. Phillips. Agriculture and Ecology in Africa, 1959.

3. C. R. Hursh. The Dry Woodlands of Nyasaland. REPT. INT. CO.OP ADMIN. 1960.

4. A. F W. Schimper. Plant Geography upon a Physiological Basis, 1903.

5. C. Gillman. Vegetation-Types Map of Tanganyika Territory. GEOG. REV./39. 7-37 1949.

6. L. J. Brass. Vegetation of Nyasaland. In Report Vernay Expedition. 1946. MEM. NEW YORK BOT. GARDENS 8.3. 161-190. 1953.

7. R. G. M. Willan. Notes on the Vegetation of Northern Nyasaland. BMP. FORESTRY JOURN. L9. 48-61. 1940.

8. J. D. Clark. The Prehistory of Southern Africa, 1959.

9. P. Topham, in J. Burtt-davy and A. C. Hoyle. Check List of the Forest Trees and Shrubs of the Nyasaland Protectorate. 1958. Govt. Printer, Zomba

SPRING FLOWERS OF BRACHYSTEGIA WOODLAND: ARUMS AND GINGERS (1987)

Compared with evergreen forest, Brachystegia woodland, which is a dominant vegetation across a greater part of eastern and central Africa, has a poor herbaceous flora, and is noticeably lacking in both a scrubby understorey and a dense growth of scandent plants. The families Compositae, Leguminosae (all the dominant tree species are legumes), Malvaceae and Acanthaceae are well represented, and as the majority are annuals, reach their optimum abundance at the end of the rains. Most of the trees are deciduous for a short period during the dry season, and during this time the woodland scene in Malawi becomes, for a botanist, somewhat depressing. The commoner herbaceous plants - Dissotis, Vernonia, Hisbiscus, Dolichos are the familar genera - shed their seed and wither. By about October the annual fires have reduced the undergrowth to ashes. But with the arrival of the first rains, or shortly before, a remarkable transformation occurs, and it is a phenomenon for which Brachystegia woodland is justly renowned. The charred embers are washed away; the earth cleansed. The trees break forth in a flush of new tree growth that has an impressive colour. And almost overnight the woodland becomes a carpet of wild flowers. As Tagore wrote; "It is the tears of the earth that keep her smiles in bloom". Besides the orchids and lilies two families are important in this floral array - the Araceae and the Zingiberaceae, and this short note gives an account of the commoner species to be found in the Shire Highlands.

ARACEAE

A large family, mostly of herbaceous plants with many species of economic or horticultural importance. It includes such plants as *taro* and *cocoyam,* as well as the arum lilies *(Zantedeschia)* and the water lettuce *(Pistia)*. Its vegetative habit is thus variable, but mainly they are herbs with aerial stems or underground tubers and rhizomes, and simple or compound leaves.

Its characteristic inflorescence consists of a large spathe (bract) which is often conspicuous and petaloid, and an enclosed spadix, which bears the numerous small flowers. Many of the family emit a foetid smell which attracts flies and beetles. Its distribution is mainly tropical with a few temperate species. About 14 species have been recorded from Malawi.

1. *AMORPHOPHALLUS MAXIMUS*

syn. AMORPHOPHALLUS FISCHERI (Engl.) N.E.Br. Williamson 1975; 37 *Chiwamasika* (dies in the dry season) Leafless at the time of flowering. Spathe large, crinkled, margin wavy, 13 cm long. Spadix protuding beyond the spathe, cylindric, black; flowers greenish yellow. Foetid smell. Leaves compound, finely divided, arising annually from a thick rootstock, 10 cm dia. Fruit, clusters of scarlet berries.
Williamson notes that the corn is pounded, and mixed with water, and used as a wash in the treatment of fever. The fruits are edible (Msonthi 1981), though like many arums, the allied *Amorphophallus abyssinicus* N.E.Br. is considered poisonous (Storrs 1982; 20). Msonthi notes that infusions of the roots are used in the treatment of headache, stomach ache and menstrual pains, though these remedies may well relate to *Ampelocissus obtusata,* which though belonging to a distinct family, shares the same name *Chiwamasika.* Locally common near riparian forest. Flowering at the break of the rains.
BM 65/150   Pwere Str Mulanje 750m November 1963

2. *COLOCASIA ESCULENT A (LO) Schott*

Williamson 1975; 145 *Mtembe, Madumbe, Koko,* Coco Yam
A cultivated aroid with large arrow-shaped leaves to 60 cm, which is widespread in certain areas. The leaves are cooked with potashes, and the „tuber provides a useful food. It seems to have become naturalized along streams in the Zomba district. No medicinal uses noted.
RKB 15612   along streams, Zomba township 960m May 1980 (no flowers or fruit noted).

3. CULCASIA FALCIFOLIA Engl.

Williamson 1975; 181

Perennial climber, epiphytic on trees and growing to several metres, stem with adventitious roots penetrating bark. Leaves elliptic-ovate, leathery, dark glossy green, petiolate, acuminate, to 30 cm long. Spathe greenish-white, rigid and waxy, 6 cm long; spadix almost as long as spathe, cream-yellow, foetid. Fruits, scarlet in clusters.

Williamson notes that the watery juice causes skin irritation and in west Africa is used as a fish poison. The leaves are reputed to be effective against leprosy, and Kokwaro notes (1976; 230) its use as a tonic - ashes taken with porridge - even though causing perspiration. Common and conspicuous on evergreen forest trees in the Ruo Gorge, Mulanje. Seems restricted to montane forests. Flowering in January.

BM 532   Ruo R. Mulanje December 1979

4. GONATOPUS BOIVINII (Decne.) Engl.

Moriarty 1975; 1 *Ndemikangongo, Mperanjiru*

Leaves arising annually, often before the inflorescence, from large brownish rootstock, bipinnately compound, pale green, leaflets ovate 5 cm long; leaf stem fleshy pale green mottled with purple, often swollen, 90 cm long. Flowers 2-3 arising at the base of leaf stem; spathe narrow pale greyish green streaked with brown; spadix creamy yellow 14 cm long. Fruits, clusters of red berries.

The rootstock and root are reputed to be poisonous (Williams 1949). Noted as a protective medicine, the roots being pounded, and the powder mixed with maize at the time of planting to keep away witches. Although considered by the Sukuma as poisonous they nonetheless use the root in the treatment of dropsy. Kokwaro (1976); 230) notes that a warm infusion of roots or stem used in the treatment of earache. Locally common near riparian forest, or fringing forest 600-800m, flowering at the start of the rains October-December.

BM 149 riparian tract, Makwawa, Zomba October 1979 850m *GONATOPUS ANGUSTUS* N.E.Br. has been recorded from Mulanje but no notes available.

5. SA UROMATUM VENOSUM (Ait.) Kunth

Herb to 30 cm long, with characteristically spreading and deeply lobed leaves, arising from a bulbous root, 8 cm dia.

Inflorescence foetid; spathe brownish-green, incurved, yellowish green within blotched with maroon; spadix brownish-green, cylindrical ,curving, 14 cm long. No cultural uses noted. Common in riparian and montaine forest on Zomba above 1300m, but rarely seen in flower. Also recorded from Thyolo Mt. Widespread in forests throughout tropical Africa and Asia.

BM 391 riparian forest, Chifundi Zomba 1350m November 1979

6. *STYLOCHITON NATALENSIS Schott* Ndemikangongo

Leaves 2-3, arising annually from rootstock, hastate, leathery, 20 cm long, with sheathing base. Flowers often appearing before the leaves; spathe pale yellowish-green, tubular, and leaf-like, completely enclosing the spadix which is cram 5 cm long. Fruit a cluster of red berries.

As with *Tacca* and *Gonatopus,* with which it shares the term *Ndemika Ngongo* (Yao"back break"), it is left untouched when the garden is hoed; to disturb it is reckoned to cause backache *(Msana).* No medicinal uses noted from Malawi, but the Zulu use a decoction of the root as a remedy for chest diseases and earache. Locally common in Brachystegia woodland, especially on hoed firebreaks 600-1200m. Flowering in late October onwards.

BM 319   Likabula path, Mulanje 1200m November 1979

The fibrous 'bracts' at the base of the leaf stem, which characterizes this species, not noted in the above gatherings.

The allied species STYLOCHITON PUBERULUS N.E.Br. has been recorded from riverine thickets at Chikwawa. An early collector (Feylet) noted that in Zimbabwe it was put in local beer which gave "it a powerful intoxicating effect, followed by dangerous depression".

7. *ZANTEDESCHIA ALBOMACULA TA (Hook.) Baill.*

Cribb and Leedal 1982; 171

Herb to 60m, leaves 3-4 arising from tuberous rootstock, hastate dark green, to 40 cm long. Spathe funnel-shaped, yellow, 12 cm long, borne on fleshy stem 30 cm long; spadix orange-yellow, 6 cm long. Root poisonous, but edible, after several boilings in water.

Locally common in 'dambo' areas, flowering during the rains January-February.

RKB 8648 in 'dambo', in Acacia woodland Lilongwe February 1970

The allied species ZANTEDESCHIA AETHIOPICA (L.) Spreng. from

South Africa has many medicinal uses, an application of the leaves being used for gout, rheumatism, sores, boils and insect bites.

ZINGIBERACEAE

A distinctive tropical family focussed mainly on SE Asia, with about 1300 species. All species have fleshy tuberous roots, or rhizomes, and ligulate or lanceolate leaves. Flowers are irregular and bisexual, and their structure complicated, a distinctive feature being the 2-3 lobed labellum. The 3 outer perianth segments are fused into a calyx tube. The family is rich in volatile oils and several species are used as condiments, species, dyes or medicinal plants - ginger, cardamom and tumeric being examples.

8. *AFRAMOMUM ANGUSTIFOLWM (Sonn.) K. Schum.*

Williamson 1975; 17, Moriarty 1975; 18 *Nthungula (Matunguru),* Wild Cardamon

Erect herb to 2m, stems arising from tuberous aromatic rhizome. Leaves distichous, elliptic, acuminate, with sheating base. Flowers growing from the rhizomes, at the base of stem, white or pink, with yellow throat. Fruits, in clusters, dark red, fleshy.

The fruits are eaten by children. The crushed leaves and stems have a gingerlike flavour. Seeds dried and used as a substitute for pepper in East Africa. Fruits also used as an aphrodisiac. Common in submontane and evergreen forests above 600m, forming gregarious patches, often covering a wide area. Flowering October-December.

AJS34   Zomba May 1963

Another species of AFRAMOMUM is locally common in riparian or fringing forest on Mulanje and Zomba but the flowers are red and yellow. No local uses noted.

BM 339   Likabula R. Mulanje 1350m November 1979

9. *COSTUSSPECTABILIS(Fenzl)K. Schum.*

Moriarty 1975; 18 Yellow Trumpet (Hoyle), *Chikau (Chikasu),* *Khokwa*

Slender herb to 20 cm. Leaves about 4, forming a basal rosette, ovate, obtuse, pale green edged maroon, fleshy, to 16 cm. Flowers arising singly, in the form of a yellow trumpet.

No cultural uses noted but leaves chewed for fevers in East Africa. Very common and widely distributed in moist Brachystegia woodland, flowering November-December.

BM 159   Makwawa, Zomba 850m October 1979

10.   *SIPHONOCHILUS AETHIOPICUS (Schweinf.) B.L. Burtt syn KAEMPFERIA AETHIOPICA Benth.*

Williamson 1975; 302 Moriarty 1975; 18

Manjanu, Mfungululu, Matunguru, Chikasu, Purple Trumpet (Holye)

Erect perennial herb to 15 cm. Leaves appearing after the flowers, alternate, distichous, linear-lanceolate, to 40 cm. Flowers at ground level, single, perianth in the form of a 'purple' trumpet, flushed yellow at the throat.

No cultural uses noted, but in East Africa tubers used as a ginger-like spice. Common and widespread in Brachystegia woodland below 1400m, flowering mainly October to January.

BM 165   Makwawa, Zomba 950m October 1979

11.   *SIPHONOCHILUS (KAEMPFERIA) DECORA Van Druten*

Moriarty 1975; 18 *Manjanu, Ntowe*

Erect herb to 45 cm, stem with sheathing leaves. Leaves, appearing after the flowers, ovate-lanceolate, acute, entire, ribbed, to 60 cm long. Flowers in terminal clustered raceme, perianth segment in the form of trumpet, yellow.

Hall-Martin (1977) records that the roots are soaked with those of *Cissamplelos mucronata,* and that the infusion drunk as a purgative. Common in moist Brachystegia woodland, though rather local, flowering November-December, mainly.

BM 65/267   Limbuli, Mulanje 800m January 1964

12.   *SIPHONOCHILUS KIRKII (Hook, f.) B.L.Burtt syn KAEMPFERIA ROSEA Schweinf. ex Benth*

Moriarty 1975; .18 *Chikasu, Kurri, Manjanu, Mbirichira,* Wild Canna (Holye)

Erect perennial herb to 45 cm, stems arising from a thick rhizome. Flowers in clusters borne on a single stem, perianth in the form of a trumpet, pink-mauve, with yellow at the throat.

The roots are used as medicine for intestinal worms. The local names *Birich-ira, Chikasu, Manjanu* also refer to the cultivated Turmeric *Curcuma longa* L. a native of Asia. This herb is widely grown near villages, and the dried, powdered rhizome used for flavouring relish dishes (Williamson 1975; 182). This herb would appear to be used for a similar purpose although no details available. Frequent in open Brachystegia woodland particularly in drier areas. Flowering November-January.

BM 252   Makwawa, Zomba 850m November 1979 All specimens indicated are deposited in the National Herbarium, Zomba.

References

HALL-MARTIN A.J. 1977 *The Influence of Man and Wildlife on Rift Valley Plant Communities of Malawi.* Nyala 3; 3-32.

KOKWARO J.O. 1976 *Medicinal Plants of East Africa.* East Africa Lit. Bureau, Nairobi.

MORIARTY A. 1975 *Wild Flowers of Malawi.* Cape Town, Purnell.

MSONTHI J.D. 1981/1 *Survey on Traditional Medicinal Plants of Malawi.* Natural Products Meeting, Mauritius pp 129-146.

STORRS A.E.G. 1982 *Don't Eat These: A Guide to some Local Poisonous Plants.* Forest Dept. Ndola, Zambia.

WILLIAMS R.O. 1949 *The Useful and Ornamental Plants of Zanzibar and Pemba.* Zanzibar.

WILLIAMSON J. 1975 *Useful Plants of Malawi* (Revised Edition). Uni. Malawi, Zomba.

MWANAWAMPHEPO - CHILDREN OF THE WIND (1991)

PART I: INTRODUCTION

Some years ago when I was engaged in studies of the epiphytic orchids it came to my notice that many of these plants were well known to local people of the Mulanje District (Malawi) and that the commoner species - *Angraecopsis parviflora, Cyrtorchis arcuata* and *Bulbophyllum sandersonii,* though morphologically distinct, were referred to by the collective name *mwanawamphepo.* It means "children of the wind". Given my ecological bias I thought it quite an appropriate term for the epiphytic orchids, many of which grew high on the outer branches of trees, and in the preface to my book (1970) I even suggested that I was tempted to call the study 'Children of the Wind'. Imagine my surprise, therefore, when undertaking ethnobotanical studies in the Zomba district during 1979-80, when I discovered that the term *mwanawamphepo* was applied to a wide variety of herbacaeous plants and was by no means restricted to the epiphytic orchids. One *sing'anga* (herbalist) I knew assured me that there were at least twenty five different kinds of *mwanawamphepo* - an estimate which, as we shall see, is close to the truth. What, then, did the term signify? In essence, it refers to those plants which are used medicinally in the treatment of a particular disease *(nthenda)* called by the same term, *mwanawamphepo.* As the disease is as compex as the plant taxon, it is the purpose of this present paper both to detail those plants which are subsumed under this rubric and to unravel the meaning of the disease category itself, for which there is no direct English equivalent.

Mwanawamphepo as a plant category is largely focussed around the family Vitaceae. Interestingly, out of twenty three species recorded as having cultural significance, only two members of the family - *Cissus rubiginosa* and *Cyphostemma kilimandscharicum - are* not referred to by this term. Thus, *mwanamphepo* virtually corresponds, as a folk category, to this botanic family. What is of course interesting about this family, which is confined mainly to the tropics and sub-tropics (and numbers about -700 species) and includes the economically important grape-vine, is that they are mainly climbing shrubs with tendrils. Having small inconspicuous flowers they are barely noticed. Thus, as these plants are neither trees nor the type of plant that would figure in Moriarty's (1975) study *The Wild Flowers of Malawi,* many ordinary people are unable to recognize them. Yet, adapted to survival in savanna woodlands most members of this family - like the gingers and yams - have developed large perennial rootstocks or tubers. By this means they survive the annual bush fires. The term *chiwamasika,* by which three of these shrubby vines are known, means 'dies in the dry season'. These storage organs contain chemical constituents that have important therapeutic properties - and these are tapped by local herbalists. In an important sense then, the Vitaceae are known only to two kinds of specialists - scientific botanists and traditional healers or herbalists. But, as I have discussed elsewhere (1983), their reflections centre on quite different aspects of the plant. For the botanist it is the inflorescence which has salience, and from a perusal of the *Flora Zambesiaca* (Excell 1960) one would hardly be aware that plants had any roots or uses! For the herbalist, on the other hand, these plants have no flowers *(palibe maluwa),* and they concentrate their attention on the tubers, which, in terms of utility, is their essence. Many herbalists have an amazing propensity or ability to recognize plants by their roots, and it would be no surprise to local herbalists to learn that the old Greek doctors were called *rhizomokoi* - root gatherers.

Although the taxon *mwanawamphepo* is focussed on the Vitaceae, and *Ampelocissus obtusata* and *Cyphostemma junceum* seem to be prototypical, the taxon is also applied to several other plants. These include several epiphytic orchids (two species are detailed below), two members of a family of mainly tropical lianes, the Menispermaceae (which includes the famous curare) and four plants which are well known throughout Malawi for their medicinal properties - *Elephantorrhiza goetzei, Adenia gummifera, Paullinia pinnata,* and *Pyrenacantha kaurabassana*. It may, on occasion, be applied to several other plants, but the above covers its main conspectus. The taxonomy of the category *mwanawamphepo* can be summarized as in Fig. 1.

Figure 1. Outline of the taxonomy of *Mwanawamphepo*

MWANAWAMPHEPO

CHIWAMASIKA	Ampeolocissus obtusata	
	Cyphostemma crotalarioides	
	C. zombensis	
MPELESYA	Rhoicissus tridetata (Mpesa/mpete)	
	Cissus cornifolia	
	C.intergrifolia	
	C.quadrangularis (Mthambe)	
	(C.rubignosa)	
NDEMIKANGONO	Cissus bucananii	
	Cyphostemma junceum (Mwinimunda/Mwanankali)	
NCHOFU	Cyphostemma subciliatum	
	Cayratia gracilis (nterevere)	
MWANAWAMPHEPO	Cyphostemma gigantophyllum	Jateorhiza bukobensis(Njoka/Kasana)
	C.rhodesiae	Tinospora caffra (Chidyakanda)
	Ampelocissus africana	Bulbophyllum sandersonii(Kalisachi)
	Rhoicissus tomentosa	
	R.revoilii(Ntutomuko/Mdyapumbwa)	Cyrtorchis arcuata (Kalisachi/Mwanamvula)
	Cissus faucicola	Adenia fummifera(Mkuta/Mlozi)
	C.producta	
	C.trothae	Elephantorrhiza goetzei(Chitete/Chalima)
	C.aristolochifolia (Kamutu)	Paulilinia pinnata(Mkandankhuku)
	C.cucumerifolia	Pyrenacantha kaurabassana (Chitupa/Nakulungundi)

Let me now turn to *mwanawamphepo* as a disease category.

One herbalist described to me the meaning of *mwanawamphepo* in these words:

"Ndi munthu amatupatupa miyendo yonse imangotupa kapena ndi nk-hope yomwe ndi manja omwe kupaka mankhwala amenewa kuletsa kuti ku-tupa kwake kuchoke. Mimbanso imatupa ndipo m'mimba mumalira nthawi zonse. Mwanawamphepo ali mitundu yambiri, pali wina munthu amatuluka msungu m'miyendo mwake ndi thupi lonse. Pali mwanawamphepo wina wotupatupa alipo wina wotupa thupi lonse pamodzi ndi mimba yomwe, uyu ndi wamtundu wina, ilipo mitundu itatu ya mwanawamphepo."

A rough translation would be:

"If a person has swollen legs or hands or face, we put on medicine so that the swelling will go. The stomache also can swell and will 'cry' all the time. There are many kinds of *mwanawamphepo*. There is one when a person has lots of sores on the legs, or all over the body. Another, when the whole body is swollen ; and yet another when the stomach is swollen. There are, therefore, three kinds of *mwanawamphepo*."

In talking to many herbalists about this complaint, the ailment appears to involve what to me seems to be three separate symptomatic manifestations. These are broadly indicated in the above quotation, though different *asing'anga* will stress particular aspects of the 'disease'. The first is the notion that the disease involves a swelling of the tissues, or in particular, a swollen stomach. An immediate response of many people when asked about the disease was that the body is *zotupatupa* (swollen). But more important the swelling seems to be localized in the stomach, and associated with other symptoms. A person is unable to eat and drink and suffers from severe abdominal pains. The person with *mwanawamphepo* also experiences a dry, burning sensation in the stomach, and the stomach 'cries' *(m'mimba mumalira)*. Many herbalists in explaining the disease will often make the sound "urrrr.." to illustrate the ailment.

"M'mimbamu mumapweteka kwambiri, mumakolera moto m'mimbamu; kulephera kutenga madzi kumwa ndiponso kulephera kudya nsima; mimbayi kusasamira: ndiye timati mwanawamphepo".

The stomach pains very much and is hot (and there is) a failing to drink water and porridge through cramps: this we call *mwanawamphepo*."

- So a woman herbalist expressed it to me.

The third aspect of the disease is that it involves a skin complaint with water blisters *(zilonda chiluka madzi)* which also give a burning sensation *(ku-fanana moto - like fire)*. Such a rash seems to be quite distinct from such *matenda* as scabies *(mphere)*, measles *(chikuku)* and chicken pox *(sabola)*.

But many herbalists associate *mwanawamphepo* (and it is usually classified as a disease, specifically affecting adults) not only with what are probably digestive disorders, but also with abdominal pains affecting women - menstrual pains and reproductive disorders especially. Several herbalists I knew well described two types of *mwanawamphepo*: (a) *mwanawamphepo_wang'ono*, which was related to skin eruptions and digestive disorders *(Rhoicissus tridentata and Paullinia pinnata* are frequently noted by this term and considered remedies) and (b) *mwanawamphepo wamkulu,* which seems to be specifically focussed on barrenness in women *(mkazi osabala,* a woman who cannot give birth). The term *mimba* in Chichewa refers to both the stomach and to the womb, and the concept *mwanawamphepo* bridges this duality. Thus, not only does *mwanawamphepo,* as a disease category, refer to a specific type of digestive ailment, but also to abdominal disorders and pains affecting women. Those plants referred to as *mwanawamphepo wamkulu - Ampelocissus obtusata* and *Elephantorrhiza goetzei* specifically - are especially deemed suitable for curing barrenness. As with many other communities depending on subsistence agriculture, rural people in Malawi place an important emphasis on sexuality and the bearing of children. The herbs referred to as *mwanawamphepo* are thought to have the property of helping a woman to conceive. As medicines *(mankhwala)* they are described by market herbalists under the treatment categories 'wosula' or 'oimikira. The verb *ku-sula* (of which there is no precise English equivalent) means 'to make someone produce a child'. It is derived figuratively from the expression to weld or forge iron (Scott 1929: 514) and is applied to both sexes. *Oimikira* is derived from the verb *ku-imika* (to cause to stand) and means to make pregnant; to hold, that is, the menstrual flow.

One final point is that the disease concept *mwanawamphepo* is viewed very much in naturalistic terms and almost as a causal agent that enters the stomach *(imalowa m'mimba).*

In exploring the concept *mwanawamphepo,* both as a plant and as a disease category, some interesting points emerge in relation to Chewa and Yao folk classifications.

Firstly, the term is polysemic, and it is quite contrary to Chewa thought to see disease and plants as exclusive domains - for medicines and plants are intimately related. Indeed, although *mtengo* and *mankhwala* are distinct concepts in Chewa, the Yao term *mtela* is polysemic, meaning both 'tree' and 'medicine'. Many African languages express the same polysemy, closely equating plants and medicines (cf. Evans-Pritchard 1937:440; Richards 1969:232; and Ngubane 1977:22 for the Azande, Bemba and Zulu respectively). Many of the folk generics noted inter in Part Two indicate the same phenomenon: for *kutupa, ntchofu, mwanamkali, chitete* and *kamutu,* though plant names, are also names for disease categories or refer to ailments.

Secondly, although it would be quite misleading to suggest that folk classifications are unsystematic, they do not imply any logically distinct categories arranged hierarchically as in scientific taxonomy - as several anthropologists seem to suggest (cf. Berlin et al, 1974). Rather the classifications indicate overlapping 'complexes' and a mode of thinking that is prototypical. *Mwanawamphepo* refers essentially to such plants as *Ampelocissus obtusata* and *Cyphostemma crotalarioides:* yet it is also a general category embracing a wide variety of plants. The twenty-nine herbs that constitute its main *focus are* detailed in Part II. But, there is no clear demarcation of the category, for the term *mwanawamphepo* may be applied, in certain therapeutic contexts, to many other plants. Prototypical thinking, it is worth noting, permeates Chewa folk classification: *mtibulo* is focussed on the plant *Mondia whyiei,* but is applied as a category to several other plants used by men as potency medicines; *napose* specifically refers *to Acalypha sinensis,* but it is also applied to many other plants that are, as it were, general-purpose medicines; the semi-cultivated *Hibiscus acetosella* is *thelele,* but the same term is employed to describe all other plants utilized in the preparation of a kind of mucilaginous relish, referred to by the same term *(Linyololo in Yao). Thus, denje (Corchorus trilocularis)* and *chewe (Sesemamum angolense) are* also categorized as *thelele.* Chewa-speakers describe the prototype by the phrase *yeniyeni* (truly this).

The 'complex' or overlapping nature of the taxonomy is indicated by examining the referents of some of the 'intermediate' taxa (Figure 2). *Kalisachi,* for example, means 'to sit on one's own'. Several epiphytic orchids are described by this term, and so are the parasitic *Loranthus* species (the Ndembu of Zambia have a similar concept (Turner 1967:132-3)). Yet, although *mtengo* (to which most plants in Malawi belong) and *bowa* (edible fungi) are quite distinct types of organisms to the Chewa, several lignicolous fungi, like *Schizophyllum commune, are* also termed *kalisachi.* Similarly *mdyakamba* ('eaten by the tortoise') is a term that is not only applied to the creeper *Tinospora caffra* (a *mwanawamphepo)* but also to the tree (shrub) *Lannea edulis* (both are *mitengo)* as well as to an edible species of Mushroom, probably *Termitomyces* sp. (Scott 1929:289). The following diagram, I think, illustrates the 'complex' nature of such classifications (cf. Vygotsky 1962:72, Friedberg 1979:85).

Thirdly, folk categories vary enormously in the degree to which they are both culturally and spatially distributed. The names of some trees, for example *mwanga (Pericopsis angolensis)* and *mlambe (Adansonia digitata) are* known over a wide area, while others have a very local distribution. And in this regard it is of interest to note that *mwanawamphepo,* both as a disease and as a plant category seems to be confined to the southern region of Malawi.

Finally, as the above discussion has indicated, and as I have explored more fully elsewhere (1983), Chewa folk classifications have an important pragmatic dimension. The taxon *mwanawamphepo,* like the life form category *mtengo,* is not simply a morphological category for it includes trees, shrubs, leaves as well as herbaceous plants. For in an important sense it is a functional category focussed on the usage of these plants as medicine.

Figure 2. Diagram of Chewa folk classification showing overlapping nature

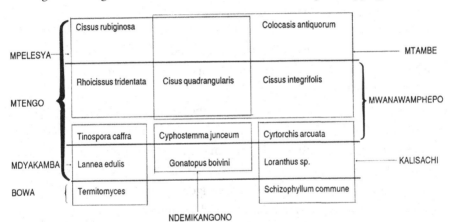

PART II: LIST OF PLANTS SUBSUMED UNDER THE TAXON MWANAWAMPHERO

VITACEAE.

1. *AMPELOCISSUS AFRICANA* (Lour.) Merr.
syn.A.GRANTII Bak

A robust climber or liane with pubescent stem. Similar to the next species, but with a broad ovate leaf, 3-5 lobed petiolate, margin serrate. Flowers small, red, in clustered cymes. Fruits red to black, 1 cm dia.

This plant is a common remedy for the disease *mwanawamphepo*. Kokwaro (1976:225) noted that in Kenya a root decoction is used for leprosy, as an anthelmintic, while the roots and flowers provide a cure for chest diseases. Widespread throughout tropical Africa, in woodland or along forest borders. Has been recorded from all regions of Malawi. [JP 5146 Rumphi, *Brachystegia* woodland April, 1972].

2. *AMPELOCISSUS. OBTUSATA* (**Welw.; Bak.**) **Planch.**

chiwamasika, chifamalimwe ('die in the dry season') - a name it shares with *Cyphostemma zombense* and *C.crotalarioides*.

An erect, robust perennial herb to 2 cm scrambling or climbing over bushes. Stem conspicuously grooved. Leaves fleshy, compound, 3-5 foliolate, each leaflet broadly elliptic with an irregular serrate margin, to 20 cm long, petiolate. Young terminal leaves have a characteristic pinkish coloration. Flowers small, in purplish-red clustered cymes. Fruits red, 1 cm dia. Roots large, with a dark brown or black scaly outer bark, white, fleshy, with red sap. Because of their shape often likened to cassava.

The plant is utilized almost exclusively in the treatment of *mwanawamphepo*, although Msonthi (1983) notes that it is also used in a cure for headaches and menstrual pains. An infusion is usually made from the roots, which are to be found on the stalls of most market herbalists. But the roots may also be dried and pounded, and the powder put in porridge. It is considered a 'senior' medicine *mwanawamphepo wamkulu* and hedged around with taboos. Both the patient and the herbalist must refrain from sexual intercourse during treatment. It is also suggested that the medicine is not active if there are clouds in the sky. Widespread throughout central and southern Africa, usually in savanna woodland or scrub, but noted in *Protea* woodland on Dedza at 1370 m. First noted on Soche Mt. by Scott-Elliott in 1893. [BM 278 *Brachystegia* woodland, Makwawa 850 m November, 1979; BM 435 same locality December, 1979)].

3. *RHOICISSUS REVOILII* **Planch,**
syn. *R. SANSIBARENSIS* Gilg.
Palgrave 1977: 561
ntutumuko, guzanyari, mdyapumbwa (eaten by bulbul)
Small tree or shrub to 3m high, with dropping branches, sometimes almost a climber to 7 m. Leaves 3-foliolate, leaflets lanceolate, apex obtuse or acute, dark glossy green, margin entire or slightly lobed, to 11 x 3cm, falling apart

when dry. Inflorescence cymose, flowers small, yellowish green. Fruits globose, black, to 1.5 cm.

Leaves or roots may be used to prepare an infusion which is drunk as a cure for *mwanawamphepo*. Alternatively, roots may be sun dried and pounded, and the powder put in porridge. Also used as a cure for infertility in women, and as a protective medicine against sorcery (the galls on the tree being especially used for this purpose). Mshiu (1979) notes its use in Tanzania for ophthalmia, while Kokwaro (1976:228) records that the sap of the roots is applied to cuts, sores and burns and has healing and anaethetising properties. Watt and Breyer-Brandwijk (1962:1060) record that the stem contains acid juice which is of value in Tanzania in times of water shortage.

Widespread throughout tropical East Africa and Southern Arabia up to 2000 m. Common in *Brachystegia* woodland especially near rocky outcrops. [BM 421 scrub *Brachystegia*, Zoa, Thyolo 900m December, 1979; BM 672 rocky hillside, Nkholonje Hill, Zomba 1000m February, 1980.]

4. *RHOICISSUS TOMENTOSA* (Lam.) Wild and Drummond.
Palgrave 1977:562

A woody liane to 20m, scrambling over high trees, with tendrils. Leaves elliptic to reniform, almost orbicular, apex obtuse, margin dentate, to 20 x 16 cm, undersurface with soft rusty hairs. Flowers small, yellowish green, Fruit almost spherical, red to black, about 2 cm dia.

Fruits grape-like and edible.

A climber of evergreen or riverine forest, noted in southern and eastern Africa. Recorded by Buchanan from Blantyre (December, 1895) but few other records from Malawi.

5. *RHOICISSUS TฦIDENTATA* (L.f.) Wild & Drummond
syn *R. ERYTHRODES* (Fresen.) Planch.
Williamson 1975:441
Palgrave 1977:563
mpesa, mpete, mpelesya

Small shrub with scandent branches, almost a climber to 10m, with tendrils. Stem reddish brown. Leaves 3-foliolate, leaflets broadly ovate or obovate, with reddish hairs, margin toothed or wavy, to 7 x 5 cm. Flowers small, greenish-yellow, in dense cymes.

Fruits black, to 1 cm dia.

Referred to especially as *mwanawamphepo wang'ono*. Fruits edible. Widely used in traditional medicine throughout Africa, although the roots are said to contain a poisonous substance which causes paralysis of the central nervous system. In Malawi the roots are either infused in a fresh condition or dried and powdered and taken with porridge as a cure for *mwanawamphepo*. Also noted as a remedy for kwashiorkor (the swollen parts of the body are washed with an infusion) and as a remedy for barrenness in women and impotency in men. Harjula (1980:127) notes that pieces of the root (which looks like a large carrot) are boiled and the solution added to soup as a tonic and to give sexual or physical strength.

Palgrave (1977) records that a decoction of the root is used as an enema by Zulu women to facilitate childbirth. Kokwaro (1976):228) likewise records many medicinal uses in Kenya: to ease indigestion and as a cure for abdominal pains during menstruation. Watt and Breyer-Brandwijk (1962:1060) record its use among the Lovedu and Maasai in the treatment of epilepsy and gonorrhoea, as well as a nerve stimulant.

Common in *Brachystegia* woodland and the margins of evergreen forest throughout tropical African to 2100m. Especially associated with rocky outcrops. Recorded from all regions of Malawi. [BM 779 scrub *Brachystegia*, Njuli, Chiradzulu, 1100m, March, 1980; BM 965 on rocks in riparian forest, Chifundi, Zomba, 1350m, April, 1980.]

6. *CISSUS ARISTOLOCHIIFOLIA* Planch.

kamutu

Distinguished from the similar *C.integrifolia* by the veins on the underside of the leaf being 'raised' and the margin toothed. Climber with tendrils sprawling over shrubs, stem with reddish purple nodes. Leaves alternate, simple, petiole 4 cm long, ovate or orbicular, apex acute, margin slightly serrate, thin and pale green, 8 x 9 cm. Flowers small yellowish in cymes. Fruits pyriform, glabrous, black 6 mm dia.

Leaves are pounded and infused or put in porridge as a cure for *mwanawamphepo* and *likango (Trichomonas)*. Also noted as a remedy for infertility in women and impotency in men.

Apparently restricted to southern Malawi and neighbouring Mozambique. The type specimen was recorded by Buchanan from the Shire highlands, where it is common in riparian and fringing forest on the hills. [BM 347 bracken briar,

Chifundi, Zomba, 1400 m, November, 1979; BM 478 riparian forest, Zomba Plateau, 1650m, December, 1979; POW 741 Zomba, January, 1951.]

7. *CISSUS CORNIFOLIA* (Bak.) Planch.
Williamson 1975:124
mpelesya, mbulumbunji (fruits)
An erect or scandent shrub to 2 m with rusty, tomantose cylindric stems. Leaves simple appearing after flowers, elliptic, acute or obtuse apex, margin dentate, 7 x 5 cm. Flowers small, in cymes. Fruits purple-black 1 cm long.
Williamson (1975) notes that the fruits are edible and eaten by children from October to December. Msonthi (1981) records that an infusion of the leaves or root is taken as a remedy for a variety of complaints: oenema, impotence, and pregnancy and menstrual complications.
Common throughout tropical Africa and in all types of woodland to 1800 m. [PT 937 Tuchila plateau, Mulanje, November, 1933.]

8. *CISSUS CUCUMERIFOLIA* Planch.
A liane with angular, pubescent stems; with tendrils. Leaves simple, elliptic to ovate, usually 3-lobed, petiole to 15 cm long, to 15 x 16 cm. Flowers small, in cymes.
There are only a few herbarium records, but it is widely used as a medicinal plant in Malawi. An infusion of the roots is noted by Hargreaves (1980) as a remedy for leprosy, rheumatism and stiff joints.
Known only from the coastal strip of Tanzania and northern Mozambique, extending inland to Malawi; found in riparian forest.

9. *CISSUS FAUCICOLA* Wild & Drummond
A large herbaceous climber scrambling over evergreen trees, to 5 m or more. Stem pale green with purplish spots, with tendrils. Leaves digitate, 3-5 folio-late, petiole to 7 cm, leaflets elliptic, apex acute to acuminate, margin serrate, Flowers small, in cymes.
The roots are sun dried and pounded and the powder put in porridge as a remedy for *mwanawamphepo*. Hargreaves (1980) notes also its use as a cure for kwashiorkor.
Noted from Zambia, Tanzania and Malawi: seems to be restricted to ever-green or riparian forest over 700 m. [BM 419 in riparian forest, Chinyenyedi Str., Thyolo, 750 m, December, 1979.]

10. *CISSUS INTEGRIFOLIA* (Bak.) **Planch.**
mtambe, nthambinthambi, mpelesya.

A large climber with tendrils, growing to the top of trees. Stem with dark red swollen nodes, exuding gum when cut. Leaves simple, broadly ovate with acuminate apex and entire margin, petiole to 5 cm long, to 10 x 9 cm. Flowers small, yellowish green, in cymes. Fruits red ellipsoid 20 mm long. Roots large with reddish sap.

Often described as *mwanawamphepo wang'ono,* the roots are used for a variety of complaints. An infusion of the roots is often to be seen on market stalls in bottles, the reddish brown infusion often taken with that of *Mondia whytei* to increase sexual potency in men. The root is also dried and pounded and the powder added to porridge for the same purpose. An extract of the root, by either method, is also taken as a cure for rheumatism, fevers, influenza, colds, urinary diseases and syphilis as well as for *mwanawamphepo* and general stomach disorders. Msonthi (1981) notes its general and anti-biotic properties. Mshiu (1979) records that it also has anti-fungal properties. John Kirk in 1858 mentioned its use in the making of ropes, while Schoffeleers notes that this creeper is an indispensable element in the *Chikwangali* spirit ceremonies, being associated with witches as a 'dirty' thing.

Widespread in central and eastern Africa, being associated with woodland or riparian forests. Common in Malawi and collected from, all regions and altitudes to 1800 m. [BM 677 *Brachystegia* scrub, Nkholonje Hill, Zomba, 900 m, February, 1980; BM 820 scrub woodland, Masuku, Namwera, 750 m, March, 1980; EAB 612 Mua Reserve, Dedza, January, 1965.]

11. *CISSUS PRODUCTA Afz.*

Climber with angular stems and tendrils. Leaves simple, petiole to 6 cm, ovate to oblong, margin entire or slightly serrate, rounded at the base, apex acute, to 10 x 6 cm. Flowers small, yellowish green. Fruits black or purplish-red, 1 cm long.

Although there are few herbarium records, the plant appears to be widely used by herbalists, particularly as a strengthening medicine: an infusion of the boiled roots being given to the expectant mother.

Widespread in fringing forest from Senegal south to Angola and Zimbabwe. [JP 4580 Lakeshore jungle, 550 m, April, 1971.]

12. CISSUS QUADRANGULARIS L
chiresya, mtambe, lunga
Large scrambling climber; stem angular, fleshy, to 5 cm dia. with tendrils. Leaves simple, fleshy and succulent, glabrous, thick, ovate, sometimes 3-lobed, petiole to 3 cm long, margin dentate, apex abtuse, 4 x 3 cm. Inflorescence an axillary cymes. Fruit ovoid, wine red, to 8 mm.
An infusion of the root is taken for infertility in women and for stomach complaints. Also the plant is said to aid the production of semen. Kokwaro (1976:226) notes that the stems are used to stop bleeding in East Africa, and that the roots are mixed with soup as a remedy for colds. Hargreaves (1980) also records its use for reproductive disorders. Watt and Breyer-Brandwijk (1962:1058) note that the plant is used throughout Africa for a variety of therapeutic procedures, the leaf or stem being used as a remedy for stomach complaints, palpitations, swellings and muscular pains, and as a dressing for wounds, ulcers and burns.
Common throughout tropical Africa and Madagascar, extending to Arabia, India and SE Asia. Widespread in Malawi, but mostly in low rainfall areas. [BM 424 Zoa Falls, 750 m, December, 1979; BM 783 *Acacia* woodland, Chikwawa, 125 m, March, 1980; RKB 8725 Mpatamanga, 230 m, February, 1970.]

13. CISSUS ROTUNDIFOLIA (Forsk.) Vahl.
Robust climber or liane to 4 m with angular stem, succulent, pubescent, with tendrils. Leaves simple, ovate to orbicular, apex obtuse, margin crenate, petiole to 1 cm long, 8 x 8 cm. Flowers small, in cymes. Fruit red becoming purplish.
No names or uses are recorded from Malawi, but Kokwaro (1976:226) notes that the leaves are pounded with oil and used in the treatment of swellings and inflammations, and that the juice is used to wash an infected ear. Roots have a purgative effect. Watt and Breyer-Brandwijk (1962:1058) note that the pounded plant or leaf is applied to wounds or ulcers, and that an extract of the root is a remedy for muscular pains and rheumatism, as well as for toothache.
Common in the drier woodlands of Malawi's Rift Valley. [RKB 8724 Mpatamanga, Blantyre, 230 m, February, 1970.]

14. CISSUS RIBIGINOSA (Welw.ex Bak.) Planch.
mpelesya
A small creeper with both stems and leaves covered in soft reddish-brown

hairs. Stem cylindric, with tendrils. Leaves orbicular and heart shaped, soft and pubescent, acute apex, margin dentate with characteristic projective teeth, 13 x 15 cm. Flowers small, whitish in cymes. Fruits black 7 mm long.

Although a common plant it is not subsumed under the taxon *mwanaw-amphepo,* and no medical uses have been recorded. Fruit said to be edible.

Widespread throughout tropical Africa from Sierra Leone south to Malawi, growing amongst rocks in *Brachystegia* woodland or in fringing forest. [BM 436 *Brachystegia* woodland Makwawa, Zomba, 800m, December, 1979; BM 659 scrub woodland Nkholonje Hill, Zomba, 1000m, February, 1980; JBC 428 Zomba, March, 1934.]

15. *CISSUS TROTHAEM Gilg.* & **Brandt.**

Small shrub arising from a perennial rootstock, and flowering before the leaves are produced. Stem cylindric, without tendrils. Leaves simple, broadly ovate or orbicular, sometimes slightly 3- lobed, margin dentate, to 23 x 22 cm. Flowers small, in cymes.

Noted by Hargreaves (1980) belonging to the taxon *mwanawamphepo.*

Only a few scattered records from Tanzania and central Africa, usually amongst rocks in *Brachystegia* woodland or near swamps.

16. *CYPHOSTEMMA ADENOCAULE (Steud.ex* **A. Rich) Descoings**

A climbing herb with a large rootstock and 5-foliolate leaves.

No names or cultural uses noted from the few Malawian gatherings but Kok-waro (1976:227) records that in Kenya the leaves are warmed over the fire and used as a poultice for swellings and also put on the chest as a remedy for pneumonia. The tubers, which are said to contain tannin, are boiled and the warm infusion drunk in the treatment of syphilis, abdominal pains in pregnancy, and in disorders of the joints. Watt and Breyer-Brandwijk (1962:1057) record that a paste of the roots is applied to swollen limbs and to abcesses and boils, as well as being *a* remedy in the prevention of abortion (Tanzania). Widespread in forests of east and west tropical Africa.

17. *CYPHOSTEMMA BUCHANANII* **(Planch.) Descoings**
syn *CISSUS BUCHANANII* Planch.
Williamson, 1975:190
ndemikangono, namwalicheche, ntchofu (colic)
Climbing herb to 2m, stems covered in reddish glandular hairs, tendrils pres-

ent. Leaves digitate, 3-5 foliolate, leaflets elliptic to obovate, apex acute, margin serrate, petiole to 5 cm with red maroon hairs, to 11 x 7 cm. Flowers small yellow/dark purple, in lax axillary cymes. Fruit ellipsoid, red with short glandular hairs. Plant dries black. Large rootstock 30 cm long.

Fruits are edible. Williamson (1975) writes that the roots are eaten by children when raw, and that an infusion of these is taken as a cure for *nyamakazi* (rheumatism and allied complaints). It has been noted as a cure remedy for dysentery *(kamwazi)* and Msonthi (1983) records that an infusion of the roots has also been said to relieve menstrual pains and to cure barrenness in women and venereal diseases. Among the Lovedu it is a remedy for sneezing.

Widely distributed in *Brachystegia* woodland and forest fringes throughout Malawi, and through central and east Africa. [BM 389 riparian forest, Chifundi, Zomba, 1100 m, November, 1979; BM 513 *Brachystegia* woodland, Makwawa, 800 m, December, 1979; SB 188 Chikala Hills, Januaty 1979.J

18. *CYPHOSTEMMA CROTALARI01DES* (Planch.) Descoings
chiwamasika

Erect herb to 1 m high, stems rather stout, covered with reddish glandular hairs, tendrils absent. Leaves digitate 3-foliolate, sessile; leaflets oblong-obovate, apex acute, margin serrate, covered with short hairs, 14 x 6 cm. Flowers with 4 petals, purplish, in terminal cymes. Fruit ellipsoid-globose, green turning red-purple, 1 cm long. Large rootstock, 30 cm or more long, flesh reddish brown with pungent smell.

The roots are boiled and the infusion drunk as a cure for stomach ailments. Hargreaves (1980) records its use also for depressions and rheumatism. The dried root is frequently pounded and the powder administered in gruel to women "for reproducing" *(ku-sula).*

Common in *Brachystegia* woodland with a distribution extending from Nigeria and Dahomey to Central Africa. [BM 382 amongst rocks near riparian forest, Chifundi, Zomba, 1200m, November, 1979; BM 498 *Brachystegia* scrub woodland, Makwawa, Zomba, 900 m, December, 1979; RKB15040 Malosa Mt. 900m, November, 1977.]

19. *CYPHOSTEMMA GIGANTOPHYLLUM* (Gilg. & Brandt) Descoings

A scrambling or climbing herb with a pubescent stem. Leaves digitate, 3-5 foliolate, leaflets elliptic, apex acute, margin serrate, 15 x 6 cm. Flowers small, creamish in lax cymes.

Fairly common in the Blantyre (Malawi) area. A woodland species found mainly in Tanzania and Central Africa. [HP 12 Blantyre, March, 1969.]

20. *CYPHOSTEMMA JUNCEUM* **(Webb) Descoings**
syn. *CISSUS JATROPHOIDES* (Welw.ex Bak.) Planch
Williamson 1975:125
mnuwakemunda, mwinimunda (owner of the garden), *mwanankali, ndemi-kangono* (a term shared with *Cyphostemma buchananii* and the arum *Gonatopus boivini*).
An erect shrubby herb, to 1 m high, with a hollow ridged stem, tendrils absent. Leaves digitate, usually 3-foliolate and sessile or with a short petole; leaflets oblong - lanceolate, often folded along midrib, apex acuminate, margin in sharply serrate, pale greyish green, 30 x 5cm. Flowers small, purplish, in lax cymes. Fruit reddish purple, ellipsoid, 1 cm long. Large rootstock with red resinous sap that has a pungent smell.
Fruits, which ripen in October-December are edible. The plants are left undisturbed in the garden, hence its name-a term it shares with *Tacca leontopetaloides*. Both plants have very erect stems and it is believed that to hoe them down will cause backache. The roots are boiled and the infusion drunk as a cure for stomach ailments and rheumatism *(nyamakazi)*. Hargreaves (1980) records its common use as a medicine for barren women, and as a tonic for expectant mothers.
Widespread in *Brachystegia* woodland throughout tropical Africa with a distribution extending from Ghana, Cameroun and Sudan south to Zimbabwe and Mozambique. Common in Malawi, where it was first recorded by Buchanan from the Shire highlands (December 1881). [BM 184 montane grassland, Makwawa Peak, Zomba, 1500m, October, 1979; RGT 259 Zomba, 900m, December, 1937.]

21. *CYPHOSTEMMA KILMANDSCHARICUM* **(Gilg.) Descoings.**
namawondo
Climber or liane with a glabrous stem. Leaves digitate, 3-foliolate; leaflets ovate, apex acute to acuminate, margin serrate, 7 x 5 cm. Flowers small, yellowish green, in lax cymes. Fruit ellipsoid, red, 1cm long.
Although not referred to as *mwanawamphepo,* Hargreaves, (1980) records that an infusion of the root, or the powdered root is utilized by herbalists in the treatment of various reproductive ailments.

A forest species apparently; recorded from Zaire and East Africa. [JDC 169 Misuku Hills, October, 1953.]

22. *CYPHOSTEMMA RHODESIAE* (Gilg. & Brandt) Descoings

Erect herb to 1.3 m tall. Leaves digitate, 3-5 foliolate, sessile or subsessile; leaflets oblong-elliptic to obovate, apex acute, margin serrate, 24 x 14 cm. Flowers small, in terminal cymes. Fruits subglobose, purple-black, 1.2 cm. long. Hargreaves (1980) records that the tubers are pounded and turned into powder which is then given with gruel for abdominal pains or "for reproducing". Confined to Central Africa and Mozambique. Found in *Brachystegia* woodland.

23. *CYPHOSTEMMA SUBCILIATUM* (Bak.) Descoings

ntchofu

Climbing herb; stem with glandular hairs. Leaves digitate 3-5 foliolate, usually sessile, leaflets elliptic, apex acute, margin serrate, 10 x 4 cm, often tinged purplish. Flowers small in terminal cymes. Fruit ellipsoid, red, 1.2 cm. long. Roots are widely used, either as an infusion (or wash) or in powder form for a variety of ailments: malaria, vomiting marasmus and impotency (Hargreaves, 1980). Widely distributed throughout Central Africa, as well as Tanzania and the Transvaal.

24. *CYPHOSTEMMA ZOMBENSE* (Bak.) Descoings

syn. CISSUS ZOMBENSIS

chiwamasika

Erect herb to 1m with pubescent stem. Leaves digitate, 3-5 foliolate, sessile; leaflets oblong-lanceolate, apex acuminate, margin serrate, 24 x 6 cm. Flowers small, in sub-terminal cymes.

The roots are boiled and the infusion is given to expectant mothers at the time of delivery.

Locally distributed in *Brachystegia* woodland. Recorded also from Zaire and Zambia. The type specimen collected by Alexander Whyte from Zomba Mt. [JGT 270 Zomba, 900m, November, 1937; JDC 44 Mulanje MT, February, 1957.]

25. *CAYRATIA GRAC1LIS* (Guill.& Perr.)

syn *CISSUS GRACILIS* Guill.& Perr.

nterevere, ntchofu

Climbing herb; stem glabrous with tendrils. Leaves 5-foliolate, glabrous; leaflets narrowly ovate, apex acuminate, margin serrate, petiole to 6 cm long, 7 x 3 cm. Flowers small, in cymes. Fruits green, globose, to 6 mm long.

As the name suggest, the roots are boiled and the infusion drunk as a cure for colic, and for other digestive disorders. Leaves are rubbed on the legs of a young child to make them grow. When rubbed and held close to the nose the leaves give off a powerful almost irritating aroma which is said to cure headaches. Hargreaves (1980) notes its use as a laxative and in the treatment of skin irritations. Not as widely used as many other members of the family. Kokwaro (1976:220) records that the roots are boiled and the decoction drunk as a cough remedy.

Widespread in tropical Africa, and found in many types of woodland up to 1600 m. [BM 263 riparian forest, Makwawa, Zomba, 1200m, November, 1979; BM 971 riparian forest, Chifundi, Zomba, 1350m, April, 1980; HP 180 riparian forest, Mulunguzi Stream, Zomba, 1650m, March, 1978.

Several other members of the family have been recorded from Malawi but cultural data on these species are lacking; they include:

Apelocissus multistriata(Bak.) Planch	C.kervoodei(Dewit) Descoings
Cayratia ibuensis(Hook.f.) Suesseng	C.lynesii(Dewit) Descoings
Cissus grisea (Bak.) Planch	C.masukuense (Bak.) Descoings
C.nigropilosa Dewit.	C.robsonii Wild & Drummond
Cyphostemma congestum (Bak.) Descoings	C.setosum (Roxb.)Alston
C.glanulosissimum(Gilg. & Brabdt.) Descoings	C.simulans (C A Sm.) Wild & Drummond

MENJSPERMACEAE

26. JA TEORHIZA BUKOBENSIS Gilg.
syn *JA TEORHIZA PALMA TA* (Lam.) Miers
catumba root, njoka, kasana (nsana, back)

Perennial climber with densely pubescent stems. Leaves large, cordate at base, and divided into 5 broad lobes, acuminate at apex, membraneous, covered in hairs, petioe to 20 cm, 35 x 40 cm Flowers small, yellowish green, in racemes. Fruits ovoid. Rootstock tuberous, yellow.

This is one of the most familiar medicines in Malawi and its yellow tubers, or bottles containing them, are to be seen on most herbalists stalls in markets.

Used for a wide variety of complaints. An infusion of the root is drunk as a cure for headache, snake bite, various stomach ailments, venereal diseases, backache, jaundice, haemorrhoids *(kanyera)* and roundworms. Githens (1948) notes its use as a bitter tonic, while Williamson (1975) records its use by the Yao as an anthelmintic. Its great therapeutic value has led to the plant being cultivated in Tanzania, and as calumba root being exported to Europe (c.f. Watt and Breyer-Brandwijk 1962:757-8 for details). Kokwaro (1976:160) reports that the roots are used in Kenya for cases of hernia and rupture and also used as a strong stomach medicine.

A liane of lowland evergreen forests and riparian tracts, to 1500 m, it has been recorded from most East African countries. [BM 145 in riparian growth Makwawa, Zomba, 800m, October, 1979; BM 601 same locality, January, 1980.]

27. *TINOSPORA CAFFRA* (Miers) Troupin
Williamson 1975:507
chidyakamba, nsirenda
Shrubby climber or woody liane; stem soft, succulent with conspicuous varicose protusions. Leaves ovate, almost orbicular, apex acute to acuminate, margin entire, fleshy, petiole to 10 cm long, 8 x 7 cm. Flowers small, in long sprays to 10 cm long, yellowish-green.

Roots are taken and roasted in fire and the ashes mixed with salt as a remedy for *mwanawamphepo*. A U.N. report (1978) notes its anthelmintic properties. Hargreaves (1980) records that an infusion of the roots is used as a strengthening medicine and for reproductive ailments. Stems are used for fishing ropes. Common throughout tropical Africa, south to Natal; mostly in evergreen forests. [BM 451 riparian forest, Makwawa, Zomba, 800m, December, 1979.]

ORCHIDACEAE
28. *BULBOPHYLLUM SANDESONII* (Oliv.) Rebb.f.
Morris 1970:41
kalisachi
Epiphytic herb. Pseudobulbs yellowish green, 4-angled, narrowly conical, 5 x 2 cm arising at intervals from a pale brown, woody creeping rhizome. Leaves 2, arising from pseudobulb, green, fleshy, elliptic-oblong, margin entire, apex obtuse, 16 x 2 cm. Flowers marron, small, borne on a fleshy purplish green rhachis.

The pseudobulbs and leaves are pounded in mortar, and an infusion used in the treatment of *mwanawamphepo.* [BM 214 riparian forest, Chifundi, Zomba, 1350 m, November, 1979.]

29. *CYRTORCHISARCUATA* (Lindl.) Schltr. subsp. *WHYTEI*(Rolfe) Summerh.

Morris 1970:105

litulo, kalisachi, mwanamvula (child of the rain)

A large robust, epiphytic herb with woody stem. Leaves distachous, strap-shaped, green, leathery and fleshy, up to 15 x 3.5 cm. Flowers white turning yellow with age, fragrant, in pendant racemes. Roots grey, aerial.

The leaves are used in the treatment of *mwanawamphepo,* as well as reputed to be a medicine that brings good luck in business and friendship *(chikondi).* Hargreaves notes that it is pounded into powder, and taken with gruel as a cleansing agent and in the treatment of diabetes and skin infections. Reputed to be a laxative. Oxalic crystals noted in dried leaves.

Occurs throughout tropical Africa. Essentially an epiphyte of riparian forests or moist *Brachystegia* woodland, being especially associated with *Syzygium* trees.

PASSIFLORACEAE

30. *ADENIA GUMMIFERA* Harms.

Williamson 1975:13

nkuta, mlozi, msambafumu (wash the chief)

Woody climber to 30 m. Stem thick, bluish green, exuding reddish pungent fluid when cut, with tendrils. Leaves orbicular to ovate, usually deeply 3-lobed, apex obtuse, dark green above, glaucous on the underside, petiole to 11 cm long, with glands at the leaf base, to 11 x 11 cm. Flowers small greenish-yellow, hanging in cymes. Fruit capsule, ovoid, green to reddish. Rootstock tuberous, very large.

Only occasionally referred to *as mwanawamphepo,* as with the allied species *Adenia digitata* (Harv.) Engl. Widely used as medicinal plant. Williamson (1975) records that the roots (which contain cyanogenetic glycoside) are burnt fresh or dried and the smoke used to stupify bees when honey is being gathered. The leaves are also put round the entrance of huts to prevent snakes entering (cf. Sweeney 1971: 23), and in Zambia the plant is sometimes used as an arrow poison or to kill fish. The roots are pounded and the infusion drunk, or reduced to ashes and then rubbed into incisions, as a cure for rheumatism. Root infusions also recorded as a tonic "adding blood" and for reproductive concerns, and in the treatment of leprosy and stomach ailments. Kokwaro (1976:171) notes the use of root decoctions in the treatment of anaemia, diarrhoea and gonorrhoea. For further details of its medicinal uses in southern Africa see Watt and Breyer-Brandiwjk (1962:828). The leaves are eaten as a vegetable*(ndiwo)*. The fruits are poisonous causing gastro-enteritis.

Widespread in forests and savanna woodlands throughout central and eastern Africa, commonly on rocky slopes and termite hills. [BM 76 scrub *Brachystegia*, Makwawa, Zomba, 800m, October, 1979; JDC 1155 Bembeke, Dedza, February, 1961.]

LEGUMINOSAE (MIMOSOIDEAE)

31. *ELEPHANTORRHIZA GOETZEI* (Harma.) Harms.
Williamson 1975:218
Palgrave 1977:259
nkhumba, chiteta, chikundulima, ntcheramila, chamina, chalima (as Entada abyssinica)

Shrub or small tree to 7 m high, without thorns, deciduous. Bark grey to dark brown. Leaves acacia-like to 53 cm long, with 10-40 pairs of pinnae, each bearing 20 - 48 pairs of leaflets; leaflets linear-oblong 1.2 cm long. Flowers small, creamy yellow, in axillary spikes to 20 cm long. Pods cylindric 45 x 2 cm, slitting in a characteristic manner, reddish brown. Roots fibrous, reddish-brown.

This species is often referred to as *mwanawamphepo wamkulu* - stressing its importance, especially as a remedy for reproductive complaints. Williamson (1975) notes: "the roots have a high tannic acid content. They are crushed and stirred into ponds as a fish poison, the seeds are also poisonous. The bark is used for string. An infusion of the roots is drunk as a cure for *chiteta,* a disease of women after childbirth." An infusion of the roots is used widely for a variety of treatments: they are pounded in a mortar and the infusion administered as a cure for post-natal pains, renal diseases and to promote fertility in women (Msonthi, 1983); for gonorrhoea and syphilis, *mauka* (a disease affecting young children-poss-ibly trichomonas - which is believed to be caused by the infant taking hold of the breast of a young girl who has not yet reached puberty), headaches, and stomach ailments. Together with the aromatic leaves of the tree *Heterophyxis natalensis* Harv., the roots are used to induce trances at *madzoka* (spirit) rituals in the Thyolo district.

Occur in various types of woodland, both *Acacia/Combretum* and *Brachystegia,* often near rocky outcrops. Widespread in central and southeast Africa. [BM 155 *Brachystegia* woodland, Makwawa, Zomba, 800m, November, 1979; BM 219 scrub *Brachystegia,* Songani, Zomba, 750m, November, 1979.]

SAPINDACEAE

32. *PAULINIA PINNATA L*

mkandankhuku, mkandanyalugwe, mapirano, chika

Scandent shrub or woody climber, with angular, pubescent stem. Leaves to 30 cm, composed of two pairs with a terminal leaf, and a characterically winged petiole. Leaflets elliptic to ovate, apex acute, margin dentate, 16x9 cm. Flowers small, white, in clusters, on peduncle to 11 cm long, which bears 2 tendrils. Fruit club shaped, red, glabrous.

The roots are scraped and pounded and the powder taken in porridge as a remedy for *mwanawamphepo.* Noted also in the treatment of *tsempho* (associated with kwashiorkor). Msonthi (1981) notes that it has diuretic properties and that the root is used in the treatment of leprosy, jaundice, wounds and snake bite.

Watt and Breyer-Brandwijk (1962:932-3) record that it is widely distributed through tropical American, tropical Africa and Zanzibar. Fairly common in Malawi, mainly in riparian and evergreen forests. [BM 420 riparian forest, Chinyenyedi Str, Thyolo, 750m, December, 1979.]

ICACINACEAE

33. *PYRENACANTHA KAURABASSANA Baill.*
Williamson 1975:435

mchende, chitupa, chibulubuda, nakulungundu

A scandent or climbing herb; stems olive green, hairy. Leaves ovate triangular, deeply 3-5 lobed, with almost a sagitate base, soft and flaccid with stiff hairs, apex acute or rounded, petiole to 6 cm long, 9 x 7 cm. Flowers small, yellow orange, 2 cm dia. Rootstock large.

This is about the only plant noted in *Flora Zambesiaca* (Excell 1960) as having medicinal value (as poultice). Widely used, particularly by women, as a cure for a number of ailments: the roots are dried and pounded and the brown powder taken in porridge as a remedy for roundworms *(njokaja m'mimba)*, stomach disorders, rheumatism and lumbago, chancroid and other venereal diseases, and infertility in both sexes. Sometimes an infusion is drunk. Williamson (1975) notes that the fruits are eaten.

Frequent in dry *Brachystegia* woodland, especially near rocks and termite mounds. Distributed throughout south-east Africa. [BM 234 scrub *Brachystegia* woodland, Makwawa, Zomba, November, 1979.]

ACKNOWLEDGEMENTS

I am grateful to many people for help and encouragement in my botanical studies, but with respect to the present paper I should particularly like to thank the following:

Bruce Hargreaves, Flocy Sande, Benson Zuwani, Simon Nkhoma, Pilato Mbasa, Hassam Patel, Elias Banda and Efie Ncherawata.

REFERENCES

BERLIN, B., D.E. BREEDLOVE & P.M. RAVEN (1974) *Principles of Tzeltol plant classification,* Academic Press, New York.

EVANS-PRITCHARD, E.E. (1937) *Witchcraft, oracles and magic amongst the Azande.* Clarendon, Oxford.

GITHENS, T.S. (1948) *Drug plants of Africa.* University Pennsylvania Press.

HARGREAVES, B.J. (1980) *Personal communications.*

EXELL, A.W. & H. WILD (1960-) *Flora zambesiaca.* Crown Agents, London.

FRIEDBERG, C. (1979) Socially significant plant species and their taxonomic position among the Bunaq of Central Timor. *In:* R.

Ellen and D. Reason (Eds.) *Classifications in their social context.* Academic Press, London.

HARJULA, R. (1980) Mirau and his practice. Tri-Med., London.

KOKWARO, J.O. (1976) *Medicinal plants of East Africa.* East African Literature Bureau, Nairobi.

MORIARTY, A. (1975) *Wild flowers of Malawi.* Purnell, Cape Town.

MORRIS, B. (1970) *Epiphytic orchids of Malawi.* Society of Malawi, Blantyre.

MORRIS, B. (1983) The pragmatics of folk classifications. *J. Ethnobiology.* 4(1):45-60.

MSHIU, E.N. (1979) *Traditional medicine and modern medicine.* OAU Symposim.

MSONTHI, J.D. (1981) *A survey of traditional plants of Malawi.* Natural Products Conference, Mauritius.

MSONTHI, J.D. (1983) *Traditional medicine research in Malawi.* UNICEF Conference, Lilongwe, Malawi.

NGUBANE, H. (1977) *Body and mind in Zulu medicine.* Academic Press, London.

PALGRAVE, K.C. (1977) *Trees of Southern Africa.* Struik, Cape Town.

RICHARDS, A.I. (1969) *Land, labour and diet in Northern Rhodesia.* Oxford University Press.

SCOTT, D.C. (1929) *Dictionary of the Nyanja language.* Butterworth, London.

SWEENEY, R.C.H. (1971) *Snakes of Nyasaland.* Asher, Amsterdam. TURNER, V. (1967) *The forest of symbols.* Cornell University Press, Ithaca.

VYGOTSKY, L.S. (1962) *Thought and language.* MIT press, Cambridge, Mass.

WATT, J.M. & M.G. BREYER-BRANDWIJK (1962) *Medicinal and poisonous plants of Southern & Eastern Africa.* Livingston,Edinburgh.

WILLIAMSON, J. (1975) *Useful plants of Malawi.* University of Malawi, Zomba.

BOTANICAL AND HERBAL FOLK KNOWLEDGE AMONGST THE CHEWA OF MALAWI (1984)

The writings of the early European administrators and settlers are replete with colonial sentiments, and often racist attitudes. Even more enlightened administrators like John Buchanan were not without such sentiments. The people of Malawi were often described superficially, and in the most derogatory terms. H. L. Duff, for example, who spent a number of years in the Zomba and Mulanje districts, spoke of the Malawian people as "lazy, squalid, incurious beings", whose mind "remains confused and feeble" (1903; 276). Such writings, which often tell us more about the mentality of the colonial administrator than they do of the people, are full of paradox; even Duff could write of their vitality, their patient toil, and their warm friendship and hospitality. They are beyond doubt, he wrote, "a most healthy and hardy people" (212). And he wrote too of their acute powers of observation and their remarkable facility for learning languages. But given the importance of hunting as a recreational activity during the colonial period — which as Duff remarked, occupied "the leisure thoughts and hours of the European exile" (1903; 140) — it is not surprising that such Europeans came into close contact with nature and with the rural population. The hunting trip (Ulendo), taken at the close of the dry season (Masika), was indeed an important ritual in colonial times.

The outcome of such experiences was, I believe, a realisation by many of these exiles, particularly when they came to write their memoirs, that local people were not only skilled agriculturalists, but possessed a wealth of botanic lore. Duff MacDonaJd, an early Blantyre missionary wrote the following:

"A great many trees are supposed to have virtues. Each native knows this, and becomes to some extent his own doctor. Pain in the stomach

93

is treated by the bark of the Mbawa; headache by rubbing externally with the ashes of Msozo, as also by certain charms put around the temples. The symptoms of cold and shivering is treated by bathing in 'water of the Mkako'. For ulcers they use the Mconde."

(1882; 45)

Around the same time, John Buchanan, a keen botanist, who made some important early plant collections from Malawi, made the following observations:

"It is interesting to notice how the natives have found names for many trees, shrubs and herbs. I have no doubt each name has its own meaning, although it would require a long time to find out one half of them. In the case of *Biophytum sensiiava* where the leaves of the plant immediately close on being touched, the natives have styled it Awile Ambujegwe, which roughly means 'his master is dead'. Then, in the case of another, Msukachuma, it means that the leaves and branches of this plant are used to disinfect the head of a deceased relative by washing all together with water. Mlimbi is the name of a species of *Euphorbia,* from which they make bird lime, and the word simply means stick fast, or hold fast. These are merely specimens of a vast number of great interest, if one (only) had the time".

(18S5;91)

The general picture to emerge from Buchanan's book on the Shire Highlands, and from other writings of the same period (of Livingstone 1887, Johnson 1922) is of an industrious people growing a wide variety of crops, and engaged in trade, cotton-spinning, and metalwork, and where there was evidently a high degree of sexual equality. Their knowledge of the plant world impressed many of these early European settlers and administrators, and Johnston's compendium of information on Malawi, published in 1897, included an essay by Harry Kambwiri on the useful trees of what was then British Central Africa. Based only on a school essay, it lists about 100 species, and includes a good deal of information on the medicinal uses of many trees. Although these Europeans seemed only too eager to highlight the more "exotic" aspects of Chewa (or Yao) culture — and contemporary anthropologists are not immune from the same tendency — such writings did indicate the wealth of knowledge that the indigenous people had of the natural world. When the Rev. Johnson records that Mombo makes the best bark cloth and rope; that Nchenga is good for hoe handles, and that the leaves of the Mbapa are pounded in a mortar and mixed with water to be used as medicine to bathe a sick child (1922; 66) he had absorbed local folk knowledge, and presented it to a wider audience.

And when Livingstone recorded Bishop Mackenzie's remark, that one of his objects of going out to Africa was to teach the people agriculture, only to discover that "they know far more about it than I do" (Livingstone 1887; 357) he was but indicating that no person or community has a monopoly of knowledge. But perhaps the most interesting observation comes from the pen of Hans Coudenhove, who lived, around 1912, in the Chikala Hills, close to where I undertook my own researches. Sensing the "beautiful harmony" with nature which local people had and which MacDonald perceived, and aware that when it came to cruelty to animals, it was the Europeans themselves who were often the "pioneers" (53), Coudenhove wrote the following about traditional medicine:

"The native pharmacopoeia, though exercised with superstitious practices, comprises many efficacious remedies for all kinds of diseases; and when the time comes for it to be investigated thoroughly and extensively, it will probably add some invaluable and quite unforeseen data to our own store of medicinal knowledge".

(1925,28)

Coudenhove was thus able to detect the substantive knowledge of plants and medicines that underpinned the traditional practices of the local herbalist.

More contemporary reports on African peoples, particularly by anthropologists, have confirmed these early findings. They give evidence of the tremendous fund of plant knowledge that such cultures hold. I will cite two examples. In his classic study of the Azande, the anthropologist Evans-Pritchard puts a central focus on their witchcraft beliefs and on the role of the doctor-diviner — and thus tends to underplay or devalue herbal knowledge and practices. In fact he consistently tended to translate the term Nguo as "magic", although it is essentially a polysemic concept meaning both "plant" (more or less equivalent to the Yao concept Mtela) and "medicine". The distinctions he makes between "magic" and "medicines", and between "medicines" and "drugs" has I think little validity in the Azande context. But although he puts an emphasis on divination and "magical rites" (even though by his own admission, they tend to be performed only infrequently (425)) — his writings indicate the degree to which botanical knowledge permeates their culture. I will quote some relevant extracts.

"Every Zande, whether old or young, whether man or woman, is to some extent a magician. At some time or other a man is sure to use some or other medicine . . .

When I walked through the bush with Azande they would often point out to me trees and plants with magical uses, since they knew I was interested in the subject. There are a vast number of such plants and trees, and they are employed in a great variety of ways. If it were possible to collect every medicine known to each individual Zande, they would probably number several thousands . . . . they possess an enormous pharmacopoeia (I have myself collected about a hundred plants, used to treat diseases and lesions, along the sides of a path for about 200 yards) and in ordinary circumstances they trust to drugs to cure their ailments and only take steps to remove the primary and supernatural causes when the disease is of a serious nature or takes an alarming turn . . .

Every illness has its medicines which are supposed to cure it. Azande must know hundreds of different plants which yield drugs. A single man, however well informed, will not know more than two or three hundred, but if the knowledge of all could be pooled I believe we could compile a list of well over a thousand different plants used as drugs".
(1937; 432–82)

Evans-Pritchard grew tired of collecting the names of the innumerable medicinal plants (few of which he could identify) and lacked the curiosity either to collect them or to see if they had therapeutic value (though he was often ill in the Field). But these extracts suffice to indicate the crucial importance of plant medicines in Azande culture"! Although Evans-Pritchard is often lauded for his phenomenological approach to cultural understanding, his focus on the "mystical", as opposed to the "empirical" aspects of Azande culture — to employ his own terminology — seriously distorts the ethnographic evidence. This is why, as many have sensed, the book is so full of paradox, and interest.

The second illustration is taken from another classic of functionalist anthropology, the Krige's important study of

the Lovedu of the Transvaal. It gives a dimension that is lacking in Evans-Pritchard's work. The Krige's write:

"A whole volume could be written on the interest of the average man or woman in the flora alone. He knows a great deal about almost every plant. Even a herdboy, as we found in discussing our list of names of plants, could mention one or two practical uses of more than half of them. Young men could add several medical or magical uses, while old men could bring the names into relation with a bewildering number of ritual, religious or other occasions, and many had specialised knowledge according to the nature of their occupations or interests. Speaking generally ... we find that of the 500 plants we have listed, 200 have merely economic uses ... over 100 are known more particularly for their edible fruits or roots and 45 are greens or relishes; 230 are well known in the everyday medical pharmacopoeia, and of these 60 are magical..."

And they continue,

"What is striking is that the ordinary man regards the flora from a most practical point of view. Only a small proportion of the well-known plants have uses which are mainly magical, and knowledge based on empirical observation overshadows that derived from mystical conceptions ... In 90 out of 100 cases, the quality of the wood, not any magical manipulation, is important for the purpose to which it is put, especially if the purpose is economic; and it is in this sense that empirical knowledge is highly developed. Even in the medical sphere, which is predominantly magical, the ordinary man places his faith in the observed action of the herb he uses ... Among doctors, of course, all sorts of magical remedies are added; but that is the sphere of the specialist. The ordinary man uses remedies of which the visible effects are empirically related to the disturbances which he conceives to be the causes of the disease".

(1943; 47-48)

In the above paragraphs we have introduced some historical and comparative ethnographical material. From this discussion several points of interest I think emerge. Firstly, all the evidence suggests that African peasant communities have a wealth of botanical knowledge, for when an anthropologist can walk but 200 yards along a village path and be informed about a hundred medicinal plants growing along it, we have I think a good indication of the crucial role that plants play in such communities. This contrasts, I think, significantly with that of many other cultures.

I have elsewhere discussed the *relative* disinterest that the Hill Pandaram, a forest community in South India have in folk classifications, and in this context it is worth noting Lee's observations on the !Kung. Like the Hill Pandaram, who are also hunter-gatherers, the !Kung are "superb botanists and naturalists, with an intimate knowledge of their natural environment" (1979, 158). Their knowledge of edible plants is particularly impressive. Yet only one species of mushroom is eaten by them, and of the two hundred species of plants known to them, only seventy are noted as having medicinal value. "Medicine" is not even listed in the index of the book. When the 'Kung suggest that their "medicine" consists of N/um, a dormant energy within the body that is activated by dancing — this contrast is significantly invoked, because for Bantu peoples, "medicines" are intricately connected with plant substances.

Secondly, and linked to this, many writers have been impressed with the eagerness and the fluency with which African peasant communities are able to discuss plant nomenclature and usage. This point struck me many years ago, when living at Zoa. It is broached by W. Gilges, who made a pioneering study of the medicinal plants of one district in Zambia. He wrote:

> "It has always been a surprise to me to find with what eagerness Balovale were ready and willing to talk about their medicines . . . Was it an exchange of information amongst colleagues? . . . Whatever the reason, the information was readily forthcoming..."

Gilges 1955; 20)

Yet Coudenhove spoke of traditional doctors as being "notoriously reticent", and many have written about the guarded secrets of African medicine. There is no contradiction really. For the important point is that there are variations in both the degree and type of folk knowledge. This leads me to a final point, namely that the literature indicates the importance of distinguishing between three levels of botanical knowledge, and consequently between three contexts in the treatment of illness and misfortune — the everyday, the phytotherapeutic and the ritual contexts. These three domains are not rigidly demarcated or separated, particularly in relation to the plants utilised as medicines, but it is nonetheless important to distinguish them. For all too easily the role of the specialist herbalist gets ignored, or as with Evans-Pritchard, considered completely secondary to that of the diviner. Indeed, in the new revised editions of that text, the material on leechcraft (herbalism) has largely been excluded.

After these introductory remarks, let me now turn to the contemporary situation in Malawi.

Having lived for more than seven years in the rural areas of Thyolo and Mulanje, and with a keen interest in botanical studies, it long ago came to my attention that local Malawians had an impressive knowledge of the local flora. Daily during the wet season one would see women collecting mushrooms in the *Brachystegia* woodlands, and it was common to see individuals, of both sexes, in the bush digging up roots for medicinal purposes. Almost without prompting people would indicate the names of certain trees or herbs, and long discussions would often spontaneously ensue about their names and usage, or potential usage as medicines. Frequently one came across trees — like *Brienadia microcephala* — whose bark clearly indicated numerous visitations by individuals looking for medicine, or one would notice recent diggings at the base of such plants as *Adenia gummifera*. Both in Thyolo and Mulanje I became aware of individuals who were locally reported to be knowledgeable about plant medicines, either as part-time specialists or as Asing'anga and several became botanical assistants, and eventually firm friends. My more recent experiences and more detailed observations have only served to confirm these general impressions, and I can strongly sympathise with Williamson's suggestion that "almost every plant that one comes across seems to have some medicinal value to the African" (1975; 305).

But extensive as local knowledge may be, it is quite misleading to assume that *every* plant in a particular locality is known to the Chewa. Chewa folk taxonomies indicate a strong utilitarian or practical emphasis, but many herbs are simply not "known" to the Chewa, although they may be common locally, even ubiquitous garden weeds. The ferns, bryophytes, inedible fungi and those grasses not utilised as thatching material remain unrecognised, while many trees, shrubs and herbs restricted to montane evergreen forests are little known, except perhaps to certain herbalists Thus although vernacular names of trees can often be used to assist identification, caution is always needed with the evergreen forest species.

To assess the degree and variations in folk knowledge of plants, I made in

June 1980 a small survey in the Zamba district. I took forty different plants, randomly gathered from the *Brachystegia* woodland, and went around the villages inquiring as to their names and usages. I had detailed interviews with some twenty individuals (only one of whom was literate and spoke English). Among those asked was a local woman herbalist, and a Sing'anga (who practised divination). What I learned was essentially what I had intuitively understood from wider contexts and observations and may be summarised as follows:

Many plants are immediately recognised and their names are known to everybody, even young children, although there may be variations in the amount of knowledge known about their medicinal properties or other usages. Such plants as *Dichrostachys cinerea, Piliosrigma thonningii, Steganotacnia araliacea* and *Side acuta* fall into this category.

Several herbaceous plants are simply not within the cultural framework, and are not known. They may be referred to as Mtengo Basi, or, if they have noticeable flowers, as Maluwa Acabe (trees or flowers of no account). In the Domasi area *Lamana camara, Tridax procumbens, Imparicns oreocallis* and *Jusricia striata* fall into this category.

But the majority of plants — thirty-eight out of forty in the survey mentioned — are known to the Chewa, but there are wide variations in knowledge according to sex, age and specialist interests. Nomenclature and folk knowledge are by no means consistent. People may know the name of a particular plant (Mtengo) but be unable to suggest any usages. They may simply denote that it was used as medicine (Mankhwala) but be unable to stipulate specifically what these uses are, or they may suggest that they are known only to herbalists (Nganga adziwa). Alternatively, a person may not know the name of the plant, but be quite familiar with its uses. A good example of this is the herb *Euphorbia hirta,* which is known by many people as an eye medicine; but very few are able to give it a name — Nakameso or Namesa (eye Disa pi. Maso). Usually it is described as "eye medicine" (Mankhwala wa Maso).

Knowledge of herbs is very much a function of age, and older men and women have a much greater knowledge of plants and their medicinal uses. This I think is largely related to experience and memorate knowledge Although clearly socio-economic change, especially increasing urbanisation, have had an important effect on the folk knowledge of plants, I doubt whether, in rural areas, this "lore" is being lost, or disregarded by the younger generation, as Gilges (1955; 1-2) implied with regard to Zambia. In rural areas of Malawi today, people are still highly conversant with the natural environment in which they live, dependent as they are on the land for their basic livelihood and health. The old continental proverb, for every illness a herb is growing, is very much a part of the Chewa cultural ethos.

Knowledge of the plant world, in kind rather than in degree, is also related to gender. Broadly speaking a woman's knowledge of plants is focused on food plants and on such folk medicines that are related to illnesses specifically affecting children and women.

Thus men know little about plants that are utilised as Ndiwo (relish) Few men are able to recognise the many species of edible fungi to be found in Malawi or such herbs as *Bidcns steppia, Crassocephalum rubcns,* and *Galinsoga parviflora*. It came as a surprise to me to find that many men did not recognise *Galinsoga parviflora* — Mwamuna Aligone. I asked several herbalists, many of whom had an impressive knowledge of plants and their medicinal uses, the names of the Bowa (edible fungi) that they knew, and invariably drew a blank. Alternatively men have a much deeper knowledge of those trees used for building purposes, or for cordage and on the whole, tend to be more conversant with the medicinal uses of the commoner trees.

Finally, as expected, specialist herbalists and diviners have a much more extensive and detailed knowledge of the plant world than has the ordinary villager. Recognition of many important medicinal plants, like those subsumed under the taxon Mwana wa mphepo — *Cyphostcmma juncfum,* and *Cissus crotalariodes* for example — seems to be restricted to those who have a specialist interest in medicines, even though they may not necessarily be a practising Sing'anga.

The importance of medicinal plants in the everyday life of the Chewa is also illustrated by simply observing a typical village setting. Although the distinction between the village (mudzi) and the woodland (thengo) has important symbolic and cultural significance for the Chewa and many other African communities, as writers elsewhere have noted, the distinction in ecological terms is by no means rigid. Moreover though the munda (cultivated garden) is a fairly distinct ecological concept in Chews thought, there is again no rigid demarcation of this domain, and as Elias Banda and I have noted in our guide to the common weeds — the concept "weed" is almost alien to Chewa thought (if I may mix metaphors). For many herbs growing in gardens that have medicinal or relish uses arc rarely "weeded" out. Thus there is a gradation of environments from the evergreen montane forests (nkalango) and untouched graveyards through to *Brachysiegia* woodland (thengo) and fallow land (tsala) to the gardens and village domain. Plants within the woodlands are utilised but not cultivated. The primary grain crops — millet and maize — and cassava are cultivated within the munda. But within the village and even within the kitchen and living quarters themselves useful plants are *allowed* to grow in a semi-wild state.

There is, then, within the village a sphere of protoagriculture wherein fruit trees like mango and pawpaw, tomatoes, chillies *(Capsicum sp.)* and *Amaranihus* herbs are given space and encouraged to flourish (see map). But within this ecological domain many medicinal plants are also to be found. Often one finds such plants as *Boerhavia rrecla, fvicandra physalodes, Cleame monophylla,* and *Chenopodium ambrosioides.* Interestingly the last species, an aromatic herb believed to keep snakes out of the house, **is** to be found growing outside the University dispensary at Zamba. But compared with communities elsewhere, herbalists in Malawi tend to gather their medicinal substances from the *Brachysiegia* woodland, rather than to cultivate them within the village surroundings (cf. Janzen 1978; 163-9 on the Kongo of Zaire. Evans-Pritchard's study of the Azande is replete with illustrations of medicines growing within the domestic domain.(1937:438.)

SKETCH MAP OF TWO HOUSEHOLDS WITHIN VILLAGE HAMLET
MASUKU, NAMWERA, March 1980

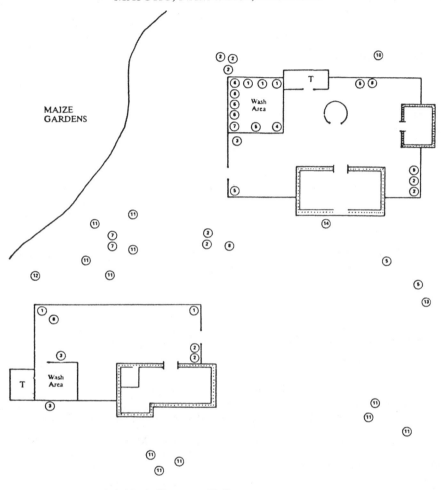

1.Capiscum annuum (Sabola) - Red Peppers or Chillies

2.Amaramhus hybridus (Bonongwe) - Pigweed or Wild Beet

3.Luffa cylindrica (Nsambira) - Dish Cloth Gourd

4.Curcuma longa (Kari) - Hidden Lily

5.Carica papaya (Papaya) - Papaya

6.Ananas comosus (Nanasi) - Pineapple

7.Sida acuta (Masache) - Mallow

8.Lycopersicon esculentum (Matamati) -Tomato

9.Oxygonum sinuatum (Seselesya)

10.Manihot glaziovii (Mpira) - Ccara Rubber

11.Mangifera indica (Mango) - Mango

12.Nicandra pliysaloides (Doza) - Shoo Fly Plant on The Apple of Peru

13.Botrhavia ertcia (Nambenawo)

14.Chenopocliuni ambrosioides (Nunkamani) - Mexican Tea

The above notes give some indication of the wealth of herbal lore possessed by the people of Malawi. The extent of this folk, knowledge is not surprising when one considers that the rural peasant still depends to a large degree on medicinal plants for his or her health care. It certainly belies the assumptions of the early colonial administrators.

References:

Buchanan. J.: *77ir Shire Highlands,* Blackwood, 1885.

Coudenhove. H.: A/\ *African Neighbours.*

Duff. H L : *Nyasaland Under the Foreign Office,* Bell, London.1903.

Evans-Priichard. E. E.: *Witchcraft, Oracles and Magic Among the Azande.* Clarendon. Oxford, 1937.

Gilges. W.: *Some African Poison Plants and Medicines in Northern Rhodesia,* Rhodes Livingstone Museum, Livingstone, 1955.

Janzen. J. M.: *The Quest for Therapy in Lower Zaire,* University of California, Berkeley, 1978.

Johnson. W. M.: *Nyasa, The Great Water,* Oxford University Press, 1922.

Krige. J. D. and E. J.: *The Realm of a Rain Queen,* Oxford University Press. 1943.

Lee. R. B.: *The !Kung San,* Cambridge University Press. 1979.

Livingstone, D.: *Expedition to the Zambesi and Its Tributaries, J.* Murray, 1887.

MacDonald, D.: *Anriorna, or The Heart of Heathen Africa,* Menzie, Edinburgh, 1882.

Williamson. J.: *Useful Plants of Malawi,* University of Malawi 1975.

BOWA: ETHNOMYCOLOGICAL NOTES ON THE MACROFUNGI OF MALAWI (1994)

INTRODUCTION

There has long been, among biologists, a kind *of* aversion towards folk classifications, and the local names of animals and plants have often been treated with derision. This is what an early naturalist wrote about the names and classifications of small mammals in Malawi. And he goes on to suggest that the sooner all vernacular terms are forgotten the better (Wood, 1949).

> "I have added a list of "native" names referable to certain species but would caution any future workers to pay little attention to them. My experience over many years has been that they are almost always unreliable. Having no knowledge whatsoever of systematic natural history, the Africans have nearly always applied a local vernacular name to "groups" of animals that may have a superficial similarity of appearance but not actually be clearly allied".

Rodney Wood was a good enough naturalist to realise the need to record common names, but as you can see, his attitude towards them is essentially a negative one. I have discussed elsewhere the nature of folk classifications in Malawi (Morris, 1980, 1984a), suggesting that there is no "great divide" between folk and scientific classifications. In the present paper I want to look specifically at folk classifications of fungi in Malawi, basing my observations on research studies focussed specifically on the Shire Highlands.

OBSERVATIONS

In his study of African religious philosophy, John Mbiti (1969) suggested that although traditional African culture is permeated with religious concepts, the orientation of this religion is essentially pragmatic and utilitarian rather man spiritual and mystical. If religious ideas have this emphasis then it is not surprising at concepts relating to everyday life have the same stress, and mere is no better illustration of this than the Chewa (and Yao) classification of fungi. In Malawi there are three general terms used to classify the 'plant" domain. *Mtengo* is a very broad category covering trees and woody plants; *Maudzu* covers the grasses and slender herbaceous herbs like the *Aathericum lilies,* while *Bowa (Uwasi in* Yao) is a general term for the edible fungi. Although it may be possible to speak of Bowa, like the English term mushroom, as a general concept for the larger fungi in Malawi, it essentially refers only to the edible species. Edibility is a defining characteristic of the taxon, and in everyday usage inedible and poisonous fungi are not considered Bowa. Any of the latter species when categorised at all, (for, apart from one or two species, they have no generic name) are usually referred to as *Chirombo* (or *Cbikoko* in Yao). The category chirombo is highly complex, but in normal usage it refers to a wild animal, a noxious insect, or a weed - any organism that is useless or harmful to humans.

I have heard it suggested that the term chirombo is not applicable to fungi or plants, but almost everyone I encountered who collected fungi made a clear categorization between edible fungi or bowa, and inedible species which were described as *chirombo.* "It is not a Bowa but a useless thing *(Chirombo)"* was an expression that women often used. Interestingly, several species which are in fact edible, but which are not eaten (as far as I could ascertain) in Malawi, have no common name. Examples are *Agaricus silvaticus* and, at least in the Zomba district, *Suillus granulatus* and *Schizophyllum commune.*

In an early report on local foods the pioneer ethnobotanist Jessie Williamson (1941:12) mentions that in classification of fungi "each district seems to have its own distinct set of names". This is true but what is significant is that not only is there wide agreement about common names within a specific locality, but mere seems to be a common pattern of categorising fungi throughout Malawi. The basic scheme is denoted in Table 4 (Appendix I).

Most women in the rural areas of Malawi have an extensive knowledge of identification and ecology of edible fungi. In my studies I recorded 53 edible species but, because of their varied distribution, few women knew all of them. Most of the women I encountered could name, without difficulty, about 20 species, and I have been on collecting expeditions with women when nine different species were garnered. In my studies of the macrofungi of Malawi I recorded 362 species, fourteen percent of which (53) were named and deemed edible (Table 2; Appendix I). The cultural significance of these fungi are discussed elsewhere (Morris, 1984b, 1987).

The category *Bowa (Uwasi)* is subdivided into many genetic terms, although there is some grouping within a particular genus, such as *Lentinus* or *Cantharellus,* but there are few intermediate categories. Some of the terms that are used to describe fungi are also applied

Figure 1 Nakasuku (Cantharellus longisporus)

to the *Mtengo* category and are in a sense overlapping taxa. For example *Chamasala* is derived from the term *Tsala* (plural Masala) meaning an old garden that has been left fallow or uncultivated. It is frequently used to denote garden weeds, but it is also a name given to *Psathyrella atroumbonata,* which sometimes grows amongst leaf litter in cultivations, as well as to species of

Mycena. Another tax on is *Kalisachi* which roughly translated means "it sits on what belongs to it". It is a term given to epiphytic or parasitic herbs and it has been recorded as a name for the white fairy club fungus *(Clavaria* cfr. *albiramea)* and *Schizophyllum commune.* Thus *Chamasala* and *Kalisachi* are terms that straddle the two main life-form categories in Chewa.

Figure 2 Chipindi (Russule schizoderma)

Figure 3 Nakambvzi (Cantharelluscongolensis)

Figure 4 Manyame (Cantharellus cibarius)

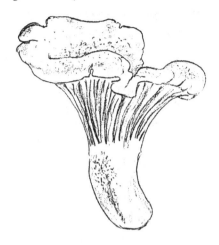

The Chewa classification of fungi does not form a neat hierarchy. Although there is abroad correspondence between folk terms and scientific nomenclature as a glance at Table 1 (Appendix I) will indicate - the same term may apply to species of quite diverse genera. Williamson (1973) earlier noted the problems here and wrote: "The specific names are legion and very confusing for the same name appears to be used for entirely different types of fungi" - different that is to the biological taxonomist. But though diverse species may be grouped together, the grounds for doing so are not arbitrary but based on real empirical knowledge. For example, many mushrooms are associated with that ubiquitous tree of secondary woodlands, *Msuku (Uapaca kirkiana),* and they bear names that indicate the ecological association - *Kamsuku, Nakasuku, Ngunda Msuku (the pipe of* the Msuku). Thus certain edible species of *Lactarius* are put in the same category as the *Cantharellus,* almough local people by no means confuse them, for they usually treat *Lactanusto* a more elaborate cooking procedure, discarding the water after the initial boiling. The names then indicate an awareness of the ecological relationship between *Uapaca kirkiana* and certain kinds of mushrooms. Likewise, two species of *Lentinus* share the same term as the bolete, *Gyroporus luteopurpureus, Kamchikuoi-* derived from the term *Nkbuni*used for firewood or sticks - as all grow on or near dead timber.

Other groupings are based on appearance or texture. *Kanchombo* is a term derived from *Mchombo,* the navel, and is indicative of a pointed or umbonate cap. It is specifically applied to *Ternutomyces eurrhizus* whose sharply pointed cap enables the fungus to push its way through the termite mound. But it is also applied to two common species of *Psathyrella,* one of which significantly bears the specific name *atroumbonata* (atro, dark,

Figure 5 Nyonzwe (Terrntomyces clypeatus)

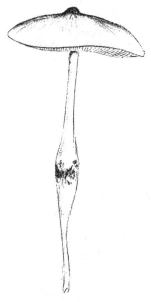

Figure 6 Nakajongolo (Amanita bingensas)

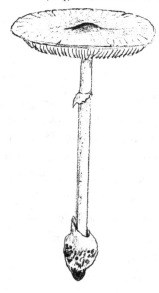

umbilicus, navel). The mycologist, D. Pegler (Pegler & Piearce, 1980), is clearly thinking along the same lines as the Chewa. But other than this feature *Ternritomyces* and *Psathyrella* are entirely dissimilar!

Another widely used term is *Msongolo wa Nkhwali(the* lower leg of the Francolin). This has been noted with reference to a number of very different fungi - *Cantharellus tenuis and Melanoleuca melanoleuca* - and almost certainly alludes to the reddish colouration of the cap, which is mindful of the red legs of this common game bird.

Like all good mycologists, women in Malawi do not put much stress on colour, but when handling and identifying fungi rely more on smell and texture. I have known many women who have suggested to me that they knew whether a particular fungus is edible or not purely by its smell. I found great difficulty, when discussing my specimens with them, to curb their natural tendency to tear the fungus apart, as they always do in verifying the identification of a particular species. If one asks a woman to "group" a collection of fungi they invariably put to one side boletes, *Clavaria* cfr. *albiramea* and specimens of *Lactariusand Lentiaus,* all of which are not highly favoured as food. Then into one category they place *Russula schizoderma,* all of the *Cantharellus* spp., *Ternritomyces schimperiand* an edible species of *Inocybe (Ulundi).* Into another group they put the three main species of edible *Amanita* and *Ternritomyces eurrhizus.* If one asks about the rationale behind this it is suggested that the second group consists of fungi with a slippery texture - *Onse Kutelela* (all are slippery). This is in accord with the folk classification, for the taxon *Katelela* is virtually a generic term for the edible *Amanita. T. eurrhiza* is known in Yao as *Nakatereysa.* Both terms are derived from the verb *Ku-Terera (Ku-Teresya* in Yao) meaning to be slippery or slimy. I never actually heard *Ternritomyces* being described as *Ka telela,* but several species of this genus are clearly associated with the viscid *Amanita.* Again, this links with an important functional category within the *Mtengo* life-forum, for *Thelele* is an important group of plants focussed around *Hibiscus* and similar mucilaginous species which are used as relish vegetables.

Folk generics (Table 1; Appendix I) can roughly be divided into two types; simple generics like *Manyame, Nakajeti, Katelela, Nyonzwe* (which may or may not have analysable roots), and those having metaphorical connotations, e.g. "drum of the baboon", "liver of the tortoise". But this division corresponds closely to the cultural importance of the fungi; all those with metaphorical names are of secondary importance as a food source, and some, like the "baboon's tobacco" *(Lycoperdon citrinum)* are considered inedible.

CONCLUSIONS

Finally it is worth noting that Malawian women see a much closer relationship between mushrooms and meat *(Nyama)*, than between fungi and either plants or vegetables. One woman I knew always categorised a basket of fungi by dividing them into two piles, *Nyama* (edible) and *Chirombo* (inedible) fungi. She almost used the term *Nyama* (meaning meat, or edible quadruped in its normal sense) as a taxonomic category for the edible species. I have often heard species of *Bowa* being referred to as *Nyama,* and many generic terms indicate this association - *Manyame, Kanyama, Mnofii wa Nkhuku* (flesh of the chicken). This association of fungi with animal life, rather than with plants *(Mtengo),* based as it is on structure and edibility rather than on morphology, is probably widespread in traditional cultures. The Chewa clearly see *Mtengo* and *Bowa* as quite distinct categories and the general notion, accepted by Europeans and many past biologists, that all living things belong to one of two kingdoms, plants and animals (with "fungi" placed in the plant "category") makes little sense to the majority of Malawian women. To suggest to them that a particular fungus belongs to the *Mtengo* category, is rather like asking an English person whether a cabbage is a kind of tree. Thus the views of Malawian women are probably closer to those of the modern taxonomist than the ideas of the great botanist Linnaeus.

ACKNOWLEDGEMENTS

This paper is based on studies made in Malawi during the year 1979-1980, and was supported by an E.S.R.C. grant for which I am grateful. I am also grateful to members of the Biology Department and the Herbarium staff at the University of Malawi for support and encouragement. I would particularly like to express my thanks to Moira and Mark Spurrier, Anne and John Killick and George and Helen Welsh. Also to Chenita Sulemani and her sister Esmie, Helen Mgomo, Benson Zuwani, Hassam Patel, Kitty Kunamano, Rosebey Mponda and Salimu Chinyangala for help and instructions in many aspects of Malawian cultural life, particularly relating to mushrooms. I would also like to record my thanks to David Pegler and Leif Ryvarden for identifying my specimens, which are deposited at the Royal Botanic Gardens, Kew and the National Herbarium, Zomba.

REFERENCES

Mbiti, J. (1969). African Religions and Philosophy. MacMillan,London.

Morris, B. (1980). Folk Classifications. Nyala 6(2): 83-98.

————, (1984a). The pragmatics of Folk Classification. J. Ethnobiol. 4(1): 45-60.

————, (1984b). Macrofungi of Malawi: Some EtnnobotanicalNotes. Bull. Br. Mycol. Soc. 18: 48-57.

————, (1987). Common Mushrooms of Malawi. Fungiflora, Oslo,   108 pp.

————, (1990). An Annotated Checklist of the Macrofungi of Malawi. Kirkia 13(2): 323-364.

Pegler, D.N. and Piearce, G.D. (1980). The edible mushrooms of Zambia. Kew Bull. 35:475-491.

Williamson, J. (1941). Nyasaland Native Foods. Times, Nyasa.

————, (1973). Preliminary List of some edible fungi of Malawi. Soc. Mal. J. 26: 15-27.

TABLE 1: Classification of the Taxon Bowa (Uwasi Y, Uwa L) in Southern Malawi

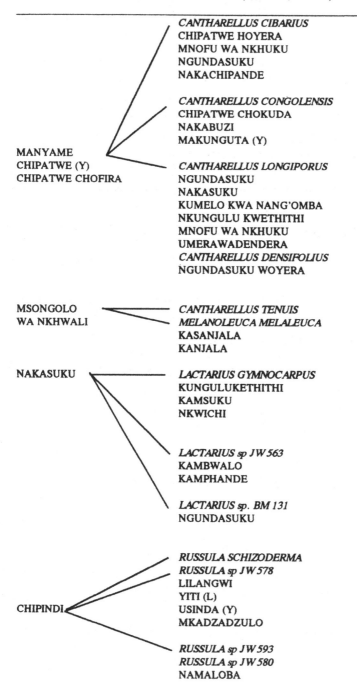

MANYAME
CHIPATWE (Y)
CHIPATWE CHOFIRA

CANTHARELLUS CIBARIUS
CHIPATWE HOYERA
MNOFU WA NKHUKU
NGUNDASUKU
NAKACHIPANDE

CANTHARELLUS CONGOLENSIS
CHIPATWE CHOKUDA
NAKABUZI
MAKUNGUTA (Y)

CANTHARELLUS LONGIPORUS
NGUNDASUKU
NAKASUKU
KUMELO KWA NANG'OMBA
NKUNGULU KWETHITHI
MNOFU WA NKHUKU
UMERAWADENDERA
CANTHARELLUS DENSIFOLIUS
NGUNDASUKU WOYERA

MSONGOLO
WA NKHWALI

CANTHARELLUS TENUIS
MELANOLEUCA MELALEUCA
KASANJALA
KANJALA

NAKASUKU

LACTARIUS GYMNOCARPUS
KUNGULUKETHITHI
KAMSUKU
NKWICHI

LACTARIUS sp *JW 563*
KAMBWALO
KAMPHANDE

LACTARIUS sp. *BM 131*
NGUNDASUKU

CHIPINDI

RUSSULA SCHIZODERMA
RUSSULA sp *JW 578*
LILANGWI
YITI (L)
USINDA (Y)
MKADZADZULO

RUSSULA sp *JW 593*
RUSSULA sp *JW 580*
NAMALOBA

114

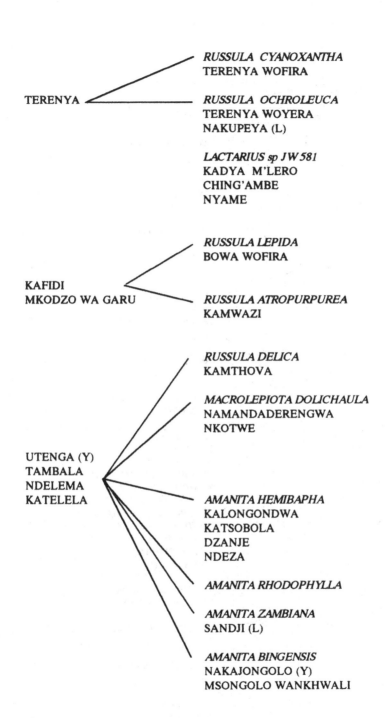

TERENYA
- *RUSSULA CYANOXANTHA*
  TERENYA WOFIRA
- *RUSSULA OCHROLEUCA*
  TERENYA WOYERA
  NAKUPEYA (L)

LACTARIUS sp JW 581
KADYA M'LERO
CHING'AMBE
NYAME

KAFIDI
MKODZO WA GARU
- *RUSSULA LEPIDA*
  BOWA WOFIRA
- *RUSSULA ATROPURPUREA*
  KAMWAZI

UTENGA (Y)
TAMBALA
NDELEMA
KATELELA
- *RUSSULA DELICA*
  KAMTHOVA
- *MACROLEPIOTA DOLICHAULA*
  NAMANDADERENGWA
  NKOTWE
- *AMANITA HEMIBAPHA*
  KALONGONDWA
  KATSOBOLA
  DZANJE
  NDEZA
- *AMANITA RHODOPHYLLA*
- *AMANITA ZAMBIANA*
  SANDJI (L)
- *AMANITA BINGENSIS*
  NAKAJONGOLO (Y)
  MSONGOLO WANKHWALI

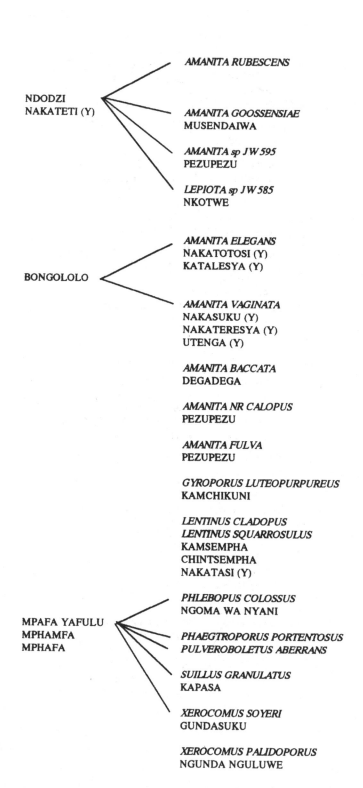

NDODZI
NAKATETI (Y)

AMANITA RUBESCENS

AMANITA GOOSSENSIAE
MUSENDAIWA

AMANITA sp JW 595
PEZUPEZU

LEPIOTA sp JW 585
NKOTWE

BONGOLOLO

AMANITA ELEGANS
NAKATOTOSI (Y)
KATALESYA (Y)

AMANITA VAGINATA
NAKASUKU (Y)
NAKATERESYA (Y)
UTENGA (Y)

AMANITA BACCATA
DEGADEGA

AMANITA NR CALOPUS
PEZUPEZU

AMANITA FULVA
PEZUPEZU

GYROPORUS LUTEOPURPUREUS
KAMCHIKUNI

LENTINUS CLADOPUS
LENTINUS SQUARROSULUS
KAMSEMPHA
CHINTSEMPHA
NAKATASI (Y)

MPAFA YAFULU
MPHAMFA
MPHAFA

PHLEBOPUS COLOSSUS
NGOMA WA NYANI

PHAEGTROPORUS PORTENTOSUS
PULVEROBOLETUS ABERRANS

SUILLUS GRANULATUS
KAPASA

XEROCOMUS SOYERI
GUNDASUKU

XEROCOMUS PALIDOPORUS
NGUNDA NGULUWE

116

NTHANDO ————————— *TERMITOMYCES ROBUSTA*
TERMITOMYCES EURRHIZUS
KACHOFU
NAKATERESYA (Y)
UTEMBO (Y)
UWUMBU
MAZUMBIKIRA
NTOROMWE (L)
NAMATOKHU (L)
KAMBVI
KANCHOMBO

TERITOMYCES MICROCARPUS
MANDA
KAMUBVI
NAMAROKOKHO (L)
KALUMWE

UJONJO
NYOZWE

TERMITOMYES CLYPEATUS
NAKASUGULI
UTOTHI (L)
CHIKUMBAKUMBA
NAKASOWU
CHANJIRA UPYA
KANCHOMBO

MICROPSALLIOTA BRUNNEOSPERMA

PSATHYRELLA ATROUMBONATA
CHAMASALA

PSATHYRELLA CANDOLLEANA
NAKASUGULI
KANCHOMBO

MYCENA sp JW 697
CHAMASALA

TERMITOMYCES SCHIMPERI
NYOZWE WANKULU
USINDA WANKULU
LILANGWI
MANANDADARENGWA
MAZUMBIKIRA
NAKASOWU (Y)
TOROMWE (L)
NAMOWE (L)

TERMITOMYCES sp *JW 602*
KANCHOMBO
KACHOFU

TERMITOMYCES STRIATUS
KASALE

TERMITOMYCES STRIATUS
CHANJIRA UPYA
NAKATERESYA (Y)

TERMITOMYCES NR TITANICUS
UTALE
BAMBOMULUZA
KATSOKOMOLE

STROBILOMYCES COSTATISPURA
MPANDO WAFISI
FISI

GYROPORUS CASTANEUS
KASANGA

OUDENMANSIELLA RADICATA
CHADWALI

XERULINA LACHNOCEPHALA
NKALANGANJI

STEREOPSIS HISCENS
KANJEDZA

CYMATODERMA DENDRITICUM
KANYAMA
NAKAKANYAMA
MAKUNGUTA
MAGUNGUGULI
MASANJALA

KALISACHI
NAKASACHI

SCHIZOPHYLLUM COMMUNE

CLAVARIA cfr *ALBIRAMEA*
KABVISAZA
KASANZA
MASANJALA (Y)
NAKAMBI (Y)

INOCYBE sp *BM 74*
ULUNDI (Y)

AGARICUS CAMPESTRIS
NKOLAKOLA

118

AGARICUS sp *JW 571*
MSOLO WA NKHWALI

AURICULARIA AURICULA
MATWE
MAKUTUKUTU
KHUTULANJOBVU

COLLYBIA DRYOPHILA
MANGUNGULI

COLLYBIA sp *JW 662*
KWASANGA

TABLE 2: Total Number of Species According to the Orders Represented *

	Total number of species	Number of species named	Number of edible species
ASCOMYCETES			
PYRENOMYCETES			
(Flask fungi)			
XYLARIALES	3	-	-
HYPOCREALES	1	-	-
DISCOMYCETES			
(Cup fungi)			
HELOTIALES	1	-	-
PEZIZALES	2	-	-
BASIDIOMYCETES			
GASTROMYCETES			
SCLERODERMATALES	2	-	-
LYCOPERDALES	10	2	-
PHALLALES	2	-	-
HYMENOMYCETES			
TREMELLALES	5	1	1
APHYLLOPHORALES	110	7	6
AGARICALES	177	27	27
BOLETALES	29	6	6
CANTHARELLALES	5	5	5
RUSSULALES	15	7	7
TOTAL	362	56	53

* Derived from the annotated checklist of the macrofungi of Malawi (Morris, 1990)

TABLE 3: Number of Named Fungal Species According to Genera.

	Total number of species	Total number of species named and edible
GENERA		
HYGROCYBE	4	-
COLLYBIA	6	1
MARASMIUS	14	-
MYCENA	4	-
AMANITA	23	11
TERMITOMYCES	7	7
VOLVARIELLA	3	1
AGARICUS	14	2
LEPIOTA	11	-
COPRINUS	7	-
PSATHYRELLA	7	2
CANTHARELLUS	5	5
LACTARIUS	6	1
RUSSULA	9	6

TABLE 4: Scheme for classification of fungi

FUNGI

BOWA (see Table One)	**CHIROMBO**
FODYA WA NYANI *(LYCOPERDON CITRINUM)*	**NO SPECIFIC NAMES** **IN THE FOLK** **TAXONOMY**
NGOMA WA NYANI *(CALVATRIA UTRIFORMIS)*	**:IT INCLUDES INEDIBLE** **AND POISONOUS** **FUNGI SUCH AS:-** *AFROBOLETU LUTEOUS* *AMANITA MUSCARIA* *HYPHOLOMA SUBVIRIDE* *LECCINUM UMBONATUM* ETC

120

NOTES ON THE
GENUS TERMITOMYCES HEIM
IN MALAWI (1986)

Termitomyces is a cosmopolitan but mainly tropical genus, occuring in Asia, Africa and the Pacific Islands. It is distinguished from all other Agaric mushrooms by its long and distinctive stem which takes the form of a pseudorrhiza. This penetrates deeply into termite nests with which this genus is intimately associated. The cap usually has a distinctive umbo, a botanical term derived from the Latin for navel; interestingly one of the common names for the members of this genus, *Kanchombo,* has the same derivation, *Mchombo* being the Chichewa for navel. The gills are free and usually crowded, and the spore print cream or pink. Most species in this genus appear to be edible, and are all highly flavoured. The genus includes the largest known mushroom *Termitomyces Titanicus* Pegler and Piearce (cf 1980 : 479-82), which has recently been described from Zambia. Its cap is up to 100 cm. (some 3 ft.) in diameter, and one specimen weighed 2.5 Kg. The fungus appears to be widespread in Zambia and is commonly sold as food in markets, and as Pegler and Piearce note, it seems incredible that such a large and well-known fungus should have remained undescribed for so long. It features in Bemba stories as a shelter for snakes and antelopes. (Piearce 1981 : 4) It may possibly occur in Malawi (see below). Eight species of Termitomyces have been recorded from Malawi to date, but many more may occur. These short notes are offered in order to stimulate further researches into this interesting group of fungi.

1. Termitomyces Aurantiacus Heim

A medium-sized species with a warm ochre-brown conical cap and a white stem, which typical of the genus, forms a long tapering tap root extending 10 cm. or more into the soil. Appears to be common in early December in cultivations and open woodlands, often near paths.

Cap to 7.5 cm. diameter, convex-umbonate to conical, becoming extended, smooth, tough and leathery, ochre-brown, splitting towards margin exposing the white flesh. Stem cylindric, white, tough, bulbous just below soil and extending into rhizomatous taproot 10 cm. or more long, splits easily, 0.6 cm. diameter. Gills free, closely packed, 0.5 cm broad. Spore print white.

BM 286 in cultivations, near Brachystegia trees, 800 m Makwawa December 12/81.

2. *Termitomyces Clypeatus Heim*

It is found growing in clusters in termite hills in savannah woodland, and appears to be widespread in Malawi. Local names recorded are *Nyonzwe* (C) and *Uzuma* (Tu) - both also recorded from Zambia as Nyanja terms (Peglier & Piearce 1980 : 478). It usually occurs early in the rains, in early December. Amongst Yao speakers it is referred to as *Nakasuguli* or *Ujonjo* which it shares with species of Psathnrella. It is sometimes referred to by terms applied to the other members of the genus i.e. *Chanjira Opya, Kanchombo.*

This species is widely distributed in tropical Africa, and has been reported from both West and East Africa as well as .Zaire. It is characterized by its silky greyish-brown cap, which has an acutely pointed umbo, of a darker brown colouration.

Concerning their edibility, Williamson writes (1975 : 328), "Cooked as *Ndiwo,* said to be delicious and much sought after in Zaire. In Malawi usually cooked with groundnuts and often given to young children because it is soft and good-flavoured." Pawek notes that the flavour is faintly nutty.

The Yao term refers to its sweet taste *(Sukali,* sugar). Usually only the cap is eaten.

Cap 5-10 cm. diameter conical, becoming convex with a characteristic pointed umbo, greyish or ochre-brown at the umbo, silky and shiny, glabrous, margin lobed or splitting. *Stem* cylindric, sometimes bulbous near soil surface, developing into a long pseudorrhiza, solid, white 10 x 1 cm., sometimes with yellowish tinge. *Gills* free, crowded, white to pink, veil absent. Context white, firm. Spore print pinkish or yellowish-brown.

JW 7linear R.C. Church Zomba, 700m, December 28/73.

BM 274'on perimeter of termite hill, gregarious, 800m. Makwawa, in pine plantation. Strong aroma. December 11/81.

3. Termitomyces Eurrihizus (Berk) Heim

A large fleshy mushroom, with a cap (usually) to about 30 cm. in diameter, which is widespread throughout tropical Africa and Southern Asia. It is a very variable species but it is recognized by its brown, smooth, viscid, cap. It appears to be common in Malawi and like others of the genus, is associated with termite hills, and is to be found in both cultivations and woodlands. It is described by a wide range of local terms. In the Zomba district I recorded the following:

TERMITOMYCES AURANTIACUS Heim Makwawa, Zomba. December 1981

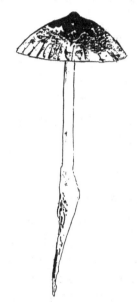

TERMITOMYECE5 CLYPEATUS Helm Makwawa, Zomba. December 1981

Utembo (noted also by Sanderson 1954 : 278), *Nakateresya* (from the Yao verb *Teesesya*, to be slippery, connoting its viscid cap), *Zumbukira* (derived from the Chewa verb Kumba - (to dig), *Uwumbu* and *Ululu*. But the most widely used term is *Nakachombo* or *Kanchombo*, alluding to its conspicuous umbo. The term *Kachofu* was noted by Scott (1929 : 169). Widely used as a food and greatly favoured. Often sold in market places. It is cooked as *Ndiwo* either fresh or dried. Illustrated on the recent 30 tambala postage stamp.

Cap 3-40 cm. diameter, conical and bell-shaped, becoming flat but with noticeable umbo, pale yellowish-brown, dark brown at disc, viscid when moist, margin irregularly splitting. *Stem* cylindric, fleshy, solid, white, pseudorrhiza long and tapering, 20 x 2 cm. covered with hairy filaments, sometimes with ring. *Gills* free to adnexed, white to cream, or pale yellowish-brown, to 1 cm broad, moderately crowded. Context white, fleshy. Spore print pale pink-cinnamon.

JW 602 (Sister Anthony) Anthill in gardens Blantyre. 1100m.

BM 2 in pines near Majiga, Chifundi Str. 1350m Zomba Mt. November 26/79.

Williamson (1975 : 328) records under *Termitomyces Eurrhizus* (lOc) a much larger fungus with a cap to 40 cm. diameter, which she suggests is well-known in Malawi and conspicuous in short grassland. It is sometimes found in large numbers, hence the name Bambomuluzu, an exclamation of astonishment, *(bambo,* father or friend, *mulu* a heap or quantity). It grows in the early rains, and is sold at markets or at the sides of the road. It is cooked fresh or dried, but as it does not soften easily, potatoes are often used. It is apparently well-liked. This may possibly be *Termitomyces Titanicus,* but from Williamson's field notes I can find no record or reference at all to any gatherings or data - apart from a collection by Sister Anthony from the Shire Highlands, December 1973 *(Utaie)*. Williamson also records the names *Katsokomole* (C) and *(Utenge* (Y) but the latter is a taxon usually applied to *Amanita Zambiana*. The *Utale* is noted by both Scott (1929 : 586) and Peglier and Piearce (1980 : 490) as a Nyanja name. Scott records the saying *Munthu wa Mphumi Aturukira Pa Boa, Utale*. A person with luck or instinct, comes upon the mushroom Utale. The name *Utale* is derived from the verb - *Tali or - Talika* distant or long. Scott (1929 : 521) also records the term Thale as an edible mushroom. It is worth noting that Scott mentions that *Utale* is a "huge mushroom" up to 2 ft. in diameter, which would seem to point to *Termitomyces Titanicus*. Williamson (1976) notes the Alomwe term as *Namtokhu*. Williamson writes to me (6th September 1981) that a large species of Termitomyces was well-known in the Likabula district of Mulanje. Discussions I had with Richard Kamphale who was born in the area, confirmed this. Women near Ruo Estate, mostly Alomwe speakers, spoke of a species of edible fungi, highly esteemed, which though sharing the same name as *Termitomyces Schimperi* (which I collected) - *Ma/Zumbnkira* (C) or *Ma/Toromwe* (AI) - was much larger. *T. Schimperi* itself is 20cm. diameter. Apparently older women who knew from long experience where the mushroom are, watch for cracks to appear near the termite hills in the early rains, and then cover the area with leaves and branches, to hide them and may even water the site. An indication of how well-liked and important the mushrooms are considered, and why naturalists hardly ever see them.

4. Termitomyces Medius Heim and Grasse

Uncommon species resembling Termitomyces Microcarpus, but it is more robust and has a well-developed pseudorrhiza. It has been recorded from Zambia, but no records from Malawi.

5. Termitomyces Microcarpus (Berk. & Br.) Heim

A very well-known fungus found throughout tropical Africa, and extending to Southern Asia. Although growing singly, it occurs in very large numbers in dense swarms often numbering several thousands, on or near old termite hills. It is a very small white species, with a cap to 2cm. diameter and lacks a true pseudorrhiza. I have heard it described as *Ujonjo,* but this term is more consistently applied to species of *Psathyrella,* but which are also often found on termite hills. The Nyanja term *Manda* means "grave", and is also reported from Zambia (Pegler and Piearce 1980 : 479). The term *Nyonzwe* is also probably applicable to this species (cf Scott 1929 : 429). In Blantyre known as *Kalumwe.*

This fungus is eaten all over Africa, being dug up and cooked fresh or dried after pounding. The *Ndiwo* made from this species is well-liked, having a good flavour and a rather crisp texture. In Zambia it is sold in markets. It is seldom abundant however, and quickly deteriorates. Thus the Bemba saying to the effect that people are like the *Samfwe* mushroom, that is, human life is short. (Piearce 1981 : 6).

Among the Yoruba people of S.W. Nigeria this fungus plays an important role in everyday life. Besides being eaten it is associated with various myths and is believed to have medicinal properties, as a good luck charm, for reproduction, and in the treatment of gonnorhoea (Oso 1977:367-8).

Cap 1-2 cm. diameter, bell-shaped to convex then expanding, often with umbo, white to cream, often brownish or ochre near centre, dry, smooth. *Stem* cylindric, slender, with bulbous base, smooth white, no speudorrhiza. 4 x 0.3 cm. *Gills* free to adnexed, white, crowded, veil absent. Context thin, white, tough. Spore print rose to pink. No distinctive smell.

JW 503 stream bank under trees, Blantyre 1100 m. Spores white turned pink overnight, not eaten. December 1/71.

BM 491 gregarious on roadside bank near Mudi Stream, near market, Blantyre 1050m. December 30/81.

6. Termitomyces Robustus (Beeli) Heim

A tropical species widely distributed in Africa. A medium to large fungus with a brown viscid cap, but unlike *Termitomyces Clypeatus* the umbo is con-colourous with the remainder of the cap. It differs from *T. Eurrhizus* in rarely having a membraneous ring, for though present in unopened specimens this quickly disappears. Single record only.

The records of *Utale* in Anthony (1973) may be referrable to this species.

As with the preceding species this fungus is important in Yoruba culture. Its name derives from an association with a mystical figure Yoruba Ogoglo, and it is used in the preparation of good luck charms and in the treatment of various social diseases. (Oso 1977 : 368-9).

An edible species cooked as *Ndiwo* and well-liked.

Cap 10-20 cm. diameter, convex with umbo, tawny to dark brown often cracking radially, glabrous, viscid when moist, margin incurved.

Stem long, solid cylindric, thickening towards base before tapering below soil surface. Cream or pink-ochre to greyish-brown, ring absent in mature specimens, to 20 x 3 cm.

Gills free, crowded, white to pale ochre. Context white to grey. firm. Spore print pinkish-cream.

Sister Anthony (JW 628 C) Blantyre. 1050m. January 1973.

7. Termitomyces Schimperi (Pat) Heim

Reported from Tanzania, Ethiopia and Zambia, this is a large robust species, the cap measuring about 20 cm. in diameter. It is easily recognized by its rough scaly cap and stem, the brown scales of the cap usually in the form of radiating concentric rings. The base of the stem is bulbous just below the ground surface, and then tapers

TERMITOMYCES SCHIMPERI (Pat.) Heim Ruo, Mulanje. December 1981

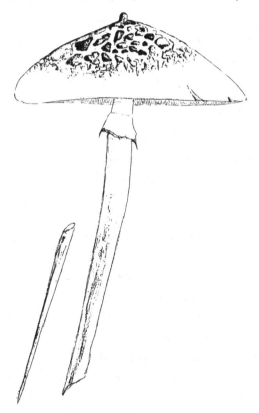

penetrating very deeply into the ground. Usually found on or near anthills. Unlike many other Termitomyces it lacks an umbo.

Several synonyms have been recorded for this species: *Liwangwi, Usinda Waukulu* and *Manandarengwa* are all probably of Yao derivation. Liwangwi is a name it shares with *Russula Schizoderma*. The association of the two species is also indicated by the term *Vsinda Waukulu*, the large *Usinda*, Williamson records the term *Nyozwe Yaikulii (Nyonzwe)* linking this Termitomyces with the genus *Psathyrella*, which as said is also associated with anthills. The names *Namowe* and *Toromwe* were recorded from the Mulanje district, both probably of Alomwe derivation.

Pegler and Piearce report (1980 : 479) that in Zambia though considered edible, it tends to be unpopular, owing to a reputed bitter taste, but this is only present in specimens that are not perfectly fresh. They also note that though it may be collected for domestic use, it is never sold in market. In Malawi however, as Williamson writes (1975 : 330) it is often on sale in markets (and my own observations confirm this) and is well-liked as *Ndiwo*.

Cap 6 - 25cm. diameter, rounded at first then becoming convex to flat, lacking umbo, surface covered with thick large persistent scales, concentric and forming plate-like covering at the disc, white with yellowish-brown scales, viscid when moist. Margin entire, often reflexed, *Stem* cylindric, swollen towards the base (4cm.) then tapering to a long pseudorrhiza 40cm. long, white staining brown, veil persistent as fibrous scales. *Gills* free to adnexed, white to cream or ochre-brown, up to 1.4 cm. wide, moderately crowded. Context thick, white. Spore print, cream with pinkish tinge.

JW 606 Limbe in Brachystegia woodland, Blantyre. 1050m. March 4/72.

BM 174 woodland, Malosa Mt. above Domas school. 1100m. March 7/80.

BM 356 in blue gum plantation, 600m. Ruo Estate, Mulanje December 1981 Specimens noted for short pointed umbo. Widely known in the Mulanje area as *Ma/Zumbukira* (C) and *Ma/Toromwe* (Alomwe) and well-liked as relish food. Zomba women referred to the specimens as Nakasowu. This gathering in having a conspicuous knob at the centre of the cap may possibly be *Termitomyces Letestui* (Pat) Heim illustrated in Piearce's small handbook on Zambian mushrooms (1981 :3).

8. Termitomyces Striatus (Beeli) Heim

Growing on or near termite hills, this species is reported to be one of the commonist Termitomyces growing in tropical Africa. A medium sized fungi with a cap to 12cm. diameter, it is very variable in colour; but it is mainly recognized by the radial lines on the cap, together with its pointed umbo. Although associated with termites it appears to grow in a variety of habitats; Acacia and Brachystegia woodland as well as in grassland or in cultivations. Appears to be frequent in Malawi. An edible species and well-liked.

Cap 4-12cm diameter, conical then convex to flat, but always with a conical umbo, grey to ochre-brown or orange darkening towards centre, with radial lines, margin often splitting, slightly viscid when moist. *Stem* cylindric, solid, expanded slightly before tapering to a long pseudorrhiza up to 40cm long, white to cream, to 2.5cm diameter, *Gills* free, crowded, cream to pink or orange; occasionally with ring. Context thick, white. Spore print pinkish cream. JW 507 Embankment near Chichiri school, Blantyre. 1100m. December 2/71.

9. Termitomyces Titanicus Pegler & Piearce

Recorded from Zambia; may possibly occur in Malawi (see discussion above under *Termitomyces Eurrhizus*). This species as described by Piearce (1981 : 4) has:

"a rough whitish or brownish cap, darker in the centre, regularly exceeding 60cm in diameter, exceptional specimens reaching 100cm or more and is usually cracked or split at the edge. The stem is thick robust and white, with (unless it has fallen off) a frill or annulus hanging from it just below the creamy densely crowded gills, and with a very long, tapering root-like underground extension called a pseudorrhiza most or all of which may have been discarded from marketed mushrooms. The pseudorrhiza is ultimately attached to the termite nest, at a depth of a metre or so, from which these remarkable fungi arise." In the Eastern province of Zambia it is called *Utale*.

Acknowledgements

This paper is based on studies made in Malawi during the years 1979-81 and supported by an S.S.R.C. grant for which I am grateful. I am also grateful to members of the Biology Department and the Herbarium staff at the University for support and encouragement. I should particularly like to express my thanks to Jessie Williamson, Moira and Mark Spurrier, and to Chenita Sulemani and her sister Esmie, Benson Zuwani, Kitty Kunamano, Rosebey Mponda and Silimu Chinyangala for help and instruction in many aspects of Malawi cultural life, particularly relating to mushrooms. I should also like to record my thanks to David Pegler who kindly identified my specimens, along with those of Jessie Williamson. All are deposited in the Kew Herbarium.

References

ANTHONY, Clara 1973 Investigation of the Protein Content of Some Mushrooms growing in Malawi. Diss. Chancellor College, Univ. Malawi.

OSO, B. A. 1977 Mushrooms in Yoruba Mythology and Medicine, Econ. Bot. 31 : 367-70.

PEGLER, David N. 1977 A Preliminary Agaric Flora of East Africa, KEW. BULL. ADD. SERIES 6 HMSO.

& PIEARCE, G. D. 1980 The Edible Mushrooms of Zambia, "KEW BULL. 35 : 475-9.

PIEARCE, G. D. 1981 An Introduction to Zambia's Wild Mushrooms, Forest Dept. Kitwe.

1981 Zambian Mushrooms - Customs and Folklore BULL BRIT. MYCOL. SOC. 15; 139-42. -

SANDERSON, G. M. 1954 A Dictionary of the Yao Language, Govt. Print. Zomba.

SCOTT, D. C. 1929 Dictionary of the Nyanaja Language, USCL, Lutterworth.

WILLIAMSON, Jessie 1975 Useful Plants of Malawi, Rev. Ed., Univ. Malawi

1976 A List of Some Fungi Collected in Malawi between 1971 and 1974 SOC. MAL. J.29 ; 46-53

MUSHROOMS: FOR MEDICINE, MAGIC AND MUNCHING[41] (1992)

I want this evening to talk about mushrooms, and to try to do three things. Firstly, I want to talk about cultural attitudes to fungi, and how these differ among different people. This is the anthropology part. Secondly, I want to address the question: what is a mushroom or fungus, and to say something about their biology, ecology and identification. This is the mycology part. And finally I want to put the two together and discuss the uses of fungi - as medicine, in ritual, and as food. And I hope in the end to get you 'hooked' on this fascinating group of organisms.

CULTURAL ATTITUDES TO FUNGI

There are, it seems, two kinds of people, or rather there are two kinds of culture. But if we are largely determined by our culture (if we are to believe the anthropologists) we find that in their attitudes to fungi there are two very different kinds of people (Morris 1987a). Some people are what you might called mycophobic. They hate and fear fungi. They don't know anything about fungi and they don't want to know. The Brahmins in India are like this, and there are other people too. But the most mycophobic tribe are the English - and those Americans who are descended from the pilgrim fathers. Apart from puffball and crampball, which they used for medicine in the past, the English only have two words to describe the fungal kingdom. Those that are edible they call mushrooms, but strange to say they only recognize and eat one kind - a species of *Agaricus*. Those that are poisonous or not eaten they call toadstools - and the English don't like toads either. One species, the fly agaric

---

4 1 Talk given to the Wildlife Society of Malawi, P.O. Box 1429, Blantyre on 8 January, 1991.

(Amanita muscaria) they consider the prototypical toadstool, and it is associated with witchcraft, fairies and other strange beings. I shall talk about the fly agaric later. If you go into an English market you'll be lucky if you find any mushrooms, and even if you do, it will only be one kind.

This cultural attitude, this mycophobia, goes back a long way. I will quote you an extract from a famous English herbal, that of John Gerard, published in 1597. This is an important book on medicinal plants, and contains descriptions of well over 2000 plants. Its chapter on mushrooms is very short, and it contains this statement.

> "Few of them are good to eat, and most of them suffocate and strangle the eater. Therefore, I give my advice unto these that love such strange and new-fangled meates, to be aware of licking honey among thorns, lest the sweetness of one do not countervail the sharpness and pricking of the other."

You can see that for Gerard all fungi are 'strange', most, he erroneously thought, were poisonous; only a few are edible and these he thinks are probably not worth the risk. Gilbert White's classic study of Selbourne (1789), is another example of English mycophobia. It is significant that this detailed observer of English country life never mentions mushrooms!

I'll give you a final example of English mycophobia, one more contemporary and closer to home. Some friends of mine have written a smashing book called *The Malawian Cookbook*. (Shaxson, Dixon & Walker 1974). It specifically tries to bring in local dishes, and includes a section on insects and such delicacies as *gumbe*. But do you know that it hardly mentions mushrooms at all - and has absolutely nothing on the many varieties of mushrooms eaten by Malawians. This is not a criticism! Annabelle Shaxson and June Walker, happen to be, like me, of English background. This antipathy towards fungi permeates English culture. Thus, it is that we have checklists of the grasses, trees, mammals, birds, epiphytic orchids, butterflies, snakes, but hardly anyone thought it worthwhile making a checklist of the fungi - until I published one last year (Morris 1990). And the only people interested in publishing it were the editors of an obscure botanical journal that only botanists read. The head of the cryptogram section at the National Herbarium, Mr. Magombo, bewails the fact that we've hardly any fungi specimens - only those collected by Jessie Williamson (1974) and myself and these you can fit in one cupboard!

We do not have a specimen at all of what is probably the largest mushroom in the world, *Termitomyces titanicus,* which almost certainly grows in Malawi.

But there are people, you know, who love mushrooms. They eat many kinds of fungi and have lots of names for the different species. In their markets you'll find lots of different mushrooms for sale. Some even use fungi for decorations, or in religious rituals. Such people are what you might call mycophilic. The Greeks and Italians are mycophiles, so are the Russians, so are the French, so are the tribal people of India, as are the people of Malawi. Over sixty different kinds of fungi are recognized as edible in Malawi (Chipompha 1985) - but more about Malawi later. You might well realize that one of the aims of my talk is to institute a kind of religious conversion and to convert most of you (I would guess) from being mycophobes to being mycophiles. And who knows, we might even get the Wildlife Society of Malawi to recognize fungi as an important and fascinating form of wildlife, certainly as interesting as the elephant, the Angola Pitta, and the bee-orchid.

THE BIOLOGY OF FUNGI

If fungi are to be seen as a form of wildlife, what kind is it? At the time of Linnaeus, natural things were divided into three kinds - animal, vegetable or mineral. They did not know where to put the fungi, so they grouped them with the plants. So today if you're interested in fungi you'll have to go to the herbarium and not the museum to find them. But you know mushrooms aren't like plants at all - they form a distinct group of organisms, different from both plants and animals. Unlike plants, they lack chlorophyll and are, therefore, unable to produce their own food. Thus, they are similar to animals since they are dependent on plants for nutrition, and their tissue structure too has affinities with animal life. Gerard referred to fungi as 'meates' and most women in Malawi associate mushrooms with *nyama,* not with plants. But fungi are immobile and obtain their food by absorption not by ingestion. Most of the larger fungi are saprophytic, feeding on decaying plant materials. One mycologist has described fungi as the great scavengers of the plant world and most plant diseases are caused by fungi of various kinds - blights, smuts, and mildews.

The kind of fungus that everybody knows - the toadstool - is not the whole organism, but only the fruiting part. It's like the tip of an iceberg, for the basic structure of the fungi consists of a mass of hyphae, microscopic thread-like strands. Collectively these are known as mycelium, and they spread in every direction in the organic substratum - leaf mould, a dead tree stump, or the soil. The fruiting bodies are special structures above the ground whose function is to produce the spores. These are dispersed by the wind, and in suitable conditions, will germinate to produce new mycelia colonies. The spores are microscopic and are of different colours and shapes - and are of critical importance in the identification and classification of fungi. For someone who does not have a microscope, and who is used to identifying birds and flowers, identifying fungi is no easy matter. One bulbul is pretty much like any other bulbul, and once you know a *Haemanthus* it's easy to find and identify another. But the fruiting bodies of fungi go through a process of change and a newly emerging *Amanita* will be completely different, in both shape and colour, from one in the last stages of decay. You can always recognize an expert botanist or ornithologist - they will tell you not only what species it is, but what subspecies it is. An expert mycologist on the other hand might tell you only what genus it belongs to! It's like an ornithologist telling you that a bird is a kind of pipit.

But in the identification of fungi, a number of features have to be taken into account. For the amateur naturalist of crucial importance are the following:

(1) the colour and shape of the cap
(2) whether the fungi has gills, spores or spines
(3) the colour, spacing, and the kind of attachment that the gills indicate
(4) the nature of the stem, and whether it possesses a ring, a cortina (a cobweb-like film) or a cup-like volva at the base
(5) The colour of the spores, indicated by making of a spore print
(6) the smell and taste of the mushroom.

Fungi are associated with plants of all kinds, being largely responsible as saprophytes, for the breakdown of decaying material. They are thus found wherever plants grow, and in all types of habitat. Often they form symbiotic relationships with plants, the most familiar of these being lichen (a fungus and an algae), and the mycorrhizoral associations between fungi and the roots of certain higher plants such as orchids and pines. Many fungi have specific associations - *Cantha-rellus, Lactarius* and *Suillus granulatus* for example, have mycorrhizoral associations with specific trees and the genus *Termitomyces,* as its scientific name suggests, is invariably found on or near termite mounds. Like plants, fungi require moisture for growth, and are thus most plentiful during the rainy season from December to April.

ETHNOMYCOLOGICAL NOTES

Let me turn to the uses of fungi which may be dealt with under three headings: as medicine, in ritual and as food.

AS MEDICINE

Surprisingly, in most cultures fungi are little used as medicine. Apart from the use of the bracket fungi, *Perenniporis mundula,* which often grows on the Mwanga *(Pericopsis angolensis)* trees, and is used in the treatment of pleurisy *(chibayo)* and potency, I found little evidence of fungi being used as medicine in Malawi. Graham Piearce (1981) found the same in Zambia - and this is of interest when you consider the degree to which plant medicines permeate the cultures of Central Africa. Dioscorides' treatise on medicinal plants, *De Materia Medica,* only discusses one fungi used as medicine, *agarikon,* the punk or tinder agaric *Polyporus officinalis.*

RITUAL USES

Over the past two decades, ethnomycological studies have taught us a good deal about the use of hallucinogenic mushrooms in various cultures. Three ethnographic contexts are worth mentioning.

The first is the reported cases of 'mushroom madness' among the highland people of Papua New Guinea (Reay 1960). Apparently at a certain time of the year, around the end of the dry season, the *Boletus* mushrooms which the people are fond of eating, have an extraordinary effect - and lots of people go into trances - become 'mad'. Interestingly when 'mad', men and women behave quite differently: the men tend to become tense and aggressive - particularly towards their own kin - while women tend to flaunt especially the norms relating to sexual behavior. Thus, the convention is no simple relationship between the induction of hallucinogenic mushrooms and certain behavioural states for the latter is always filtered by and dependent on cultural norms.

A second example are the mushroom cults of Mexico (Mapes 1981). When the Spanish conquerors reached Mexico in the sixteenth century they found the Indian communities practising several religious cults in which the sacramental rites involved the use of hallucinogenic mushrooms. The Aztecs called mushrooms *(Psylocybe, Conocybe, Stropharia* and *Panaeolus* were the main genera involved) *Teonanacatl,* a term meaning 'flesh of the gods'. The Catholic church tried to suppress the indigenous cults, and, thus, mushrooms were banned. In recent years anthropologists have rediscovered the existence of such mushroom cults among many Indian communities of Mexico. The mushrooms have a hallucinogenic effect, and are used in a ritual ceremony involving an all-night seance, which includes an elaborate curing rite with chants and prayers. What kind of psychological state is induced by the mushrooms is best described through the words of one Mazatec shaman, Maria Sabina (Wasson 1974).

"There is a world that is beyond ours, a world that is far away, nearby and invisible. And there it is where God lives, where the dead live, the spirits and the saints, a world where everything has already happened and everything is known. That world talks. It has a language of its own. I report what it says. The sacred mushrooms take me by the hand and bring me to the world where everything is known. It is they, the sacred mushrooms, that speak in a way that I can understand. I ask them, and they answer me. When I return from the trip I have taken with them, I tell what they have told me and what they have shown me."

Such rites have, therefore, both a curing and a divinatory aspect. Throughout Central America many remarkable archaeological artifacts known as 'mushroom stones' have been unearthed, and they are believed, like the mesolithic dolmans elsewhere, to be associated with past mushroom cults (Manilal 1981).

The ritual use of the well-known fly agaric, *Amanita muscaria,* in the shamanic ceremonies of the tribal people of Siberia has been known for a long time (Eliade 1951). The shamans, as traditional healers, induced an ecstatic state by the induction of the mushrooms and by rhythmic drumming and dancing. While in a trance they would communicate with the spirit world, and attempt to ascertain the reasons for a particular misfortune or disease. The mushroom was taken fresh or dried, but experienced shamans drank their own urine which contained the hallucinogenic properties of the mushroom in its concentrated form, and without the adverse side effects. Subsequent researchers have tried to show that the fly agaric had a ritual significance in many other cultural contexts outside of Siberia. The Norsemen were supposed to go 'berserk' through consuming the fly agaric and Wasson (1971) has argued that the soma of the Vedic scriptures and rituals was also this fungi. Soma was regarded as a special kind of divinity by the early Hindus: it was drunk infused in milk and had special visionary effects - the worshipper had strange experiences of power and was alleged to have passed beyond heaven and earth. Then there was the association, in Britain, of the fly agaric, the toadstool, with fairies. I've written a little poem on how you can see fairies. The poem was written for a friend, but I am sure I can share it with you.

HOW TO SEE FAIRIES
Do you seek the road to fairyland?
It's a secret, but I'll tell it you tonight.
Collect those mushrooms which I showed you
That are red and flecked with white.
Then, if no evil power be nigh to thwart you out of spite,
You put them in condensed milk and brandy
And if you get the formula right,
Drink it, and you'll see lots and lots of fairies
Before the morning light.

Then there is the legend of Father Christmas with his red and white coat, his team of flying reindeer, his coming to the hearth to put presents in stockings - all this has been seen as cultural vestiges of Siberia, or at least Eurasian shamanism. John Allegro, in his study *The Sacred Mushroom and the Cross* (1970) has even suggested that the religions of the Near East, including Christianity, were based on fertility rites focussed around the *Amanita* mushroom. The mushroom was seen as a microcosm of the world, with God the seed, the mushroom the phallus, and the earth the receptacle or womb. In terms of this conception of the universe as an androgynous organism, Allegro interprets a good deal of the Biblical tradition - the Tree of Life and the Garden of Eden,

Ezekiel's vision, Jacob's ladder, Joseph and his 'coat of many colours', and the imagery of the serpent.

Allegro's study has been subject to much criticism by Biblical scholars - but one real problem with the thesis is that *Amanita muscaria* is a north temperate species and is not found in the Near East. Two points in favour of Allegro's thesis are worth noting. One is the fact that sexual imagery is in fact an important aspect of many tribal and peasant cosmologies. The other is the existence of a fresco, dating from the thirteenth century on the wall of a church in Plaincourault in France. It depicts Adam and Eve on either side of the 'Tree of Life' - which is clearly depicted as *Amanita muscaria*.

I have a feeling too that western philosophy and science may have had its origins in a mushroom cult. Plato, for example, had the audacious theory that the world of our sense perceptions, the phenomenal world, was in a sense unreal, a world of appearance, and that the real world, was the domain of Eidos - of forms or ideas. Knowledge was the perception of these external, un-changing forms. And in his classic political treaties, *The Republic,* he has the allegory of the cave, and the world as we experience it being but the shadows on the wall of the cave. The idea of a 'world' beyond phenomenal existence, whether expressed in forms or in the laws of nature, was a crucial insight in the advancement of human knowledge, and may well have come from Plato eating mushrooms in the cave.

AS FOOD

Throughout the world mushrooms are gathered as food. Of 134 species of fungi collected by one researcher in Mexico, 43 (34%) were recognized as food, and of these, ten were regularly sold in the market place. In Malawi, over 60 kinds of edible fungi are recognized, and this number in itself gives some indication of their cultural relevance (Chipompha 1985, Morris 1987b). As in other African cultures mushroom *(bowa)* are an important source of food, and are used as a relish dish *(ndiwo)*. During the rainy season (mainly December to March) there are stalls selling a variety of fungi in most markets in Malawi, and impromptu stalls are set up by roadsides. Who has not seen women and young boys holding *utenga (Amanita zambesiana)* aloft on the Liwonde road? In all rural areas women regularly gather mushrooms from the *Brachystegia* woodland and at favourable times make almost daily expeditions to the woodland, as the early rainy season tends to be a lean season for relish food. Jessie Williamson (1974) long ago noted the important role that mushrooms play in the diet of local people. Vast amounts must be gathered annually, and the value of *Brachystegia* woodland has long been ignored by economists and administration alike.

The gathering of mushrooms is undertaken almost entirely by women who usually forage in groups of 3 to 5, often accompanied by young girls and children. Each carries a basket and they may traverse several miles in the course of the day. Older women may forage alone and I have come across elderly women several miles from the village and sometimes high on the slopes of Mulanje and Malosa mountains. Gathering begins at the break of dawn, for humans have to compete with other forms of animal life for the mushrooms – how early can be illustrated if I recall my experiences at Ruo Estate, Mulanje.

In January 1991,1 went looking for mushrooms in the woods on Ruo Estate. I set off with my basket around daybreak (around 5 am). I could find no edible species at all, although occasionally I found some broken pieces of mushroom and this seemed strange. All of a sudden I came across two young girls gathering mushrooms. On seeing me they ran. I ran after them calling them to stop. They were joined by other women, and the outcome was me chasing a group of about 12 women and girls through the woodlands. They outpaced me, and my shouting in Chichewa for them to stop was to no avail. I picked up some of the fungi that had bounced out of their baskets. The next morning I left the house well before dawn, about 4 am. I walked quietly through the same woodland. Then I heard some rustling of leaves, for the women brushed away the leaves with their feet when searching for mushrooms. *Muli bwanji?* (How are you?) I said, in the most gentle way possible, as I approached some young women gathering mushrooms. "Don't run", I said, "I want to see the bowa" (mushroom). We soon got into conversation, and I ended up sitting under a tree with my basket and notebook surrounded by about a dozen women and young girls. The eldest was in her sixties, the youngest about 5. I proceeded to help myself to all the best fungi specimens from their baskets, while at the same time questioning them on their names and preparations. I filled my basket with about six different species, and then came the dilemma, how to reward them. As I had gathered lots of information and lots of good specimens for the Herbarium I decided to give them five kwacha. In those days it was equivalent to about three days wages weeding on the estate. I gave the money to the old lady, with explicit instructions to share it between them. An amazing scene then unfolded, as the group of women danced about the track ululating, the older women leading and holding the K5 note aloft.

There is a sequel to this. A couple of weeks later I was invited to a Sundowner at Mulanje Club. And there, as they were drinking Zoa coffee, I overhead one Malawian tea planter converse with another about a crazy European who paid K5 for some mushrooms at Ruo Estate. Such foolishness, he said, as for only 10 tambala he could have bought some in Mulanje market.

Most women in the rural areas of Malawi have an extensive knowledge of fungi both with regard to their identification and ecology. Some have a real eye for mushrooms. Although I have recorded over 60 edible species, few women are able to name and identify all of these because of their varied distribution. But many rural women have no difficulty in naming about 20 species and I have been on collecting expeditions when nine different species were gathered. Many women were able to separate edible and inedible *Russula,* which look very similar, without hesitation, and when I questioned one woman about how she did this so effortlessly she replied, "I grew up with them."

Within Africa there are wide variations as to what is considered edible by different people. The Split-gill fungus, *Schizophyllum commune,* is commonly eaten in Zambia, (Piearce 1981) but rarely touched in Malawi. In Madagascar, *Boletes* are eaten in great quantities but *Cantharellus* ignored, while in Zaire (Parent & Theon 1977) and Malawi, the reverse is the case. In fact, along with *Termitomyces and Amanita,* the genus *Cantharellus* is highly favoured in Malawi, while *Boletes* are only eaten infrequently. Knowledge of fungi in Malawi is largely confined to women, and apart from the commoner species, there are few men who know anything about them. Although vast quantities of mushrooms are consumed each year in Malawi, there are very few cases of fungus poisoning. The only case that came to my notice concerned a group of forestry workers - all men - who had to be admitted to Zomba Hospital after eating some fungi from a pine plantation.

I hope that what I have had to say about the fungi, has stimulated your interest in this fascinating form of wildlife, and I would like to end the talk with a Latin quotation.

Argentum atque aurum facile est, laenum togamque mittere; boletus mittere difficile est.

Roughly translated this means: It's easy to despise gold and silver; but who can refuse a plate of mushrooms?

REFERENCES:

ALLEGRO, J. (1970) *The sacred mushroom and the cross.* Hodder & Stoughton, London.

CHIPOMPHA, N.W.S. (1985) *Some mushrooms of Malawi.* Zomba Forestry Research Record No. 6.

ELIADE, M. (1951) *Shamanism: archaic techniques of ecstasy.* Princeton University Press.

GERARD, J. (1975) The herbal, or general history of plants. (Original date of publication 1597.) Dover, New York.

MANUAL, K. S. (1981) *An ethnobotanic connection between mushrooms and dolmens.* In: S. K. Jain (Ed.). Glimpes of Indian ethnobotany. Oxford University Press, New Delhi, pp321-5.

MAPES, G. (1981) *Ethnomicologia purepecha.* Inst. Biol. Univ. Mexico.

MORRIS, B. (1987a) *Common mushrooms of Malawi.* Oslo University, Fungiflora.

MORRIS, B. (1987b) Mushrooms and culture, *Man and Life.* Calcutta, 13: 31-48.

MORRIS, B. (1990) An annotated checklist of the macrofungi of Malawi. *Kirkia,* 13: 323-64.

PARENT, G. & D. THOEN (1977) Food value of edible mushrooms from Upper-Shaba Region (Zaire). *Econ. Botany* 31:436-45.

PIEARCE, G. D. (1981) *An introduction to Zambia's wild mushrooms.* Forest Department, Kitwe, Zambia.

SHAXSON, A., P. DIXON & J. WALKER (1974) *The Malawi cookbook.* Government Print, Zomba.

REAY, M. (1960) Mushroom madness in the New Guinea Highlands. *Oceania* 31:137-9.

WASSON, R. G. (1971) *Soma: divine mushroom of immortality.* Harcourt Brace, New York.

WASSON, R. G. (1974) Maria *Sabina and her Mazatec Velada.* Harcourt Brace, New York.

WHITE, G. (1789) *Natural history ofSelbourne.* Scott, London.

WILLIAMSON, J. (1974) *Useful plants of Malawi.* Revised and extended addition. Government Print, Zomba.

A DENIZEN OF THE
EVERGREEN FOREST (1962)

It was late October and the grass fires were everywhere. Mlanje Mountain 9,800 ft., sixty miles away to the North East, which throughout the winter months could be seen daily towering above the Luchenza Plain, was now barely visible through the grey heat haze that hung about. The destructive fires had begun and would go on unceasingly for the next three or four weeks until the break of the rains. But these fires were not considered destructive to an African who made his way, hoe on shoulder, down one of the steep pathways that connect the villages of the this part of Nyasaland.

Certainly not! Are not fires necessary things? Are they not an important means of securing the needed meat supply? Meat makes a welcome change to the beans and wild herbs which are the usual relish taken with the maize porridge which forms the native's basic meal. But meat is scarce, for there are few cattle in the area owing to the steep nature of the land, and fish, brought up from Chiromo on the River Shire are eagerly bought.

Not surprisingly, in the heavily populated and cultivated area in the vicinity of the Zoa Estate, 30 miles south of Cholo, there is very little game, although Bushbuck, Duiker, Mongoose and Jackal and some of the smaller mammals are to be seen near streams or in the patches of Brachystegia woodland still existing; and the occasional leopard, which seems to thrive near human habitations, is still to be encountered.

Only one group of mammals has survived the pressure of the human population—the rodents, which have not only survived, but actually thrived and multiplied, for the area with its abundance of canes and fodder plants is a veritable paradise for rodents. It was in order to obtain these rodents—the rats (most of the species being edible, the Giant Rat *(Cricetomys)* "Kuve" especially so, being considered a great delicacy, as a supplement to the meat supply) that the grass fires were initially started. Usually begun in the form of a large half-circle the fire invariably got out of control, but this matters little as few rats are taken fleeing in advance of the fire—the harvest begins after the fire has passed when, armed with hoes and sticks, the local population proceed to dig out the rats which have taken refuge from the fire in shallow holes. Two species are normally taken this way, the Bvumbwi *(Pelomys)* which is especially common in the lower areas and the Mpera *(Lemnis-comys)*, a small rat with a dark vertical line down its back. Both these species normally live amongst grass and rank vegetation and

View of Zoa Estate

rarely burrow, making their nests of grass at ground level. At other seasons they are taken in small spring traps set in their runways in the grass.

But the African was not concerned with the grass fires that blazed all about him. He had another task on hand and made his way down to one of the stream valleys that bisect the very hilly and uneven country, passing through one of the many bamboo plots — old garden sites deserted when, due to the run-off of top-soil through primitive cultivation, they became unproductive and now completely taken over by the common bamboo *(Oxytenantherd)*— he entered one of the riverine tracts, the small patches of evergreen forest bordering some of the streams in the area. These evergreen tracts are, so the foresters tell us, the last remnants of the extensive evergreen forests that once covered this part of Africa, and which, through many hundreds of years of shifting cultivation, have degenerated into the many grades of Brachystegia belts that are now to be found.

This patch of forest, covering the stream gully, is the haunt of a rare species of Tree Mouse, *Beamys major,* a little known animal which has survived in this part of Nyasaland. Only very few specimens of this rat have been collected and these were caught on Mlanje Mountain and on the Nyika plateau, and nothing is known of the habits and life-history. An allied species *Beamys hindei* was collected from Taveta in Kenya many years ago.

The *Beamys* is a handsome rat, about five inches in length. It is uniformly Oswald grey above and has a pure white forehead patch and underparts — its feet and the tip of its tail are pink, the tail, which is about 80% of the length of the head and body, is very unusual, being rather square in structure and is quite unlike that of any other rat; it is semi-prehensile and used as a balancing organ by the rat when climbing.

But our friend allows nothing to divert his attention and makes his way to a small Strychnos tree covered in creepers and searched about amongst the undergrowth at its base. After half a minute or so he found what he was searching for — a small hole that was the entrance to the burrow of the Yunkurukuve, the native name for the *Beamys major*, which his children had found that morning while playing in the forest. He realised immediately that it belonged to the Beamys owing to its oval shape, for the multimammate rat Mbewa *(Rattus natalensis),* the commonest rat in the area (in fact the most abundant rat in Nyasaland), and most other burrowing rats make a circular or near-circular hole.

He began to dig. No precautions in digging out the "Yunkurukuve", he thought to himself, for they have but one opening to the burrow and no escape hatches, like most of the other burrowing rats; no need either to smoke the burrow beforehand to render the occupant helpless and unable to dash for safety, as with the Kuve, its larger relative. Such a stupid animal the Yunkurukuve he thought — why even the Pygmy mouse *(Mus minutoides)* often has an escape hole. He dug vertically for some three feet for the burrows of most *Beamys* have a vertical shaft. The burrow then became horizontal and after digging a short distance, the passage was found blocked with soil, which was so tightly packed that he found difficulty in penetrating it with his fingers. This was the "chiseko" or door, the animals' way of keeping out snakes and other unwanted visitors, especially the Hissing Sand Snake which is particularly fond of rats. He knew the animal was at home and proceeded to dig further and following the tunnel along horizontally some five feet he came to a small chamber some ten inches in diameter containing the remains of some mango seeds, for which the *Beamys* has a great liking; and a little further on another chamber containing a large pile of assorted fruits and seeds on top of which was placed a nest, saucer-like in shape, of leaves. A little further in one of the side tunnels, he found the rats' latrine. The *Beamys,* like most rats and mice, and contrary to what most people think, are clean in their personal habits, placing their droppings in the

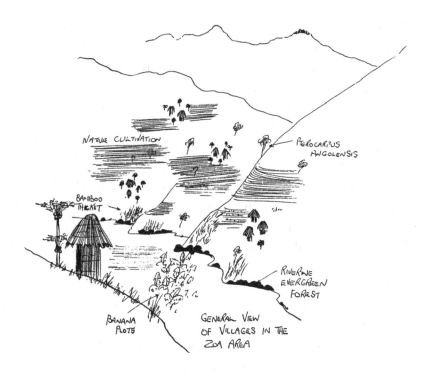

General view of villages in the Zoa area

same special position, and regularly cleaning out their burrows and storage chambers, removing all waste material and changing their bedding material as it becomes fouled. When a storage chamber eventually becomes fouled with small chippings etc., which it does in time, then the animal proceeds to make itself another chamber. The age of a burrow, and the animal it contains, can be roughly estimated by the extent of the burrow, and the number of chambers it possesses. A juvenile animal usually has but a single tunnel, at the end of which is a small storage chamber; whereas an old specimen, especially a female, may have three or four chambers and extensive burrows extending in many directions and sometimes these may have an escape hatch — a burrow reaching to within an inch or so of the ground surface and used in an emergency.

The *Beamys* is also very particular about its bedding material, always taking large leaves like the mango and mbawa *(Khaya nyasica)*; grass has never been found in its burrow. The *Beamys,* as expected, washes itself regularly in a most elaborate fashion. Its food consists mainly of seeds and fruit gathered from its evergreen home. They will in captivity, though, take almost anything, from pieces of meat to cheese and quaker oats, and when maize and Cassava gardens be close by, they naturally help themselves to the available foodstuffs, but they never do the damage as other rats do, in native gardens. The Giant Rat in particular plays havoc with the native crops, being especially fond of Grant beans *(Arachis)* and whole cobs of maize have been found in its burrow. Among the many wild fruits and seeds taken by the *Beamys*, the following are amongst the most common:- the seeds of Grant bean *(Voand-zeia Erythrophleum (Mwabvi)*, Avocado Pear *(Persea americana)*, Bengal bean *(Mucuna aterrima)*, Mango *(Mangifera indica)*, Tea *(Camellia sinensis)*, Hibiscus species, Cassia species, Yellow Oleander *(Thevetia nerifolia)* and the fruits of *Cordyla africana*, Granadilla *(Passiflora* species), Persian Lilac or bead tree *(Melia azedarach);*

Author's sketch of a Beamys Major.

Strychnos and many other wild berries. Among its food store, the peculiar wingless parasite, Hemimerus, allied to earwigs, and a smaller type than that found on Giant Rat, are often found. It is not a blood sucker and appears to live solely on the waste stores gathered by its host. This food store may sometimes contain a considerable quantity of foodstuffs —in one burrow 1,383 Mwabvi seeds were found, weighing 2 lbs. 11 ozs. As expected the *Beamys* is an agile climber, able to climb high trees in its search for food.

But to return to our friend. With great care he removed the final earth from the tunnel's extreme end, and the rat came forth. But not like the Mbewa or even the Matongondo *(Tatera afra)* which takes the place of the multimammate rat in the drier areas, which would have shot out of its hole at great speed in a desperate dash for safety. The *Beamys* came out at a walking pace and was gently picked up by the man (the *Beamys'* maximum running speed, by the way, is 1 and a half miles per hour — compare this with the *Acomys (Spiny Mouse)* which is much smaller, and able to do four miles per hour). He placed the rat in a bamboo cage and left the forest in triumph. Certain it is that he would not have picked up a Mbewa so casually, they, always ready for a fight, would very likely have taken a portion from his finger, so readily will they bite. But not so the *Beamys,* one of the most docile and friendly of creatures.

It is unusual to record that this creature, which is so tame and easy to handle, shows towards his own kind such antagonism. They fight each other continually, even without provocation, rearing up on their hind legs, with forepaws clasped and attacking each other with open jaws. If two individuals, especially two males, are put together overnight in a confined space, it is not unusual to find one of them dead or badly mutilated the next morning. Not surprisingly, they are completely solitary in habits; never more than one in-dividual found per burrow, except perhaps during November and December when a female may be found with her few young ones. The *Beamys* is com-pletely nocturnal in habits, venturing out only after dark and then only when necessary to replenish its foodstuffs, after not leaving its burrow for 4-5 days. This accounts for the fact that it is so rarely caught in the native stone fall traps, in which its relative the Tugu *(Saccostomus)* is taken regularly.

The *Beamys* are a dying race — the evergreen tracts found at Zoa, on the Nyika and elsewhere, hold the last of nine species, unable to meet the chang-ing conditions; a type on the path to extinction. But it is not the traps or the diggings or the fires that have brought the *Beamys* population to such a low ebb; the Mbewa and Mpera are facing the same conditions and they are, as in the past, continuing to thrive and multiply. A far more destructive agent is at work against the *Beamys* —the axe; those horrid men, never satisfied with their lot, ever hungry for more and more land, are cutting down those ever-green forests that are its homeland. And without a home, without an environ-ment providing all its needs, no creature can survive —not even man!

NOTES ON THE GIANT RAT
(CRICETOMYS GAMBIANUS) IN
NYASALAND (1963)

Although considered by most authorities to be catholic in its choice of habitat, and found in all types of country (including brachystegia savannah woodland). *Cricetomys gambianus,* the Giant Pouched Rat, is confined in Nyasaland to evergreen forests and riparian thickets along watercourses at an altitude of over 2,000 feet. It is common and wide-spread in Nyasaland, absent only from mountain plateaus and the low-lying rift valleys. In the Cholo district of the Southern Province, where gallery forests are particularly common, several of the large rodents were excavated during 1961-62 and the following short notes on their habits may be of interest.

The Giant Rat seems completely solitary by nature, never more than one individual being found per burrow, although in suitable localities several rats may be found living within a small area, especially so in pairs. It is by no means communal as suggested by some naturalists. These burrows are always in shady thickets where the soil is moist. They can often be detected by the presence of small mounds of recently excavated earth. The soil of these mounds is composed of small pellet-like particles and it is probable that the rat burrows by means of its front incisors in the manner of mole rats, pushing the earth behind with the fore-paws. The claws are, in fact, small and weak, ill-adapted to digging. The burrows invariably follow a set pattern: A vertical shaft, often sealed with a soil 'door' of 2-3 inches (sometimes small stones) to keep out unwanted visitors; a separate latrine compartment; several chambers, one of which contains a shallow nest of evergreen leaves — commonly from mango or mahogany *(Khaya* sp.) trees, never grass — beneath which is the food store; several tunnels ending within a few inches of the ground surface forming "escape hatches."

Two interesting facts come to light when one digs out these rats :

(a) The rat never uses the "escape hatch" at all, but rather tends to dig deeper into the soil to evade capture.

(b) On being caught (usually by the tail) it displays great strength in anchoring itself to the sides of the burrow, and it requires quite a "hefty" pull on the part of the digger to extract it.

The Giant Rat seems to be purely vegetarian in habit. Among its stores of food the following have been recorded : velvet beans *(Mucana aterrima)*, cow-peas *(Vigna ungulcucata)*, pumpkin seeds *(Cucurbita maxima)*, ground nuts *(Arachnis hypogeae)*, mango seeds*(Manifera indica)*, maize grain *(Zea mays)* — including whole cobs, tea seed *(Camellia sinensis)*, fruits of the kaffir orange *(Strychnos spinosa)*, pods of *Bauhinia petersiana* and the fruits of the tree *Vitex mombassae.* Several pieces of unidentified roots, have also been found, part eaten, among the stores. Two further items of fare were found in the nest of a female containing young — they were several empty snail shells (of a small species about an inch in length) and part of an old dog bone. I believe myself that they are eaten by the rat to obtain necessary minerals. The only other possible explanation for the presence of these items among the food stores is that the Giant Rat, like the American Pack Rat, is by nature just an inveterate collector!

Large fruits of the kaffir orange, lying in the vicinity of a burrow, have often been found opened, with pulp and seeds extracted, so it is likely that only a portion of its diet is brought back for storage. By placing small sticks across the entrance of a burrow it has also been shown that the rat ventures abroad very regularly each evening. As food is so abundant, especially with the expanding cultivations, its storage seems unnecessary, and it is probable that the habit is a deeply ingrained one, acquired long ago when food was less plentiful. I have never myself actually seen a rat carrying food in its cheek pouches, nor have I found any food remains in the pouches of a dead speci-men, as one so often does with the allied species *Saccostomus campestris* (the Cape Pouched Rat). One must conclude that the cheek pouches are not so well developed as in this latter species.

As is well known the African population have a great liking for the meat of the Giant Rat, which is considered a delicacy, and expend much energy dig-ging (and smoking) them from their burrows. On such occasions it is interesting to note, they are often disappointed, finding at the end of a long period of toil, not the desired rodent, but a Zorilla or Cape Polecat *(Ictonyx striatus)*. Several specimens of this animal brought to me, were taken from the burrow of a supposed Giant Rat. Whether the burrow was taken over on desertion or whether the rat was evicted (and eaten?) is uncertain. The late Rodney Wood, a pioneer naturalist who made a collection of mammals in Nyasaland in the early 1920's, recorded that the Giant Rat was often taken by Africans in 'dead fall' traps. I have never seen such a trap set for *Cricetomys* and it seems that the custom has died out although cane rats are often trapped by the same method.

The breeding of *Cricetomys gambianus* in captivity has been fully recorded by the distinguished French biologist, Professor Francois Bourliere. My own observations substantially follow his. The young are naked and helpless at birth (unlike *Saccostomus campestris* and several other African muridae, *Aethomys chrysophilus* (Red Veldt Rat) and *Mastomys Natalensis* (multimammate rat) for instance, which are born with hairs) with their eyes and ear passages completely closed. At the age of five days, their skin, which at birth is a pink, almost rosy, coloration, begins to darken on the upper-parts and head, the muzzle, ears, limbs, and underparts remaining pink. It is not until the young are two weeks old, at a stage when they squeal incessantly (much like other young animals), that their eyes open. Weaning is complete by the fifth week.

In Nyasaland the young have been recorded in September, January, March and May (a female with well-developed embryos was taken in October) so it would appear that breeding takes place mainly during the rainy season. Three or four young is the usual number, although, oddly enough, the female possesses four pairs of teats. Traite de Zoologie records the gestation period as 42 days.

For so large an animal, *Cricetomys* has extremely small, almost beady eyes, which seems unusual for a creature so exclusively nocturnal. Perhaps this is offset by the large and very sensitive ears, and the comparatively long whiskers (3 and a half inches) which seem ever to be in motion. It is quite probable, too, that its sense of smell is highly developed. The rat also has strangely marked feet, mottled pink and dark grey. There are six plantar pads on the rather broad hind foot. Another distinctive feature is the glandular (?) swelling at the base of the tail.

The Giant Rat, or Bwampini, as it is known in Nyasaland, is the largest of the muridae, and is, in many details of its anatomy, distinct from all other rodents. Measuring a little over two feet in

Plan of the Giant Rat burrow

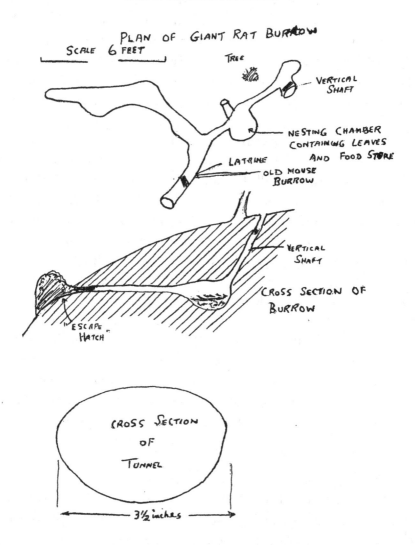

total length, it weighs about 2 and a half lbs. Copley records the size in East Africa as from 2 and a half to 4 ft. This last figure seems exaggerated as one of the largest specimens noted in the British Museum, measured 380 mm H.B. and 465 mm Tail — a total length of about 35 inches. Its fur is either rough or smooth in texture and its coloration on the upper parts varies from a pale grey to dark grey-brown. Whether this variation is purely an individual trait is uncertain. A series of specimens taken from one locality at all times of the year may prove that this species, like the Sun Squirrels *(Helio scunus gambianus)* and the smaller pouched rat *(Beamys major),* both riparian species, undergoes a seasonal colour change? The undersurface and chin is pure white. The tail which is slightly longer than the head and body is scaly and clothed with short hairs, while the distal portion is without pigment. It is held in a very characteristic way quite unlike any other rodent with the exception of the allied *Beamys* — it is carried horizontally several inches clear of the ground.

The Giant Rat is distributed throughout the forest and savannah country of Africa (to which continent it is confined) from Gambia, Bahr-el-Ghazal and Kenya, south to the Zoutpansberg range of Northern Transvaal. Within this range it is confined to hilly regions above 2,000 ft. and is essentially a creature of the evergreen forests or the riparian growths and thickets along the watercourses in brachystegia woodland. It has been recorded at 9,500 ft. on Mt. Elgon, Uganda.

Much has been written by old writers concerning the ferocity of this rat. Sir Harry Johnston for instance writes in "British Central Africa" (1897) . . . "There's one rat which is an appalling creature to look at ... in captivity it is ferocious to a degree and looks a thoroughly evil animal." One must admit that when first captured they do look formidable creatures, and when first taken from their burrows in a frightened state they never hesitate, given the chance, to bite the would-be intruder — as any creature would. At least this has been my experience. But in captivity they soon become tame, and on the whole are very docile, friendly animals. Though generally appearing slow and lethargic in their movements — if I am allowed a little anthropomorphism: they seem extremely dull-witted creatures! Their personality seems to change suddenly after darkness has fallen, for they then become extremely active, able to leap several feet off the ground, and find no difficulty in climbing small shrubs and trees. Copley records that they are able to swim. They thrive well in captivity, feeding on anything in the vegetable line, having a particular liking for groundnuts, cheese water-melons and root vegetables. They drink a good deal and in the wild state are never found far from permanent water. I have also noted that they sleep in some rather strange attitudes, all very human-like, their heads often turned sideways. Bourliere records one living in captivity for 41 years.

It would seem that the habits of *Cricetomys gambianus* follow an identical pattern to those of the smaller pouched rat *Beamys major.* The behaviour pattern of both appears to be a very rigid one. It is likely therefore that with the destruction of its natural habitat which is sure to take place over much of its range in the coming years, the Giant Rat will tend to become even more localised in its distribution.

The Giant Rat is infested with lice, fleas and a peculiar ectoparasite *Hemimerus deceptus* (Rehn). This last insect is not a parasite on the animal itself but feeds on the rodent's accumulated food stores. Several books have termed them "cockroaches", but this is incorrect. They are in fact, very primitive earwigs *(Derrnaptera)* which are blind and wingless. Several species of Hemimerus have been described.

John Kajaiwiche with Epiphytic Orchid Cyrtorchis Arcuata.
Zomba MT. September 1989

Heronimo Luka, Blantyre herbalist at stall, Blantyre market December 1990

Roadside vendors selling mushrooms. Kasupe January

Daughter of Shay Busman with Termitomyces mushrooms Makwawa, December 1990

Zoa v illages looking towards Zoa tea estate, September 1979

Davidson Potani on Mulanje Mountain, November 1990

Sketch of Elephant Shrew Zoa 1959

Sketch of Pouched Rat Beamys Hindei Zoa December 1961

Sketch of Rock Dormouse: New record for Malawi Zoa March 1961

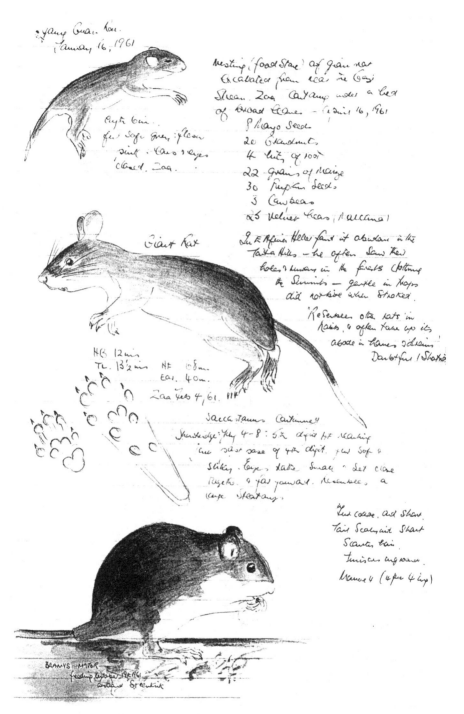

Page from my Zoa journal with sketch of Giant Rat February 1961

Sketch of Giant Rat

Photograph of Beamys Hindei Pouched Rat Zoa 1960

Bulbophyllum Malaiense Thyolo September 1965

Aerangis Pachyura Mulanje, February 1956

Cynorchis Kirkii Soche MT. January 1965

Tridactyle Tricuspis Soche MT. March 1965

Holoyhrix Johnstonii Mulanje MT. July 1965

Eulophia Horsfalli Makwawa December 1979

Tail piece: Pouched Rat

MBEWA: ETHNO-ZOOLOGICAL NOTES ON THE RATS AND MICE OF MALAWI[5] (1993)

To the memory of Peter Hanney

Among the many modes of thought and reflection, there are two kinds of knowledge that are of particular importance. The first is the knowledge we call science. It is knowledge that is written down, and is developed by criticism and by testing it against controlled experience. It belongs to no particular culture, and over the centuries people of every nation have added to the sum of scientific knowledge. Then there is the knowledge of a particular culture. It is a kind of local knowledge that is handed down from generation to generation. It is usually not written down and is largely based on direct experience. In Malawi it is called *nzeru wa makolo,* the knowledge of the ancestors, and forms a part of what is referred to as *miyambo* - customs or traditions. Science of course is also a tradition, but it has its locus in a community of scholars not in a particular ethnic group. Both kinds of knowledge are important and should be respected and both have their practical uses; both also have their limitations.

In this article I want to try and bring together these two kinds of knowledge, and to discuss *mbewa,* which is a general category the Chewa of Malawi

---

[5] In June 1962 *African Wildlife* published an article by Brian Morris, the first he ever wrote, called *Denizen of the Evergreen Forest* which described the habits of the Pouched Rat, *Beamys hindei.* He was then a young tea planter working in the Thyolo District of Malawi. Now a Reader in Anthropology at Goldsmiths College, University of London, he returned to Malawi in 1990 - to undertake ethno-zoological studies, and the following article is based on a talk given to the Blantyre Branch, Wildlife Society of Malawi, 6 August 1991.

use to describe rats, mice, shrews and elephant shrews. In Yao the equivalent term is *lipuku;* in Lomwe, *mtoro.* These terms are general categories covering many different species, but they have as their prototype the ubiquitous Multi-mammate Mouse, *kapuku, (Mastomys natalensis).*

Although mbewa includes shrews and elephant shrews, and may at times be used to cover also the bush squirrel, *gorogoro (Paraxerus)* the category essentially refers to the small rodents, the rats and mice. It excludes the porcupine, *nungu.* So *mbewa* is not exactly co-terminous with the zoological order of rodents (Figure 1.). Here I shall concentrate on the rats and mice.

Figure 1. An outline of the 'taxonomy' of the mbewa in Malawi

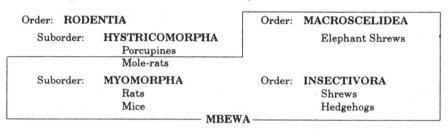

The rodents, the *mbewa,* are the mammals. They are the vertebrates which suckle their young and are covered with fur, and they constitute the largest order of mammals. There are about 5,500 species of mammals in the world; about half of these are small, nocturnal creatures - the bats (985 species) and the rodents (1685 species). Of the latter, the majority are rats and mice - the other important rodents being the porcupines and squirrels: so that about 1 in 5 of all mammals in the world is a rat or mouse. In Malawi 187 species of mammals have been recorded (132 of which are terrestrial) - of these 52 are rodents. So the category *mbewa* in Malawi covers almost half of the terrestrial mammals found in the country (58 out of 132). And like the mushrooms *(bowa),* the *mbewa* has great cultural significance to many rural Malawians. This can be gleaned from Scott's *Mang'anja Dictionary* where he lists the names of 63 species of mammals - significantly 25 of these are the names of rats and mice. He also gives descriptions of eight different kinds of traps that are used to catch them. Another important early missionary-scholar, the White Father, Fr. Louis Denis, in his *French-Chewa Dictionary,* lists 36 names relating to the category *mbewa.* This alone gives you some idea of the cultural importance of *mbewa* in Malawi.

What distinguishes a rodent from other mammals is that at the front of their mouth they have two pairs of incisors, one upper and one lower, which are separated from the molars or cheek teeth by a wide gap. They do not have any canine teeth. Nearly all rats and mice have excellent learning abilities and have acute senses of hearing and smell. Most also have good eyesight. They are found almost everywhere. They are in fact the most successful (apart from humans) and the most numerous of all mammals - both in the number of species, and in their general abundance. In Malawi they are found in every kind of habitat. We find *mbewa* (rats and mice) in *Brachystegia* and *Acacia* woodland, in dambos, in our houses and grain stores, in sugar-cane fields, in maize cultivations, in evergreen forests, and in grassland at the top of the mountains like Mulanje and Zomba.

Table 1. Main habitats of various spicies of *mbewa* found in Malawi (see text).

Species	dambo	riverside	woodland	Riparian forest	Montane grassland	Montane forest	cultivation	Human habitation
mchenzi	x	x						
Namfuko			x		x			
thiri	x	x			x			
phanya			x			x		
bwampini				x				
jugu			x			x		
yungurukuve				x				
nambalala			x			x		
gwede			x					
chinyerere			x	x				
vumbe	x	x						
mphera	x		x			x		
nthukwi	x	x						
sonthe			x	x				
fingi	x					x		
chitwa					x			
kapuku			x					x
mpakadzi			x					
Khoswe								X
Kadyamamu			x					x

Most rats and mice are terrestrial and are mainly nocturnal. Some are adapted to life underground, some are semi-aquatic, and some are very adept climbers. They are predominantly herbivorous and they are, therefore, our greatest competitors for many thrive on the plants and crops domesticated by humans. It is estimated world-wide that rats and mice are perhaps the greatest pests, taking from our gardens and grain stores about 20 per cent of our food crops. And rats and mice have played a crucial role in human history, for they carry the fleas which are the vector of the dreaded disease the bubonic plague. This disease, known in Europe as the 'black death', is estimated to have killed a quarter of the population of Europe in the fourteenth century, and was thought to have been brought there by the Black Rat, *khoswe, (Rattus rattus)*. This rat, which has now spread all over the world, also brought the plague to Africa.

But rats and mice also play a beneficial role; they destroy many harmful insects, help to eradicate many garden weeds, and form the main food supply of many mammals, birds and snakes, thus playing an essential part in sustaining the intricate balance of nature. Rats and mice are also widely used for experiments in medical research and in psychology. In extrapolating behavioural patterns from rats to humans, psychologists like Skinner, while downplaying the linguistic and cultural attributes of humans, seem to be paying the rodents a great compliment. And as someone has said, the rats have their experimenters well-conditioned, for the rats invariably get rewarded with food.

What makes rodents so successful- apart from their cleverness - is that they are such prolific breeders. They mature quickly, and often have lots of young - the *kapuku,* for example, on average gives birth to between 10 and 16 young at a time. However, they don't usually survive much more than a year, and so rats and mice generally live a short, productive and hectic life. But such prolific breeding among many species often gives rise, in favourable circumstances, to what are known as 'rodent explosions'. Their numbers rise to unprecendented levels and then, as the late Reay Smithers put it, they 'literally eat themselves out of house and home' and soon their numbers return to normal.

Let us now survey the commoner rats and mice that are to be found in Malawi. There are about twenty species that are common and widely distributed and these are detailed in Table 2. There are some twenty-five other species recorded from Malawi but many of these have a local distribution, or are restricted to montane grassland. With the Rock Dormouse *(Graphiurus platyops)* and the Giant Mole Rat *(Crytomys mechowi)* we have only a single record for each species from Malawi

- from Zoa and Rumphi respectively.

The *mbewa* in Malawi range in size from the diminutive *Pygmy Mouse pinji,* weighting only 7 or 8 grammes, to the Cane Rat, *nchenzi,* weighing in the males up to 9 kg.

But when one discusses *mbewa* with local Malawians the emphasis is less on morphology - although the different species are well-known and clearly recognized - than on their habitats and ecology. Thus, rats and mice are associated with particular habitats, and we can here perhaps follow the same line of reasoning in our presentation.

There are first those species associated with *dambo* areas and with environs close to water. The most aquatic of these is a fairly local species, never found far

Table 2. Twenty common and widely distributed species of mbewa found in Malawi

Chewa	Yao	Lomwe	English	Scientific name
nthukwi chitukwi			Water Rat	Dasymys incomtus
thiri	liulukusi	ntwiri	Vlei Rat	Otomys angoniensis
vumbe mende	lilende	pholochi nihumbe	Creek Rat	Pelomys fallax
mphera lingwere mphoni mphinzi	ngwawi	nyima	Single-striped Grass Rat	Lemniscomys rosalia
nchenzi nchezi	ngungusi	ethechi	Cane Rat	Thryonomys swinderianus
kabwanda gwede kapeta nsana	chingowe kangowe	lambe	Fat Mouse	Steatomys paatensis
kapuku mpuku nthika	liwindo lipuku	mtoro malupamtoro	Multimammate Mouse	Mastomys natalensis
dondwe phanya	lipanya	nivala tong'ondo	Cape Gerbil	Tatera leucogaster
pinji pïdo tsibwe tilonje	katolo	nantikwa nangwandu	Pygmy Mouse	Mus minutoides
jugu chitute tsambe	dugu	napuso nahuram	Pouched Mouse	Saccostomus campestris
		yungurukuve	Long-tailed Pouched Mouse	Beamys hindei
bwampini kunda	ngwime	kuve nawili	Giant Rat	Cricetomys gambianus
mpakadzi mputsa		kwetu chiradzulu	Red Veld Rat	Aethomys chrysophilus
chinyerere sakachenzi	chanasa	namulukwi tarakali	Spiny Mouse	Acomys spinosissimus
sonthe sontho jelela	lichambili	mulele chinkole	Long-tailed Forest Mouse	Grammomys dolichorus
sonthe wang'ono nambalala		Chinkoli mungole	Lesser Climbing Mouse	Dendromus mystacalis
namfuko mfuko	uko	nahuwo	Mole Rat	Heliophobius argenteocinereus
chitwa	liulwa		Brush-furred Mouse	Lophuromys flavopunctatus
khoswe	likhoswe	nikhule nsilu	Black Rat	Rattus rattus
kadyamlamu	kasapembe	mpandari	Dormouse	Graphiurus microtis

from water, the Water Rat, *nthukwi*,. It is in fact semi-aquatic, being a good swimmer. It has a long shaggy coat - as its Latin name, *Dasymys* incomtus, suggests (*Dasys*, shaggy) - though it is rather soft in texture, and it makes distinct runs through the swampy vegetation radiating from its domed nest of cut grass. It usually has a refuge hole nearby. The Vlei Rat, *thiri*, also stays close to water but it is not as aquatic as the *nthukwi,* and has much shorter tail - only about 90mm long. They are very compact little animals, vole-like, with shaggy fur and large ears. Their Latin name, *Otomys angoniensis,* means 'ear mice' *(otis,* ear). They are very common in montane grassland on Zomba and Mulanje, where spring-traps are set in their well-defined runs. They do not burrow, and neither normally does the Greek Rat, *(Pelomys fallax) mende* or *vumbe,* which is another rat associated with dambos and the fringes of streams. It also has rather shaggy-looking fur, which is distinctly grizzled, and in some lights has a distinct greenish sheen. Its feet are well-developed with strong claws. It sometimes has an indistinct dark stripe along its back - but it is faint - and not as pronounced as in the other dambo mouse, *mphera,* the Single-striped Mouse, *Lemniscomys rosalia.* This mouse has a clearly marked black line running down the centre of its back. The *mphera* is not confined to dambos, however, but is more catholic in its habits and is found wherever there is good grass cover. It seems common in abandoned cultivation and scrub *Brachystegia* woodland, is terrestrial and to a larger extent diurnal. It has well-defined runways and breeds in grass nests at the ground level. But it will take refuge in burrows during fires or when harassed.

A final animal associated with *dambos* - another non-burrowing rodent - is the Cane Rat, or *nchenzi.* Its Latin name, *Thryonomys swinderianus,* means 'rush mouse' *(Thyron,* rush). It is a rather larger rat, usually weighing 5-6 kg., the male being much larger than the female. It prefers semi-aquatic vegetation like reedbeds, is quite common in sugar-cane fields, and is primarily a veg-etarian. During the rainy season, however, it may wander far from permanent water and, unlike the other four species, is prone to take garden produce such as groundnuts, maize and sweet potatoes. One of its local names is *kaphanz-imbe,* the cutter of sugar-cane.

Five species are particularly associated with scrub *Brachystegia* woodland and abandoned cultivations and all appear to eat a diversity of plant food, helping themselves even to garden produce. All are well-known to local peo-ple. One is the attractive little mouse, *gwede* or *kapeta,* the Fat Mouse, *Steato-mys pratensis,* so called because of the accumulated layer of fat beneath its skin. This enables it to become inactive during times when food is scarce. Its Latin name *Steatomys* means 'fat mouse'. It is reddish in colour, with a white belly, and has a short tail. It lives in a fairly deep burrow, the entrance of which is usually sealed. Only one or two mice are found in a burrow in direct contrast to that of the *kapuku*, the Multimammate Mouse, *Mastomys natalensis*, whose burrow may contain 30 or 40 individuals. These mice are commensal (i.e. co-existence) with humans and in rural areas often live in houses - until, that is, the *khoswe*, the Black Rat, arrives on the scene and drives them out. Both its English and Latin name of the mouse refer to its breasts, for the female has 10-12 teats on each side of her belly. As they live close to humans, these mice do a lot of damage to crops and stored grain.

Another mouse common in abandoned cultivations, particularly in sandy areas, is *phanya*, the Cape Gerbil, *Tatera leucogaster*. These mice are of a reddish-brown colouration, with pure white underparts, long hind legs, and a long tail which has a terminal tuft of hair. They live communally in burrows and their presence is often indicated by small mounds of earth outside the entrances. They often use the cavities of old termite hills as does *pinji*, the Pygmy Mouse, *Mus minutoides*. This is truly a diminutive creature, with a body never more than 60mm long. It does not really burrow but tends to live under things - under debris, fallen trees, grass cuttings, and there it makes a nest. It eats insects such as termites and grasshoppers as well as vegetable matter.

The last species which can be described as a frequenter of scrub woodland and abandoned cultivation is the Pouched Mouse, *jugu*, (*Saccostomus campostris*). This is a barrel-shaped creature, grey above with pure white underparts and a short tail. It is a truly pouched mouse, with large cheek pouches in which it carries food back to its burrow for storage. It eats a diversity of food - but is especially fond of seeds and fruit.

There are two other pouched rats to be found in Malawi. Both are mainly restricted to riparian and evergreen forest and make deep elaborate burrows with a number of separate cavities for defecation, nesting and the storage of food. One is *yungurukuve*, the Long-tailed Pouched Rat. *(Beamys hindei)*. It is the same colour as *jugu*, but is larger and more robust, with a long erect tail which has a characteristic pinkish-white tip. It is a smaller version of the *bwampini*, the Giant Rat, but has a much more local distribution. The Giant Rat, *Cricetomys gambi-anus*, on the other hand is quite common and is even found, if there is a suitable habitat near streams, in the centre of towns like Zomba and Lilongwe. The *bwampini* or *kunda* (the name is derived form the Chewa term *ku-kundika*, to store or collect) is a large rodent, of similiar coloration to the other pouched mice, and may weigh up to 1.5 kg. It has a reputation for being a ferocious creature. Although it will bite if roughly treated, it is in fact rather docile. Whereas the *phanya* seems to be entirely independent of water, the *bwampini* is never found very far from a water source.

Turning now to those mice which are associated with woodland, two seem to be particularly fond of rocks. One is *mpakadzi*, the Red Veld Rat *(Aethomys chrysophilus)*. It is superficially like *kapuku*, but is much larger, more reddish-brown in colour, and has a long scaly tail. The female also has only 3 pairs of teats. Although it can burrow, what the *mpakadzi* is fond of doing is finding a suitable rock crevice for a home and filling the cavity with grass and bits of debris. It seems to feed largely on grass seeds, fruits and nuts.

The other mouse which seems to live around the vicinity of rocks in *Brachys-tegia* woodland is the Spiny Mouse, *chinyerere, (Acomys spinosissimus)*. It is easily recognized by its reddish-brown spiny fur, and pure white underparts. It is a small species, common in dry *Brachystegia* woodland. It feeds on grass and other seeds, but also like *pinji*, will eat a variety of insects. Peter Hanney recorded that it was rarely taken by owls.

There are two species that are found in woodland and in other suitable habitats where there is plenty of rank vegetation, which are truly arboreal. In the Thyolo area both are referred to as *sonthe*. The larger species, the Long-tailed Forest Mouse, *Grammomys dolichorus,* is well-known for it often moves into cultivations and builds it grass nest in amongst bananas. It is an attractive mouse, a rich chestnut brown in colour, with white underparts, and has a long tail over 150 mm in length. The other species, the lesser Climbing Mouse, *nambalala* or the *sonthe Wang'ono, (Dendromus mystacalis)* is similarly coloured, but it is a much smaller creature, the head and body only about 60mm long. It is truly arboreal and often frequents disused birds' nests. Like the other species, it is often found in gardens, particularly where there is shrubby vegetation. It feeds on grass seeds mainly, but will also eat insects.

Common in *Brachystegia* woodland, as well as in montane grassland - though rarely seen - are Mole Rats, *Heliophobius argenteocinereus.* The presence *of namfuko* (their name is derived from the verb *ku-fukula*, to scrape or dig up) is indicated by heaps of soil *(thuthu)* on the surface. But, interestingly, there is rarely more than one animal per burrow, and their burrows go down quite deeply, with elaborate bolt holes. They are curious creatures with soft silky grey fur, tiny eyes, a short tail, and extremely large incisors which they use for digging. They can excavate at a very fast rate and so much engenuity is required to dig out a *namfuko.*

At higher altitudes in Bracken Briar or at the borders of evergreen forests the *chitwa* or Brush-furred Mouse, *Lophuromys flavopunctatus,* is found. It is an attractive mouse with chocolate brown upperparts and a black tail and feet. It is often taken by local forestry workers in stone fall traps.

As the Black Rat, *khoswe (Rattus rattus)* is so well-known, it remains only to mention the Dormouse, *kadyamlamu (Graphiurus microtis)* to complete this brief survey of the common rats and mice of Malawi. *Kadyamlamu* means literally 'it eats its cousins', and refers to the aggressive habits of the Dormouse, which do not tolerate intruders on their territory and often fight to death. The fur of the Dormouse is soft and thick, a uniform grey, and it has a long bushy tail. Often there is a black stripe around the eyes. They are agile climbers and though largely vegetarian will also eat termites, millipedes and insects. They are usually to be found around rocks in woodland, but often they enter human habitations and build their nests in the rafters. Unlike most of the other species, *kadyamlamu* is not well-known among Malawians.

Table 3. Results of interview of 100 people on the edibilty of some selected mbewa found in Malawi.

Species	Did not know	Eaten	Not eaten
nchenzi		93	7
namfuko	1	64	35
Thiri	36	51	13
Phanya		83	17
Bwampini		79	21
Jugu		82	18
Vumbe	14	69	17
Mphera	22	51	28
Sonthe	21	51	28
Khoswe		8	92

In rural areas, many Malawians have an extensive knowledge of the biology and ecology of *mbewa*. This is because in many areas rats and mice form an important part of people's diet, a valuable source of protein, and are eagerly sought after. But they are not universally eaten. In a survey I made in the Mulanje and Zomba districts (Table 3) there was always a substantial minority who did not eat *m bewa*, although significantly most people seem to be fond of *nchenzi*, for the Cane Rat is considered a great delicacy. In peoples' responses to my questions there was not a great deal of difference between Yao -, Chewa -, and Lomwe-speakers. This is reflected in the fact that all three languages have an extensive vocabularly relating to rats and mice. But it runs against the common opinion in Malawi that it is only Lomwe-speakers who eat mice. The differences rather lay in peoples' religious affiliation. For, generally speaking, Moslems and many members of independent African churches have a rule against the eating of rats and mice and this is generally adhered to. Given its strong association with human habitations the Black Rat, *khoswe*, is almost universally not eaten. And many express a dislike for the *namfuko* and *sonthe* which are said to cause headaches if eaten. Significantly, as with the shrew, *sunche* and the hedgehog, *chisoni* (neither of which are eaten) both *namfuko* and *sonthe* are widely used as medicine *(mankhwala)*.

Given the importance of rats and mice in their diet - and this is particularly pronounced in Mulanje, Thyolo, Dedza and Dowa Districts (at least this has been my experience) - it is hardly surprising that this interest is deeply reflected in both the language and the culture of the people of these regions. In the northern region of Malawi, among Tumbuka-speakers, there seems, for some reason, to be little focus on rats and mice. Many Tumbuka-speakers, even people extremely knowledgeable about wildlife, seem to recognize only three categories - *fukuzani*, the Mole Rat; *sezi*, the Cane Rat; and *mbewa* which seems to cover all the other species of rats and mice, including the Black Rat.

Among Chewa-speakers there is a rich vocabularly specifically focussed around the category *mbewa*. Not only are there widely recognized names for all the common species (Table 2), but terms are used that specifically relate to mice, and have no direct English equivalents.

The loose earth or clay with which a mouse shuts up its hole is called *chifule;* to leave a thin layer of earth to hide an escape hole making the escape easier is *ku-Nenekeza;* the escape hole itself is called *mduli* or *mbuli* (from the verb *ku-bulika*, to break-out); rat/mice tracks or marks are *mdzimbe, mleka* or *mpita;* while mouse droppings are *nchimbiri.*

People who regularly trap and dig-up mice have an extensive knowledge of their ecology and habits. By observation and by smelling the soil they are able to detrmine the presence or not of particular species of mice, and there are a variety of traps to catch, them. The setting of these indicates great skill and ingenuity. Among the more important of these are: the *diwa*, the stone-fall trap which is baited and has fried bran *(chigaga)* put near to attract the mice; the *msampha*, the spring trap set in the runs of such species as *mphera* and *thiri;* the *chigwenembe*, another spring trap made from a hollowed root of a tree bearing the same name, *Albizia antunesiana* (also known as *mpefu)* - the trap is baited and has a noose; the *goba* or *ngombera* which is made of plaited bamboo in the form of a narrowing tube with sharpened pieces of bamboo set around the rim to prevent the retreat of the mouse once it has taken the bait; and the *nkoka,* a large spring trap with a log that is baited to catch cane rats. You will recall that two of the hills in the Dedza area famous for their rock paintings bear the names of mouse traps - *diwa* and *chigwenembe* - and you will almost certainly find mouse traps in these localities. During the dry season you will also see around Dedza youngster's selling mice on sticks along the roadsides - *kapuku* and *phanya* being the two principal species that are sold on this split-sticks *(mpani).* Most of these mice - At Kl-00 per stick - seem to be bought by passing motorists, indicating perhaps that these youngsters cater for the needs of an urban elite.

As regards the capturing and cooking of the mice I can do no better than quote an extract from a school essay - by a young standard 8 pupil from the Lilongwe District. He writes, and I quote him verbatim:

"When we were digging with my friend I saw a mice jumping in our school garden and I told my friend that there was a mice and we ran away and it started to run fast than anyone could not reach it. And fortunately we reached it and it entered in its hole and we went to our class and took the hoe and we started to dug the hole and after dug we saw it jumping on my left foot and I was huppy that it was beside me. I took a big stick and hit on its back and after hitting it I saw that it was died and when it was died I took it and put in my big pocket and go to our class. And when the teacher said that we can go at home, I ran away with my friend and took a smallest stick and I started to remove its hair and after that I remove all the wastes in its stomach-ache and I went and throw them in our pit. And I went to the tap and I pulled water from the pot and I started to washed it and when it was clean I took it and put in the pot and I went again to the tap and pulled water from the pot and I started to cooked it and cooked it side by side and when it was well cooked I took it from the pot and put in between two sticks called *mpani* in Chichewa. And I ate it with a food food called *msima*, I was with my uncle, my sister, my aunt and my father and I cut it into four parts and I divided it from them. We were happy because we have a good super at that time."

Because of their cultural significance rats and mice often figure prominently in proverbs. Among the Chewa the following proverbs are worth noting:

Buluzi kuthandiza mbewa kuthawa
The Lizard helps the mice to run away.

Dzenje la pinji lidziwika nkuunjika.
The burrow of the *pinji* is known by its little heap (of stones).

Kapinji mayenda-yenda kasiya anzache asewera.
The *pinji* was always going around leaving his friends to play.

Khoswe akakhale pankhate sapheka.
The rat who sits on the clay pot is not killed.

Kudzinga ngati thiri, tionera mende kutha.
To be quiet like the *thiri*, we see the mende getting killed

Mbewa zikachuluka zilibe mala
If there are too many mice they have no nest.

Nchenzi inamva mau oyamba.
The cane Rat heard the first words.

Wakwatira mende waleka chitute
He marries the *mende*, and left the *chitute*.

Besides being an important source of food, rats and mice are also used as medicine *(mankhwala)* and for a variety of purposes. For example, the soil from a mole rat's burrow is used as a remedy for bed-wetting and to cure constipation; the leg bones of the Giant Rat is used for infertility or birth problems, or to assist a young child to walk. Usually parts of the *mbewa* are mixed with the leaves and roots of various trees, and often constitute the *chizimba*, giving power and strength to the medicine.

Rats and mice also figure prominently in the spirit rituals of the Alomwe - the *nantongwe* ceremonies. A chronically ill person, usually a woman, may dream of a particular animal and this animal is then used as a sacrificial offering in a healing ritual. Such animals as the Gerbil, *phanya*, the Pouched Rat, *jugu,* the Mole Rat, *namfuko,* and the Creek Rat, *mphera* are used in such rites and are referred to as *mankhwala wa mutu waukulu* (medicine of the 'large' head - severe headache).

Many rural people in Malawi, as I have intimated, have quite a profound knowledge of the biology and ecology of rats and mice. I remember many years ago telling Peter Hanney, the first curator of the National Museum in Blantyre, who was then undertaking research studies into the Muridae, that people at Zoa had told me that many mice were very clever in that they not only made separate latrines in their burrows, but also built tunnels with 'escape hatches'. He didn't believe me! I had, to invite him to Zoa Estate and, with some Malawian local experts, dig up the mice so that he could examine their burrows. The sketches we made then found their way into his M.Sc. thesis and subsequently, I discovered, into some famous texts on the ecology of small mammals. But I owe to Peter my only true claim to fame. For I discovered a creature new to science - and this he described and named *Hemimerus morrisii.* It is not many people who have named after them a primitive, flightless, parasitic earwig that lives on rat droppings. Like that young lad from Lilongwe, I have ever since retained an affection for that most interesting and fascinating group of wildlife - the *mbewa,* the rats and mice of Malawi.

ANIMALS AS MEAT AND MEAT AS FOOD: REFLECTIONS ON MEAT EATING IN SOUTHERN MALAWI (1994)

In recent years, with the rise of vegetarianism, there has been an increasing interest in the sociology of meat eating. Two texts in particular (Adams 1990; Fiddes 1991) have been especially noteworthy, as they have both emphasized the "barbarity" of meat eating and have both received glowing reviews in academic journals. The present paper has two concerns. The first is to offer some brief but critical reflections on these two texts. The second is to offer some ethnographic material from southern Malawi that may counter some misleading generalizations about meat eating that stem from these two important studies.

PROLOGUE

In a much acclaimed post-modernist text on the sexual politics of meat, Carol Adams (1990) sees the eating of meat—a "blood culture"—as a "symbol of male power." She also argues that meat eating is an "index of racism" and homophobia and is intrinsically related to aristocratic rule and to warfare. Her study focuses on texts, and it has a decidedly Eurocentric bias. In the early chapters she draws on anthropological material, but her data is highly selective, focusing largely on various food taboos that affect women. A rather Manichean perspective also infuses the text, which views meat eating (but not, it seems, the eating of plant foods) as a negation of life; thus the hunting of animals for food is seen in an essentially negative fashion, even as an evil. The outcome of her study is to imply that meat is universally a male prerogative and that there is a simple and direct relationship between meat eating and gender, class, and racial hierarchies. She virtually equates meat eating with hunting and fails to distinguish between the various modalities of hunting, for food, as sport, and as a form of ritual. That many aristocratic elites have been vegetarians, that many aristocratic women in Europe have been active participants in ritualized hunting, and that women have often been actively involved in subsistence hunting are all issues that are beyond Adams's purview. What would she make of Chris Knight's (1991) thesis that the origins of culture essentially involved an exchange of meat for sex, initiated by a grouping of matrilineally related women?

In stressing the association of meat eating with "male power" and with European (or aristocratic) hegemony, Adams makes two rather misleading assumptions. One is the idea that meat eating and hunting are not important aspects of preliterate or clan-based societies. She even suggests that the biblical "garden of Eden" was vegetarian (p. 112), although as Mircea Eliade (1968) long ago suggested, the "nostalgia for paradise" was widespread in "archaic" societies, and referred to a mythical epoch when food was abundant and people lived in peace with each other and with the animals and knew nothing of death. Such myths probably referred to the memories of a golden age of hunting and gathering, when an egalitarian ethos prevailed and meat eating coexisted with a close and respectful relationship between humans and animals.

Secondly, Adams suggests that even where hunting is found, it is men, not women, who eat the meat. Anthropological evidence suggests that throughout human history, the diet of human beings has largely consisted of plant food, and this is the case even among hunter-gatherer societies. In this sense humans have always been near-vegetarians,1 although Marvin Harris (1990: 154) may well be correct when he suggests that humans, like baboons and chimpanzees, are primarily omnivores. Nonetheless, hunting is an important aspect of almost all clan-based societies, even though, as I tried to show in my study of a south Indian foraging community, the Hill Pandaram, they may tend to gather animals from the forest rather than systematically hunt them (Morris 1982: 79). And even though meat may be intrinsically associated with men and deemed by some to be a more prestigious food than vegetables, women in most preliterate communities are avid eaters of meat. Though many preliterate people feel a sense of kinship with the natural world and indicate an awareness that sustaining human life paradoxically involves the taking of life (including the life of plants), to universalize vegetarian sentiments is hardly conducive to cross-cultural understanding. Smoholla, who belonged to a largely hunting culture, the Nez Perce, even refused to participate in agricultural activities. "Shall I take a knife," he said, "and tear my mother's breast?" (McLuhan 1971: 56). Yet he was a meat eater.

Adams's study makes an important and stimulating contribution to feminist theory, in providing a feminist history of vegetarianism and in drawing out the important connections between meat eating and gender and class hierarchies. But her account is highly colored by her own perspective—that of urban middle-class literati—to the degree that she verily denies the importance of meat eating among "people of colour" (p. 30), as she refers to non-Western people, both men and women. In stressing, too, the analogical relationship between slavery and meat eating, she also oblates entirely the fact that the African populations who were taken as slaves were themselves meat eaters. Such arguments may serve to bolster the ethical superiority of vegetarians, but they do scant justice to the cultural integrity of African people, the people who were enslaved.

Nick Fiddes's lucid and stimulating account of meat as a "natural symbol," in contrast, essentially adopts Mary Douglas's symbolic approach to dietary customs. I have earlier made some critical reflections on this approach, highlighting the inadequacies of Douglas's interpretation of the Leviticus prohibitions (Morris 1976; 1987: 206-9). Fiddes, however, continues to follow this rather cultural determinist mode of thinking. His essential argument is that meat eating "symbolizes" or "represents" a specific world view, one that involves the Promethean ethic of "human control of, and superiority over, nature" (1991: 6). Meat eating implies the notion of "environmental control" and "power over nature." His focus is largely on the European context, but he implies that all "civilized" humans have long characterized themselves as "predators and conquerors" (p. 63). Fiddes sees vegetarianism as a "reaction" against this ethos of domination, one that entails a biocentric attitude to nature.

Although there is substance in Fiddes's analysis of western capitalist culture, I wish to highlight a number of problems with his analysis.

Firstly, to give meat eating an essentially monovalent interpretation is highly misleading. The dualistic premise that meat eating reflects an anthropocentric attitude and abstinence a biocentric one is questionable. Levi-Strauss

(1966: 107-8) indeed suggested that as humans recognized their essential affinity with animals, food taboos were a means of stressing their separateness, and, as Fiddes observes of Christian ethics (p. 205), abstention from meat does not necessarily reflect a biocentric attitude to the world. To the contrary, it may reflect a theocentric one. The vegetarianism of Buddha, Plotinus, and Porphyry, for example, does not express an ecological attitude but rather involves the distancing of humans from the empirical world and their "ascent" to the Godhead (whether conceptualized as "spirit," "one," or nirvana).2 If Elias's thesis of the "civilizing process" is tenable, as Fiddes seems to suggest it is, vegetarianism could reflect the increasing adoption of "urbane" values, and a further distancing of humans from their intrinsic and symbiotic relationship to the biological world. Thus, in continuing to maintain a value hierarchy and in virtually denying that plants are a form of life (is it not Speciesist to eat/kill them?), vegetarians are expressing attitudes that are neither anthropocentric nor biocentric but rather theocentric. Fiddes hardly touches upon the close association between vegetarianism and new-age religion.

Secondly, in many clan-based societies, particularly of hunter-gatherers, meat eating coexists with a close spiritual relationship between people and their natural environment. James Frazer highlighted this relationship many years ago in his reflections on sacred animals (1922: 678-79), as do such contemporary writers as Nelson (1983) and Brown (1992) on the Koyukon and Oglala Sioux, respectively. Meat eating may reflect, therefore, not power over animals but rather identification with them.3

Finally, Fiddes relates the British abstinence from eating primates and carnivorous animals to the fact that these animals are seen as akin to humans; the first in terms of morphology, the second in being predators "like us." These explanations are hardly tenable. Throughout the world almost all people recognize the similarity between humans and primates, yet dietary prohibitions hardly reflect this recognition directly. As Fiddes acknowledged, many people eat monkeys. That people see themselves as predators is also open to challenge. Throughout the world herbivores tend to be eaten; carnivores (from lions to shrews) tend not to be. Material factors surely influence our diet, for many people — and certainly Malawians — consider shrews to be unpalatable. Even animal predators recognize this, which is one of the reasons cats and dogs normally deposit shrews on the door mat!

The studies of Adams and Fiddes are well researched and provide stimu-lating reading.4 While their focus is largely on the European context, they both tend to see their observations about meat eating as having wider cross-cultural relevance. In the present paper I address three of these generalizations and refer to the Malawian evidence in an attempt to counter them.

My first objection is to the notion that meat eating is a "barbaric" custom that plays only an insignificant role in clan-based or preliterate countries. On the contrary, meat eating is important in Malawi and carries no such negative connotations. "Meat" is seen in a positive sense as an essential and important ingredient to food intake, one that is conducive to health and well-being.

Secondly, in stressing the role of meat as a "symbol" of male power, Ad-ams suggests that meat eating is the prerogative of men. I argue that among Malawians meat is as important to women as it is to men, even though men are symbolically associated with animals and men tend to be given more than their fair share of meat (as well as of other foodstuffs).

Finally, I question whether meat eating simply reflects the Enlightenment ethic of "power over nature" since, far from universal, this ethic is certainly not articulated in the Malawian context. I am loathe to follow the lamentable tendency of many anthropologists and radical ecologists to describe cultures or even entire epochs in terms of a single motif or paradigm, for cultures are complex and often indicate diverse and contrasting ontologies. Malawian culture is no exception; social attitudes toward animal life in Malawi are com-plex, diverse, and multidimensional. I have explored these issues elsewhere and do not highlight this theme in the present paper.5 Meat eating in Ma-lawi does not reflect an attitude of opposition or control over nature; to the contrary, it implies the incorporation of the intrinsic powers of nature. Such powers are associated with the Brachystegia woodland *(thengo),* with men as an affinal category, and with animals—but the harnessing of these powers (through food, medicine, and ritual) is seen as essential for human well-being, both individual and social.

The following three sections present ethnographic material on meat eat-ing in Malawi, focusing respectively on the role of meat as food,6 on the ani-mals that are customarily eaten as food in the rural areas, and on the nature of the various food taboos relating to wild mammals.

MEAT AS FOOD

Throughout Malawi the term for food *chakudya* (from the verb *ku-dya*, "to eat") implies only one thing: a solid meal consisting of a thick porridge *(nsima)* and a savory side dish or relish *(ndiwo).7* The porridge is made of fine white flour *(ufa)*— most often of maize *(chimanga)*, although other cereals such as finger millet *(mawere)*, sorghum *(mapira)*, and rice *(mpunga)* may also be eaten. The stiff maize porridge is "the staff of life of every Malawian" as the recent cookbook of the Chitukuko Cha Amayi M'Malawi (the national women's organization) puts it (CCAM 1992). Malawians who do not get a meal of nsima at least once a day will not consider themselves properly fed. They may have eaten large quantities of such filling foods as sweet potatoes *(mbatatd)* or green maize *(mundokwa)*, but they will still feel unsatisfied and say that they will "sleep with hunger" *(ndigona ndi njala)*. However, if they have eaten sufficient porridge Malawians will declare themselves full or satisfied *(wakhuta)*. The expression wakhuta has a deep emotional resonance. It indicates a feeling of well-being; only someone whose own life is focused around basic subsistence can fully appreciate its meaning. The term can also refer to a general satisfaction of heart or mind, or to a pregnant woman *(ali ndi mimba,* "she is with stomach," is the more familiar expression). Malawians in rural areas usually eat two meals a day, around midday and at sunset, though snacks are also taken. Surveys have shown that many households have only one meal a day (Burgess and Wheeler 1970). What makes a meal satisfying is that enough porridge is eaten to feel really full. This is possible only if there is an adequate and appetizing side dish. The side dish is therefore a crucial component of the meal, which is usually eaten communally, as a family, or according to gender or age. A group of people will sit around a bowl or basket of porridge and one or more side dishes. Each person in turn will break off a lump of porridge, roll it in the fingers to form a small ball, and then dip it into one of the relishes. If the ndiwo is a poor one, owing perhaps to its bitter flavor or to a lack of groundnuts or taste, then there will be little enjoyment in the meal; little porridge will be eaten and there will be no real satisfaction.

For a Malawian the ideal relish should be well seasoned and of a good flavor, neither insipid nor bitter. It should contain a certain amount of liquid or gravy and be of a soft consistency so that it will stick to the lumps of porridge dipped into it. Groundnut flour *(nsinjiro)* is important in this respect. Not only very rich in oil, it forms a sauce that is very appetizing when mixed with leaves or mushrooms. The flavor of the relish depends very largely upon adding the right amount of salt *(mchere)*, usually bought locally. Failing this ingredient, women will resort to salt derived from plant ashes (potashes, *chidulo)*, while if neither is available, they use tomatoes to provide flavor in place of salt. A side dish without salt is said to be *za madzi* (of water) and is scorned by everyone.

In her truly pioneering studies of nutrition in Malawi, Jessie Williamson (1942, 1972,1975) outlined in detail the various food plants that are used as a relish. It is important to realize, however, that not all vegetables are suitable as side dishes. While, for example, yams and sweet potatoes constitute important snacks between meals, they are not used as a relish. There are four main kinds of vegetables that are used as ingredients in the relish dish, namely, leafy vegetables such as the leaves of Chinese cabbage *(mpiru)* or various Acanthes *(bonongwe);* beans and pulses (the kidney bean *[mbwanda]* being the most popular), edible fungi *(bowa),* and the tubers of certain ground orchids.

Two points are worth noting here. The first is that there are seasonal variations in the availability of food. During the early part of the rainy season in rural areas there is often a severe food shortage, and this period is often described as a time of hunger *(njala).* Williamson observed in 1940-41 that children in villages showed a consistent loss of weight from December to February, due to a shortage of staple food (1942: 13).

The second point is that although women are owners of the granary and have a good deal of autonomy in domestic affairs, the distribution of food within the family is by no means equal. In a normal year, there will be enough maize porridge for all, but the distribution of relish is always very unequal. When a woman is serving out the food, she will invariably send the lion's share of the side dish to the men, keeping back only a small amount for herself and the young children. In the case of meat or fish, she will invariably see to it that the men of the household get not only a larger share, but often the choicest morsels.8 Consequently, women, as well as girls and younger boys, on the whole eat many more snacks. Williamson (1942: 16) observed that it was young boys, between eight and fourteen years old, who probably fared worst with regard to food. Not old enough to work or earn money, not yet strong enough to force or entice their mothers to give them food, young boys are very much left to their own devices.9 Thus young boys spend an inordinate amount of time searching the bush for food morsels, gathering fruit and wild foods, digging up mice, and collecting insects.

Although fish *(nsombd)* and insects (particularly locusts *[dzombe]* and flying termites *[inswa]*) are almost universally liked and form a regular constituent of many side dishes, to a Malawian meat is the relish *par excellence.* Williamson suggested that if the supply of fish and meat were sufficient they would willingly be eaten daily (1941: 14). Many early observers spoke of the craving that Malawians have for meat (Young 1877: 5; Drummond 1889: 115-16), and Malawians use the terms *nkhuli* or *nkhwiru* specifically to refer to this craving for meat or fish (see also Richards 1939: 56 on the related Bemba of Zambia). The Malawi data certainly do not bear out Carol Adams's suggestion that "on an emotional level everyone has some discomfort with the eating of animals" (1990: 66). Her notion that meat eating is a white male prerogative indicates a rather dismissive and prejudicial attitude toward African people, for the evidence suggests that they highly value meat eating. Although hunting and animals are associated with men — and correlatively agriculture and plants with women — in Malawi both men and women eat and enjoy meat.

The suggestion by the same author (1990: 40-41) that concepts used to describe meat tend to deny that such food is derived from living animals is certainly not the case in Malawi. For the concept *nyama* is a polysemic term meaning both meat and edible quadruped. Nyama is a term that covers all mammals that are eaten as food and by extension also refers to fungi and to the roots of certain orchids, which are seen as having a similar texture and taste to that of meat. The term has a functional contrast in the concept of *chlrombo,* which covers the carnivores — lion and hyena are prototypical — and all animal organisms that are useless, noxious, or dangerous to humans. Again, by extension, chirombo covers weeds and inedible fungi. The term nyama does not include domestic fowls *(nkhuku)* or the many wild birds *(mbalame)* that are eaten, nor does it cover fish.

Williamson remarks that "more or less anything in the way of animal flesh is eaten" (1942: 8). To some extent this is true, as there is hardly a creature great or small that may not be eaten; but, as we shall see, there are wide variations in which mammals are eaten in Malawi that reflect a variety of factors, both cultural and personal. Although it is considered unseemly for women to show any eagerness for meat — for animals are intrinsically connected with male virility (seen as essential for societal well-being) — women do in fact eat meat. There appear to be no food taboos relating to mammals that are specifically gender-linked, although there are certain circumstances when women are prohibited from eating specific animals.

Meat (or chicken) is the side dish *par excellence*. Almost all parts of the animal or bird are eaten and practically nothing is wasted, except for the bones that are too hard to be chewed. Meat may be eaten whatever the state of decay.10 The meat is invariably boiled until the flesh is very soft and comes away easily from the bones. The pot may be refilled many times during the cooking, depending on the toughness of the meat. Salt is always added, and sufficient liquid is always left to form a gravy. In urban areas meat tends to be fried initially in cooking oil, onions and tomatoes are added, and the dish is then cooked in a casserole (Williamson 1942: 62; CCAM 1992: 175).

Apart from the Ngoni and the Nkhonde of the northern region, none of the Malawian people has a pastoral economy. In a survey of a hundred families in the Mulanje and Zomba districts (see Table 1), hens and goats were the principal domestic animals, with a few families owning pigs, sheep, and cattle.

Table 1. Domestic animals

	Mulanje		Zomba		Total	
	No. of familes	No. of domestic animals	No. of families	No. of domestic animals	No. of families	No. of domestic animals
Cattle	10	65	2	14	12	79
Goats	23	115	9	60	35	175
Sheep	-	-	4	15	4	15
Pigs	4	16	-	-	4	16
Rabbits	5	15	2	15	7	30
Guinea pigs	1	2	-	-	1	2
Cats	35	41	14	15	49	56
Dogs	7	17	12	18	19	35
Doves	7	108	5	14	12	122
Hens	44	267	30	221	74	488
Ducks	3	10	1	6	4	16

Total number of families =100

All the families were essentially subsistence agriculturalists, describing themselves as *alimi* (cultivators) who augment their incomes through various trades and occupations. Although most — but not all — families own hens, only a few households possess domestic animals, 12 percent of the families have cattle, 35 percent goats, 4 percent sheep, and 4 percent pigs. No pigs are owned in the Zomba district, where Moslem Yao-speakers form a high percentage of the population. In both areas — as in most parts of Malawi — wild mammals are confined to wooded hillsides; they are only infrequently captured as food, although trapping and hunting are widely practiced. The principal animals captured are monkeys, duikers, hyraxes, and various species of field mice. In rural areas, domestic animals and poultry are rarely killed for food, unless there is good reason, such as a feast for a wedding or funeral or to honor an important visitor with good ndiwo. The suggestion of many vegetarians that people would not eat animals if they had to kill them themselves gets no support at all from the Malawian context. People who kill animals invariably eat them. But it is worth reiterating that meat is only infrequently taken as ndiwo, even though highly valued. Nutrition surveys indicate that meat (goat, hens, or wild animals) forms only a small percentage of the dietary intake of most Malawians — about 15 percent of the family/days on which food was used, amounting on average to between eight and fifteen grams per person per day. Meat eating is no higher in urban areas (Burgess and Wheeler 1970; Williamson 1972). Beef *(ng'ombe)* and goat *(mbuzi)* are the most popular as meat relishes, although the latter can often have a strong unpleasant smell. Mutton is less well liked: it is said to be lacking in taste *(ku-zizird)* and not to have as good a smell as the other two meats. But in Moslem areas, among Yaos, it seems to some extent to supplant goat flesh in popularity. The Ngoni have elaborate rules for the distribution of cattle meat *(nyama ya ng'ombe)*, and some of the choicest parts, which are considered delicacies, are reserved for men or for the owner of the beast. These include the heart *(mtima)*, the kidneys *(mpsyo)*, the head *(mutu)*, and the tongue *(lilime)*. The intestines *(matumbo)* of domestic animals are very popular and are eaten by both sexes, young and old. In market stalls, they are often sold rolled around meat ready for cooking *(ntumbwana)*. Chicken is universally eaten in Malawi and well liked, particularly by women. The hens are usually killed only when there is some occasion to celebrate. The greatest welcome you can give to a visitor, suggests the CCAM cookbook, "is to produce a whole chicken deliciously prepared" (1992: 161).

DIETARY PROHIBITIONS RELATING TO ANIMALS

Throughout Malawi there are wide variations in which wild animals are eaten as food and which species are specifically prohibited. But generally speaking, because animal food is seen as energy giving (in modern parlance), as conducive to the activation of "heat" *(otentha)*, meat eating — like sex — is considered potentially harmful in certain contexts. Thus a menstruating or pregnant woman will not eat meat during these vulnerable periods — particularly meat of animals that are seen as highly "potent," such as bushpig, hippopotamus, and elephant (Mikochi 1938: 21). All rites of passage *(chinamwali)* have similar restrictions, and so do occasions involving the administration of medicines *(mankhwala)* or offerings *(nsembe)* made to the spirits of the dead or to rain deities. Early missionaries and administrators, particularly those who had ethnological interests, frequently remarked upon food taboos relating to animal life. In a discussion of prohibited meat *(nyama zosald)* the Blantyre missionary David Clement Scott wrote:

Certain people, and varying duties, are supposed to require to abstain *(ku-sala)* from certain meats. Hence those who offer sacrifice don't eat rats (rats are supposed to be specially uncanny); girls at a particular age won't eat eggs or drink milk; the Yao mostly abstain from milk and eggs; each tribe or family has its particular abstinence from certain foods. . . . Hence a great many refuse swine's flesh; very few eat crocodile; still fewer eat fox (jackal), leopard, lion, hyena; a good many eat zebra, hippopotamus; most eat mice, elephant; almost no one refuses buffalo, fish and game of all kinds; though some few actually do not eat fowl. (1929: 492-93)

Scott lived mainly among the Mang'anja of the Blantyre area. Hugh Stannus, however, spent many years as a medical officer at Zomba, working among Yao-speakers. He was a man of wide interests and sympathetic in his approach to local culture. In his important study of the Yaos Stannus wrote regarding their food prohibitions:

The flesh of all the antelopes, of oxen, sheep and goats is eaten greedily; only bushbuck is avoided by some people as it is said to cause a skin eruption. Elephant is shunned by many on account of its rough skin, also rhinoceros because of the ulcers which it often has on its body, and hippopotamus on account of its marks on its back which are often thought to be akin to leprosy. People eating the flesh of these animals are supposed often to sicken with leprosy.. . .

Few will eat pig or warthog on account of the digging habits of these animals. It is thought they may sometimes grub up bodies from graves. These flesh taboos may be due to Mohammedan influence. The lion, hyena and fox (jackal) no one would touch, as they are supposed to be connected with *usawi (ufiti,* witchcraft), but the heart of the lion might be eaten to acquire courage. Few will touch leopard flesh. . . . All will eat the flesh of the serval cat but very few of the common wild cat. The rock rabbit (hyrax), *ngangawira (mbira),* is refused by most Yao as it is a "beast without shame" having no tail to hide what should in decency be hid. Very few will partake of the baboon, but monkey is acceptable to many. A few reject porcupine, supposing they will break out in spots, while the zebra may cause stripes and none will touch the skunk *(zorilld).* No one eats *sunje,* a mouse (shrew) that is believed to die if it crosses a path. All kinds of rats are eaten, but the shrew-rat (elephant shrew) and cane rat only by boys. Snakes no one will touch. With the exception of carrion birds such as the crow and hawk, most birds are considered fit to eat. (1922: 347-48)

These early accounts indicate the selectivity and variability in the kinds of animals that Malawians eat. They counter the crude stereotype, reflected in the writings of the colonial administrator Coudenhove, that local people have a palate so "absolutely devoid of taste" that they eat anything left by the raven and hyena and have a bill of fare so extensive that they eat "everything that breathes" — though Coudenhove did note that Yaos did not eat birds of prey or the ground hornbill (1925: 42-43).

Table 2. Ethnic and religious affiliations

	Male (57)				Female (43)			Total
	Yao	Ngoni	Lomwe	Nyanja	Yao	Lomwe	Nyanja	
Protestant churches	8	1	14	10	12	3	12	60
(C.C.A.P., Anglican)								
Roman Catholic	1	-	4	1	-	2	1	9
African Independent	-	-	8	3	-	6	-	17
churches (P.I.M.,								
Topia Church, Faith								
in Action)								
Islam	5	-	-	2	6	-	1	14
Total	14	1	26	16	18	14	14	100

Oral traditions confirm the early observations of Scott and Stannus (see Nkondiwa et al. 1977) and suggest that religious, totemic, and personal factors all play a part in determining food prohibitions relating to animal life. I interviewed a hundred people in the Zomba and Mulanje districts concerning their dietary preferences, as these specifically related to sixty-four of the more common mammal species." Table 2 shows the religious and ethnic affiliations of these people. I draw from these interviews the following observations concerning the edibility of wild mammals:

Firstly, there were a number of animals that people generally did not know. These included the night ape *(kamundi)*, the roan antelope *(chilembwe)*, and the dormouse *(kadyamlamu)*, all of which have a limited or local distribution.

Secondly, many species are generally recognized as food (see Table 3). What is of interest is that although antelopes are widely recognized as meat, and almost everyone eats mammals such as buffalo, common duiker, and kudu, in all categories there are a significant number of people who do not eat the meat. (We shall explore below several possible reasons for this.) It is also noteworthy that most people seem to eat the hyrax, hare, and bushbuck, even though these animals are mentioned in the literature as being of ill omen. The bushbuck antelope, a beautiful creature with a spotted coat, is of particular interest, since the eating of its meat is often associated with the skin disease *chiwengo*. Yet almost all of our respondents said that they used bushbuck meat as ndiwo. Though a shy animal, plenty of bushbuck still survive even near populated areas, and I have many records of their being hunted on all the hills of the Shire Highlands. Both Duff (1903: 268) and Stannus (1910: 323) suggest that the bushbuck is not eaten because it is said to frequent graveyards. A variety of mammals—giant rats, duikers, hares— frequent the woodland thickets that constitute such protected graveyards *(manda)*, however, and they are all regularly eaten, though never hunted in the manda itself. A large number of people—on personal grounds—do not eat elephant, impala, hippopotamus, bushpig, and several other species that they associate with *chiwengo*. Moslems generally do not eat bushpig or warthog, with the men tending to be more strict in the observance of this dietary restriction, as Table 4 indicates.

Table 3. Animals generally recognizied as food

Species	Not known	eaten	Not eaten	% of people knowing mammal who eat it
Ungulates				
Elephant njobvu	6	72	22	77
Rhino chipembere	12	67	21	76
Zebra mbidzi	24	63	13	83
Hippo mvuu	6	74	20	78
Warthog njiri	14	69	17	80
Bushpig nguluwe	1	82	17	84
Hartebeest ngondo	48	37	15	71
Red duiker kadumba	66	26	8	76
Impala nswala	23	43	34	56
Waterbuck nakodzwe	55	35	10	78
Duiker gwape	1	97	2	98
Klipspringer chinkoma	12	80	8	91
Sable mphalapala	7	87	6	94
Buffalo njati	7	90	3	97
Kudu ngoma	11	87	2	98
Bushbuck mbawala	2	98	-	100
Eland ntchefu	12	87	1	99
Reedbuck mphoyo	22	71	7	91
Non-ungulates				
Rock hyrax zumba	10	79	11	88
Yellow-spotted hyrax mbira	-	93	7	93
Hare kalulu	-	98	2	98
Serval njuzi	25	65	10	87
Antbear nkumbakumba	39	45	16	74
Civat cat chombwe	23	47	30	61
Genet mwili	4	71	25	74
Grey mongoose nyenga	2	66	32	67

Thirdly, there are around sixteen species of mammals that the majority of people do not consume as a relish (see Table 5). This rather dispels Coudenhove's suggestion that people of southern Malawi eat all forms of animal life. None of the larger carnivores is eaten, including the cheetah *(kakwio)*, which has a very limited distribution in Malawi. Several of the smaller carnivores are, however, eaten: genet, civet cat, grey mongoose, and serval, which some consider to be a delicacy, *ndiwo yabwino* (good relish). People avoid eating any animal species associated with witchcraft *(ufiti)*, including jackals, hyenas, snakes, and various species of owls *(kadzidzi)*. Although the civet cat is considered to have a bad smell *(kununkha)* and its meat to give rise to headaches, about 60 percent of the people eat it nonetheless. Many of the animals that are not considered sources of food

Table 4. Edibility of bushpig and warthog

	Male		Female		
	Islam	Christian	Islam	Christian	Total
Bushpig					
Eaten	-	46	3	33	82
Not eaten	7	4	4	2	17
Not known	-	-	-	1	1
Total	7	50	7	36	100
Warthog					
Eaten	-	42	4	23	69
Not eaten	7	3	1	6	17
Not known	-	5	2	7	14
Total	7	50	7	36	100

Table 5. Animals generally not eaten

	Not known	Eaten	Not eaten
Non carnivores			
Shrew sunche	2	-	98
Hedgehog chisoni	-	1	99
Fruit bat mleme	-	2	98
Insectivorous bat nanzeze	-	17	83
Banana bat chuchu	18	2	80
Pangolin ngaka	50	11	39
Black rat khoswe	-	7	93
Carnivores			
Jackal nkhandwe	-	3	97
Zorilla kanyimbi	4	3	93
Hyena fisi	-	10	90
Leopard nyalugwe	-	4	96
Lion mkango	-	3	97
Wild dog mbulu	21	5	74
Water mongoose	44	21	35
nkhakhakha			
Banded mongoose msulu	29	11	60
Wild cat bvumbwe	29	16	45

— relishes — are widely used as medicine *(mankhwald)*. The civet cat, hyena, and zorilla are typical examples.

Fourthly, the *mbewa* (rats, mice, shrews, and elephant shrews) is an important local category of animals that consists largely of edible species. In many rural areas they constitute a major source of relish; toward the end of the dry season young boys sell them dried on sticks to passing motorists. In this category only the shrew

Table 6. Edible mbewa species

Species	Not known	Eaten	Not eaten	% of people knowing mammal. Who eat it
Elephant shrew sakhwi	4	64	32	66
Mole rat namfuko	1	64	35	67
Vlei rat thiri	36	51	13	80
Giant rat bwampini	-	74	26	74
Gerbil phanya	-	83	17	83
Pouched rat jugu	-	82	18	82
Long-tailed forest mouse sonthe	21	51	28	65
Single-striped rat mphera	22	63	15	81
Creek rat mende	14	69	17	80
Spiny mouse chinyerere	4	74	22	77
Fat mouse kapeta	-	82	18	82
Cane rat nchenzi	-	93	7	93

Table 7. Edibility of ambiguous animal categories

Species	Not Known	Eaten	Not eaten	% of people knowing mammal, who eat it
Otter katumbu	8	46	46	50
Bush squirrel	3	38	59	39
Porcupine nungu	1	66	33	66
Baboon nyani	-	57	43	57
Vervet monk5ley pusi		57	43	57
Black monkey nchima	8	57	35	62
Bushbaby changa	5	51	44	57

(sunche) and the black rat *(khoswe)* are not eaten—the first because of its

offensive smell *(kununkha)*, the second because of its association with human habitations (see Table 6).

Finally, there is a group of mammals with a rather ambiguous status (see Table 7), that many people eat, but not everyone. These animals include the primates, along with the otter, bush squirrel, and porcupine. All these animals have important uses as medicine.

In sum, then, of the 61 mammal species recognized, 18 ungulates, 8 non-ungulates, and 12 of the mbewa category are widely considered to be food; 16 species are not eaten as food; and 7 species have an ambiguous food status.

We turn now to three factors that may be relevant in guiding dietary prohibitions—gender, ethnicity, and religious affiliation. Tables 8 and 9 detail the perceived

Table 8. Edibity of giant rat *(bwamini)* according to etnic group and religios affiliation

Ethnicity		Male	Female	Total
Yao & others	Eaten	10	14	24
	Not eaten	5	4	9
Lomwe	Eaten	20	8	28
	Not eaten	6	3	9
Nyanja	Eaten	12	10	22
	Not Eaten	4	4	8
	Total	57	43	100
Religious affiliations				
Protestant Churches	Eaten	28	23	51
	Not eaten	5	4	9
Roman Catholic	Eaten	6	3	9
	Not eaten	0	0	0
African Independent Churches	Eaten	7	4	11
	Not eaten	4	2	6
Islam	Eaten	1	2	3
	Not eaten	6	5	11
	Total	57	43	100
	Total eaten	42	32	74

Table 9. Edibility of baboon(*nyani*) according to ethnic group and religious affiliation

Ethnicity		Male	Female	Total
Yao & others	Eaten	7	7	14
	Not eaten	8	11	19
Lomwe	Eaten	21	6	27
	Not eaten	5	5	10
Nyanja	Eaten	7	9	16
	Not eaten	9	5	14
	Total	57	43	100
Religious affiliations				
Protestant Churches	Eaten	23	16	39
	Not Eaten	10	11	21
Roman catholic	Eaten	6	2	8
	Not eaten	-	1	1
African Independent	Eaten	6	1	7
Churches				
	Not eaten	5	5	10
Islam	Eaten	-	3	3
	Not eaten	7	4	11
	Total	57	43	100
	Total eaten	35	22	57

edibility of two species, the giant rat *(bwampini)* and the baboon *(nyani),* and show that neither gender nor ethnicity are crucial factors in determining which mammals are eaten as ndiwo, though women are less inclined to eat baboon meat.12 Although throughout Malawi, Yao and Chewa speakers tend to suggest that Lomwe people eat anything, from leopard and snakes to field mice *(Lomwe amadya,* "the Lomwe eat them," is a common phrase that comes out spontaneously in many discussions about food), my studies did not indicate a great deal of difference in the dietary preferences of the different ethnic groups. Lomwe people, like other people in Malawi, do not normally eat hedgehog, pangolin, shrews, leopard, jackals, or wild dog, and, more generally, not just the Lomwe but all ethnic communities in southern Malawi enjoy eating the giant rat and field mice. Of the seven people who admitted that they ate the black rat, only three were Lomwe speakers. Religious affiliation, however, is an important factor in dietary attitudes. Moslems (particularly men) and members of Independent African Churches (Topia Church, Providence Industrial Mission) (particularly women) refrain from eating the mbewa category and such mammals as baboons, monkeys, squirrels, and the smaller carnivores (which other people may eat). It is of interest that none of the Moslems interviewed owned a domestic dog. Chikanza (1980: 4) noted that members of the African Full Gospel Church, who reject traditional medicine and beer drinking, also do not eat bushpig and mice.

As elsewhere in Africa, Moslems *(Asilamu)* in Malawi have elaborate rites relating to meat eating, clearly distinguishing between edible and non-edible animals. Any animal that dies of its own accord *(nyama yukufa yokha)* is not eaten, and only animals whose throat has been cut by an Islamic teacher *(Mwalimu)* or someone recognized by him can be eaten. It is stressed that the individual performing the slaughter must be circumcised *(wodulidwa nsonga s ya mbolo yoke)* and must never have been bitten on the body by either a dog or a snake. When undertaking the ritual slaughter, the Mwalimu must have ritually bathed his body beforehand and be barefoot though wearing his cap *(chisoti)*. When the throat is cut, a prayer is said praising God *(Mulungu)* and asking for his compassion. God is referred to as great *(wamkulu)* and as grandfather *(ambuye)*. "There is nothing to fear, but only you God" *(Palibe wina woyenera kumuopa koma inu Mulungu)*, runs one prayer to be said when a cock *(tambala)* is killed. Animals that most Moslems consider to be unclean *(haramu)*—which are referred to as *nyama zo detsedwa* (dark to soiled animal)—include the elephant, hyrax, the category mbewa (rats, mice, and elephant shrews), hare, monkey, baboon, bushpig and warthog, jackal, hippopotamus, and caterpillars *(mphalabungu)*.

Two other factors are important in determining which animals are not eaten as food—clan affiliation and personal dietary preferences. We shall consider these in turn in the next section.

TOTEMIC CLANS AND CHIWENGO

In precolonial times the many African communities living north of the Zambesi essentially constituted a clan-based society. Social identity focused less on the local politics — the various Maravi states—or ethnic categories than on clan membership. In the early period ethnicity was related primarily to language and to bioregional criteria and had little political or even cultural significance. The area was, as many early writers have hinted, characterized by an underlying cultural unity. Antonio Gamitto, who accompanied the 1831-32 expedition from Tete to Chief Kazembe, recorded in his narrative the names of the various people living north of the Zambesi (Chewa, Mang'anja, Makua, Bororo, Nsenga, Yao), but suggested that "it is beyond dispute" that they belong essentially to the same Marave people in having the same habits, customs, and language (Cunnison 1960: 64). Linden's essay on Nyau societies in the Mua area, which specifically emphasizes "Chewa" identity, nonetheless quoted a local headman named Njoro, who, when asked his tribal affiliation, identified himself not as a Chewa but as belonging to the Banda clan (1975: 36).

In Malawi the term *mtundu* is a general category meaning variety, kind, or tribe and is akin to the concept of *gulu*, which means grouping, assembly, or type. These terms are used to refer to different kinds of plants and animals. When people are asked what mtundu they belong to they will often respond with an ethnic category, Nyanja, Chipeta, Yao, or Chewa. These terms have an essentially geographical connotation or refer to place of origin; they often have pejorative associations and tend to be used more by neighboring people (Nurse 1978: 16). In the past, however, clan affiliation was of more social significance. Although many people still recognize clan membership and clan names serve as surnames, it is nowadays socially less important. The matrilineal people of Malawi inherit clan membership through the mother. The terms usually employed to describe clan affiliations are *pfuko* (pi. *mafuko)* or *mfunda* (Yao *lukosyo)*, and this clan name is distinguished from the praisename *(chiwongo)* which is inherited patrilineally (Mwale 1948: 33-34; Nurse 1978: 25). Clans in Malawi do not have any corporate functions, either economic or ritual, nor do they carry out communal tasks. In the past they were strictly exogamous units, and a person was not allowed to marry *(saloledwa kuk-watira)* anyone of the same clan, since clan members were viewed as kin *(mbale wake)*. Clan exogamy these days seems to be less strictly observed. As one woman said, *Masiku ano anthu amangokwatira mfunda uliwonse,* "These days people may marry [someone] from any clan." What was important about clan membership in the past was that it enabled people to establish substantive relationships, interpreted as kinship, with people in distant places. It thus facilitated the movement of populations. For over a wide area clan names are the same, or the clan names of the different ethnic groups are identified or considered to have the same meaning (Soka 1953: 35-36).

In the present context what is significant is that clans have totemic associations. Many clans are in fact named after animals, as, for example, the *nguluwe* (bush-pig), *mbawala* (bushbuck), *chitolo* (multimammate mouse), *nchima* (blue monkey), *nchenzi* (cane rat), *njuzi* (serval), *njobvu* (elephant), *ngoma* (kudu), *chinkoma* (klipspringer), *ng'ombe* (cattle), and *kunda* (giant rat). Each of these clans has dietary restrictions with respect to the clan "totem." The Malawian data certainly do not bear out Levi-Strauss's (1966) suggestion that there is no connection between totemic clans and food taboos. The term nyama itself is a clan name (Mwale 1948: 35). My own researches in the Phalombe area do not confirm Nurse's suggestion that the Lomwe do not observe any totemic clan avoidances, but throughout Malawi many people these days are rather vague about the specific dietary restrictions associated with clan membership. I shall now examine some of the more important clans among the matrilineal peoples of Malawi and their associated totemic (animal) avoidances.

Phiri

This is one of the most important clans in Malawi and the one to which the early Maravi rulers belonged. The term means "hill" and is said to derive from the early migrants to Malawi who slept on top of a large hill. Clan members are forbidden to eat animals that are associated with the hills, such as baboon, porcupine, klipspringer, and hyrax. The genet cat and the zebra (associated with the Ngoni clan Tembo) also formed a prohibited category.

Zimbiri

This clan is seen in the Mulanje district to be related to the Phiri through cross-cousinship *(chisuwani),* having long ago been their domestic slaves and iron workers. The usual meaning of the term Zimbiri is "rust." Bushpig, chameleon, nthonga (the blind burrowing snake), and porcupine are animals that members of this clan do not eat. Stannus (1910: 308) notes that the clan name means puff adder *(lipili* Yao, *mphiri* Ny).

Banda

This clan is also related to the Phiri clan as cross-cousins *(usuwani),* and together they constitute an implicit moiety system that is basic to Marave culture. The Banda are, in oral traditions, seen as the original inhabitants of the country; they are thus closely linked with the land and are credited with rain-making powers (Marwick 1963: 378). Associated, in tradition, with the country at the foot of the hill, their name is said to derive from the fact that they had to level the grass *(ku-wanda,* "to beat down grass") (Ntara 1973: 6; Hodgson 1933: 144). Apart from the common duiker, no food taboos were recorded for this clan.

Mwale (Ngondo)

This clan is said to derive from a group of people who went out hunting *(kukasaka nyama).* They picked up a dead hartebeest *(ngondo),* cut it up, and shared the meat among themselves, but they disagreed about the brain *(ulembe,* "poison"). Because of the fighting that occurred they were thereafter nicknamed Mwale (from *ku-mwalira,* "to die"), as well as being known as hartebeest (Ntara 1973: 6). Members of this clan eat neither this animal nor the bushpig.

Nkhoma

According to Lomwe people, this clan is named after a flat-topped moun-tain and is also called Nakumwe. Members may not eat zorilla *(kanyimbi).* Hodgson (1933: 144) notes that the term refers to the yam bean *(Sphenostylis marginata),* a root eaten by baboons (and also by humans), but not, therefore, by members of the clan.

Mbewe

According to Ntara (1973: 7) people belonging to this clan are called Mbewe because their work was to hunt mice *(kusaka mbewa).* Accordingly, they may not eat this category of mammals which includes elephant shrews as well as rats and mice. In addition, the Mbewe do not eat bushpig (Phiri et al. 1977: 70).

Table 10.Ngoni clan totems

Mvuu	hippopotamus
Shumba	Lion, zebra, and all members of the cat family
Mbizi (mbidzi)	Heart (members of the clan do not eat the animals heart or liver, both associated with life)
Manyoni	Common duiker (nyiska), field mice (mbewa)
Chirwa	Porcupine
Nkosi	Zebra
Ndlovu (njobvu)	elephant
Jere	(mean "bangle") domestic pigieon, elephant
Mkandawire	Hippopotamus
Kumwenda	Hippopotamus
Maseko	(means "pebble") elephant , domestic fowl, rhinoceros
Ngulube	Bushpig
Soko	Baboon, bushgpig, monkeys
Nungu	porcupine
Newa	Lion, genet, wild cat, leopard
Honde	Hippopotamus
Nqumayo	Hippopotamus
Hara	Zebra
Nyangulu	Python
Shaba (shawa)	Eland, buffalo
Shonga	Buffalo
Tembo	Zebra
Nyati	buffalo

Sources: Rangeley n.d: papers 2/1/2; Chipeta 1977

The patrilineal clans of the Ngoni *(Isibongo)* are even more explicitly linked with totemic animals than are those of the matrilineal people. Table 10 lists some of the Ngoni clans and their associated food taboos, as these relate specifically to animals.

Many of the clan names are the names of animals and are sometimes archaic names, such as *soko* for *nyani* (baboon), *nyati* for *njati* (buffalo). It is of interest that few of the totemic species are carnivores. Generally speaking, the taboo *(ku-sala)* implies not only that the animal must not be eaten, but that a person should not harm the animal in any way, wear its skin, or eat the roots associated with a particular species like the baboon or bushpig. Eating the meat of the tabooed animal, whether intentionally or unintentionally, is said to give rise to the disease chiwengo.

Chiwengo is a skin ailment that results from eating certain kinds of meat. The term derives from the verb *ku-wenga,* "to bring out in spots." Although Scott (1929: 411) notes that it also covers nettle rash and eczema, it is essentially associated with meat eating, and as a disease *(nthenda),* it is usually distinguished from scabies *(mphere),* leprosy *(khate),* sores *(mphere),* and smallpox *(nthomba).* My researches do not confirm the suggestion made in Yao oral traditions (Nkondiwa et al. 1977) that eating porcupine will cause leprosy; but it may lead to the skin disease chiwengo. Although this disease is specifically associated with animals that are tabooed on religious grounds or in terms of clan affiliations *(nyama zosala* 'prohibited meat')—animals such as bushpig, porcupine, bushbuck, and domestic ducks *(bakha)* are frequently mentioned in this connection—there is also the belief that a skin rash (chiwengo) may result from eating any animal whose meat does not accord with a person's own physical constitution. As one woman put it, *"Zima-wenga malinga ndi thupi lamunthu"* (You develop spots or skin eruptions according to the body of the person). A game guard expressed it in similar fashion: *"Nyama kapena ndi nyani sanagwirizana ndi thupi lache apezeka agwira matenda achiwengo, ndiye chiwengo chimakhala chakutiumu mutuluka timibulu-mbulu tachonchi ndiye pokhanda pakhonza kumatuluka magazi"* (Meat/animal, perhaps a baboon that doesn't accord with their body, they contract the disease chiwengo, then spots [sores] come out and if scratched will cause much bleeding).

It may be noted that the wild hunting dog is called *mbulu.* It has a spotted, patchy coat, and very few people eat it. Medicinal herbs are mainly used to treat chiwengo, but the meat and skins of certain animals (such as the buffalo, spiny mouse, and fat mouse) are also thought to be a cure for this skin ailment.

CONCLUSIONS

This review of empirical data relating to meat (as food) in southern Malawi suggests not only that meat eating is important to Malawians, but, contrary to what Adams implied, that both men and women eat and enjoy eating meat. Although cultural representations in Malawi symbolically associate men, or rather affinal males, with mammals and both with the Brachystegia woodland, meat eating is by no means restricted to men. These categories (woodland, animals, affinal males) form a complementary opposition to the domain of the village, the cultivations (munda), and matrilineal kinship (for in an important sense kinship in Malawi subsumes and takes priority over the gender categories). There is thus an essential kinship between male affines and wild mammals, and in the ritual context they are virtually identified. By their symbolic logic, therefore, and consonant with Fiddes's own mode of reasoning, men — the affinal males — ought not to eat meat. But of course they do, as well as eating the porridge that derives from the domain of matrilineal kinship (agriculture). Likewise, a symbolic opposition exists between women (kinship, agriculture) and animals (male affines, hunting). In Malawi the in-marrying affine is frequently referred to not only as tambala (cock), but also as a hyena, which is the prototypical wild animal. The Malawian cultural logic creates, therefore, oppositions that are not radical but complementary and that may be summarily expressed by the following symbolic equations:

Earth substance	+	*Rain* "fertilizing" agency	=	*Agricultural productivity*
Agriculture	+	*Hunting* (fishing)	=	*Communal life*
Blood substance	+	*Semen activation form*	=	*Human child*
Herbs (mitengo)	+	*Activating animal substances* (chizimba)	=	*Curative medicines* (mankhwala)
Kinship banda clan	+	*Affines phirir clan*	=	*Collectivity of ancestral spirits* (mizimu)
Village (mudzi)	+	*Wooded hills* (thengo)	=	*Country* (dziko)

Human life and well-being involve the sustaining and harmonious union of the two contrasting domains. Thus it is, following the same cultural logic, that the ideal basic meal consists of two distinct components, namely, the porridge (nsima), which is derived from agricultural work focused around a group of matrilineally related women (kin), and a relish (ndiwo). The latter, ideally, consists of meat (nyama) that an affinal male has obtained by hunting in the woodland. Neither nsima nor ndiwo, on its own, constitutes a "meal" (chakudya) by Malawian reckoning. Both are necessary and both men and women need the two components for health and well-being, the porridge giving the sustenance or the substance to a meal, the meat relish supplying its strengthening quality. In fact, besides meaning meat or wild animal, the term nyama also refers to vital energy or to the essential property of a thing. Given a gender hierarchy, implicit even within a matrilineal context, men invariably take prominence in the distribution of the valued relish, but it would be misleading to see meat eating as simply reflecting "male power." Nor can meat eating be viewed as a simple consequence of a Promethean ethic or a social attitude of domination over nature. It does indeed reflect a philosophy of power, for it is through meat eating — as well as alternatively through animal medicines and rituals — that men and women are able to harness the powers inherent in wild nature, in the woodland, abode of both wild animals and the ancestral spirits. Ultimately it is from the woodland that fertility derives, in the form of rain or semen, which are, in Malawi, symbolically associated.

Food prohibitions concerning meat are subject to wide individual variations and are not specifically related to either gender or ethnicity. Religious affiliation, however, is an important factor, as are totemic associations. The eating of meat of a totemic species is thought to give rise to the skin disease chiwengo, even though this ailment is also seen in terms of an individual's physical constitution. Given the wide variations in individual dietary preference — although I did not meet any Malawian who was a vegetarian — the explication of dietary prohibitions simply in terms of cosmological or classificatory schemas is clearly inadequate.

NOTES

I have spent almost ten years in Malawi, including two extended periods of anthropological fieldwork in 1979-80 and 1990-91. Research notes for this paper are based on my own studies. Many Malawians have given me their help and support, but with respect to the present paper I should particularly like to thank the late Jessie Williamson, Pat Caplan, John Kajalwiche, Davison Potani, and Kitty Kunamano. I should also like to thank the Nuffield Foundation for supporting my anthropological studies in Malawi and the Centre for Social Research, Zomba, for institutional support.

1. This is, of course, a generalization. In specific historical contexts and in certain locales — as in the Eurasian context during the Pleistocene — there was a high reliance on animal foods.

2. In a recent text on "ecological" thought Peter Marshall (1992) seems to suggest that because of their vegetarianism, religious mystics through the ages, such as Buddha, Plotinus, Porphyry, and Sankara, were ecological thinkers. This is somewhat misleading, for their salvation ethic implied a theocratic perspective and a radical devaluation of the empirical world. Nothing could be more unecological, for the "unity" they conceived was spiritual, not organic and symbiotic.

3. Fiddes warns against romanticizing such cultures and stresses that all ("most"?) people must exert some degree of control over their natural surroundings (p. 107). But such reflections should put us on guard against making monolithic characterizations of cultures, whether our own or that of people like the Oglala Sioux, which always indicate a diversity of attitudes toward the world. Malawian attitudes toward animals are complex and diverse and incorporate both a pragmatic and a sacramental attitude toward other animals (see also Guenther 1988).

4. I substantially agree with some of the more general arguments of these two studies as they relate to specific aspects of modernist culture. I highlight here only the more problematic themes, as I see them, in the context of Malawian ethnography.

5. I have explored such issues in two unpublished papers: "Chirombo: Opposition to the Animal Estate in Rural Malawi," and "Skins, Horns and Tails. Reflections on the Use of Mammals as Medicine in Malawi."

6. In this paper I am not concerned with hunting or with the use of animals as medicine (mankhwala) in Malawi. Of interest is Fiddes's reference to the witches' brew in Macbeth (1991: 18). As in Malawi, the animals mentioned in the chant (bat, toad, snake, newt, owl, wolf) are not normally eaten as food, but were of course clearly important as medicine during medieval times.

7. A basic meal consisting of a thick porridge accompanied by a relish dish is, of course, common throughout much of south-central Africa. Both constituents of the meal are deemed to be essential (see Richards 1939: 46-48).

8. Men, as well as older women, invariably get more than their fair share of meat, and women are publicly frowned upon for openly showing an enjoyment of meat. This undoubtedly reflects the public affirmation of the affinal male's supremacy in Malawian society. But it is well to bear in mind that men are also given more of the valued plant food — it would be deemed very unseemly if a man ate a porridge that included bran *(gaga)*, which women commonly eat when there is a shortage of maize — and that meat eating, specifically of bat and chicken, forms an essential component of the girls' initiation rites *(chinamwali)*, which are entirely under the auspices of women.

9. Williamson's reflections have been questioned for their accuracy, but my own experiences have certainly confirmed such observations. Young boys are soon distanced from their mothers, given the pattern of uxorilocal marriage.

10. Early writers invariably commented upon the fact that meat was often eaten in an advanced state of putrification (MacDonald 1882: 27; Coudenhove 1925: 44). From my own personal experience this is still the case.

11. These interviews, conducted in Chewa, focused specifically on the edibility (or otherwise) of the commoner species of mammals to be found in Malawi. Some mammals have a local distribution within Malawi—many being restricted to wildlife sanctuaries—and, though familiar to me, many species were unknown to local people in Mulanje and Zomba.

12. Baboons are widely recognized as being like humans, both in the care of their young and in their use of medicines, and it is widely believed that the males may have forced sexual relations with Malawian women. Nevertheless, many people will eat them as food.

REFERENCES

Adams, C. 1990. *The Sexual Politics of Meat*. Cambridge: Polity Press.

Brown, J. E. 1992. *Animals of the Soul*. Rockport, Mass.: Element Books.

Burgess, H. J., and E. Wheeler. 1970. *Lower Shire Nutrition Survey*. Blantyre: Ministry of Health.

CCAM [Chitukuko Cha Amayi M'Malawi]. 1992. *Malawi's Traditional and Modern Cooking.* Lilongwe:C.C.A.M.

Chikanza, J. C. 1980. *Annotated List of Independent Churches in Malawi 1900-1980.* Zomba: Chancellor College. Religious Studies Publ. No. 10.

Chipeta, O. J. 1977. *M'Mbelwa Ngoni Traditions.* Zomba: Chancellor College, History Department.

Coudenhove, H. 1925. *My African Neighbours.* London: Cape.

Cunnison, I. G., trans. and ed. 1960. *King Kazembe and the Marave, Chewa . . . and other Peoples of S.Africa.* (ACP Gamitto. Expedition 1831-32). Lisbon: Estudios de Ciencias Politicas e Sociais.

Drummond, H. 1889. *Tropical Africa.* London: Hodder & Stoughton.

Duff, H. L. 1903. *Nyasaland under the Foreign Office.* London: Bell.

Eliade, M. 1968. *Myths, Dreams and Mysteries.* London: Collins.

Fiddes, N. 1991. *Meat: A Natural Symbol.* London: Routledge.

Frazer, J. G. 1922. *The Golden Bough.* London: MacMillan.

Guenther, M. 1988. "Animals in Bushman Thought, Myth and Art." In *Hunters and Gatherers,* ed. T. Ingold et al., 2: 192-202. Oxford: Berg.

Harris, M. 1990. *Our Kind.* New York: Harper & Row.

Hodgson, A. G. O. 1933 "Notes on the Achewa and Agoni of the Dowa District." *Journal of the Royal Anthropological Institute* 63: 123-65.

Knight, C. 1991. *Blood Relations.* New Haven: Yale University Press.

Levi-Strauss, C. 1966. *The Savage Mind.* London: Wiedenfeld & Nicolson. Linden, I. 1975. "Chewa Initiation Rites and Nyau Societies." In *Themes in the Christian History of Central Africa,* ed. T. O. Ranger and J. Weller, pp. 30-44. London: Heinemann.

MacDonald, D. 1882. *Africana, or the Heart of Heathen Africa.* London: Dawsons.

McLuhan, T. C. 1971. *Touch The Earth.* London: Garnstone Press.

Marshall, P. 1992. *Nature's Web.* London: Simon & Schuster.

Marwick, M. 1963. "History and Tradition in East Central Africa through the Eyes of Northern Rhodesian Chewa." *Journal of African History* 4: 375-90.

Mikochi, J. C. 1938. Notes on African Food Crops. Unpublished ms. 31 pp.

Morris, B. 1976. "Whither the Savage Mind?" *Man* 11: 542-57.

————. 1982. *Forest Traders*. London: Athlone Press.

————. 1987. *Anthropological Studies of Religion*. Cambridge: Cambridge University Press.

Mwale, E. B. 1948. *Zaacewa*. London: MacMillan.

Nelson, R. K. 1983. *Make Prayers to the Raven*. Chicago: University of Chicago Press.

Nkondiwa, G., et al. 1977. *Yao Traditions III*. Zomba: Chancellor College, History Department.

Ntara, S. J. 1973. *The History of the Chewa*. Wiesbaden: F. Steiner.

Nurse, G. T. 1978. *Clanship in Central Malawi*. Acta Ethnologica et Linguistica, Ser. Africana 12. Vienna.

Phiri, K., et al. 1977. *Amachinga Yao Traditions II*. Zomba: Chancellor College, History Department.

Rangeley, W. H. J. n.d. Papers and Correspondence. Manuscript collection in Society of Malawi Library, Limbe.

Richards, A. I. 1939. *Land, Labour and Diet in Northern Rhodesia*. Oxford: Oxford University Press.

Scott, D. C. 1929. *Dictionary of the Nyanja Language*. London: Lutterworth Press.

Soka, L. 1953. *Mbiri Ya Alomwe*. Limbe: Malawi Publ.

Stannus, H. S. 1910. "Notes on some Tribes of British Central Africa." *Journal of the Royal Anthropological Institute* 40: 238-335.

————. 1922. "The Wayao of Nyasaland." *Harvard African Studies* 3: 229-372. Williamson, J. 1941. "Nyasaland Native Food." *Nyasaland Times,* 1-25.

————. 1942. Nyasaland Nutrition Survey. Unpublished ms. 76 pp.

————. 1972. "Notes on Some Changes in Malawi Diet over the Past 30 Years." *Society of Malawi Journal* 25: 49-54.

————. 1975. *Useful Plants of Malawi*. Zomba: University of Malawi.

Young, E. D. 1877. *Nyassa: A Journey of Adventures*. London: J. Murray.

WOODLAND AND VILLAGE: REFLECTIONS ON THE ANIMAL ESTATE' IN RURAL MALAWI (1995)

Introduction

The purpose of this article is to discuss social attitudes towards the woodland domain among people of rural Malawi. I shall specifically focus on their attitudes towards wild mammals, for both practically and symbolically, mammals are fundamentally identified with this domain.

Malawian[1] attitudes towards mammals - and more generally towards the natural world - are diverse, complex and multi-dimensional. Thus an 'ethic of antagonism' towards wild animals, which as we shall see below has been suggested by some writers as characteristic of agricultural peoples, co-exists with other very different social attitudes and perspectives. These include the empirical (in terms of knowledge structures), pragmatic (with respect to the uses of mammals as food and medicine), aesthetic (incorporating the 'friendship' expressed towards the domestic cat and dog and the role that animals play in moral education through folk tales and proverbs), and empathetic (expressed in certain contexts where a fundamental affinity and close inter-relationship is seen to exist between living humans, animals and the spirits of the dead - an attitude that is basically similar to that found among hunter-gatherers). But my focus in this article is on the dialectical opposition between humans and mammals that is pervasive in the culture and social practices of rural Malawians. This opposition reflects an ambivalent attitude towards the woodland, and specifically towards mammals. On the one hand, in terms of the village community and agriculture, wildlife from the woodlands is seen as fundamentally hostile and antagonistic to human endeavours; while on the other hand, the woodland domain is seen as the external source of life-generating powers. Mammals are seen as prototypical of the woodland in this respect. They are regarded as the embodiment of 'power' and fierceness, and are seen as essentially opposed to humans (as wild beasts *[chirombo]);* but they are also seen as the source of meat *(nyama),* of activating medicines *(chizimba)* and, in being closely identified with the spirits of the dead and affinal males, as the essential source of fertility, and thus the continuity of the kin group (and village). Wild mammals, then, form a crucial part in the ongoing cyclic processes of life and of social reproduction. These processes are expressed in a complementary or dialectical opposition between two facets of Malawian social existence, namely between the woodland and the village, between hunting and agriculture, between the in-marrying male afFine and the kin-group focused around a core of matrilineally-related women, and between spirits and wild animals (the two of which are closely identified with one another) and living humans.[2]

To facilitate the later discussion, this complementary dualism may be outlined in the following schema, though this should not be interpreted as some totalizing cosmology that systematizes all aspects of Malawian culture:

Woodland	**Village**
(Thengo)	*(Mudzi)*
Hunting	*Agriculture*
Dry season	*Wet Season*
Affinal males	*Matrilineal kingroup*
(semen)	*(blood)*
Spirits of the dead	*Living humans*
(mizimu ya makolo)	*(anthu)*
Wild animals	*Domestic animals*
(chirombo)	*(chiweto)*

My discussion is divided into four sections. In the first section I discuss two contrasting attitudes towards nature, and specifically towards wild mammals: the egalitarian, sacramental attitude, and the oppositional and controlling one. Some scholars have identified these with hunting-gathering and agricultural modes of subsistence. My suggestion is that historically, Malawian culture has always, in a sense, combined these two contrasting attitudes, for both hunting and hoe agriculture have been important and complementary facets of Malawian socio-economic life.

In the second section I discuss the familiar dichotomy between culture and nature. After briefly looking at some of the cross-cultural material, I outline one of the fundamental distinctions in Malawian culture between the village *(mudzi)* and the woodland *(thengo)*. I suggest that this dichotomy is not simply homologous with the gender division, although symbolically it is the affinal male who is identified with the wild animals that frequent the woodland and female consanguines who are identified with the village. Although I stress the dichotomy between the woodland and the village environs in this section, in the section that follows I explore the association of the woodland with the spirits of the dead, and suggest that the two domains are intrinsically connected so as to constitute a cyclic process that is fundamentally concerned with life and its renewal.

In the final section I examine the concepts of *chirombo* ('wild beast') and *nyama* ('game animal' or 'meat') and suggest that these concepts indicate the ambivalence or the 'dialectical opposition' that Malawians express towards the wild mammals of the woodland.

Contrasting attitudes to animals: foragers and horticulturalists

The past decade has seen a growing interest in social attitudes towards animal life, both from an anthropological and a social-historical perspective (Serpell 1986; Ritvo 1987; Ingold 1988; Willis 1990). This interest, however, has reflected a tendency, especially when scholars make global contrasts across cultures, to take a rather monolithic view of specific cultures. Thus pre-literate communities are seen as having only a 'sacramental' vision of nature, in stark contrast to that of Western culture, which is rather misleadingly equated with the mechanistic philosophy of the Enlightenment with its rigid dualism -including the rigid dualism between humans and animals — and its ethic of domination, thus completely ignoring the diversity and the changing nature of the Western cultural tradition. Indeed many scholars (eg Merchant 1992: 59) write as if historically there are only two possible 'world views', the mechanistic (anthropocentric) and the organismic (ecocentric). The latter is a conceptual 'rag-bag' for a diverse collection of ontologies, old and new. Not only does this ignore the fundamental fact that many religious systems are theocentric rather than ecocentric, but also it assumes that in Europe little has changed since the seventeenth century. This ignores the fundamental re-orientation of thought initiated in the nineteenth century by Hegel and Darwin, by the rise of the biological sciences, and by the development of historical understanding, anthropology and the social sciences more generally — quite apart from the theoretical developments within physics itself. The writings of Jonas (1966) and Mayr (1982; 1988) present a much more balanced view of the history of Western thought than do many contemporary writers on ecology.

What is of particular interest in recent writings on the 'animal estate' is a growing recognition that cultural attitudes towards animals among hunter-gatherers and among agricultural societies contrast markedly. Having undertaken anthropological research in both kinds of social context, this contrast has been confirmed by my own studies.

The Hill Pandaram of south India are a foraging community, though they have long-established trading contacts with wider Indian society. They are entirely nomadic, living in small forest camps of never more than twenty people, and apart from the dog, have no domestic animals. But, importantly, the Hill Pandaram do not make a stark contrast between themselves and the environment in which they live, being intrinsically a forest people. They are largely hunters of small game - bats, flying squirrels and tortoises - and as I described in my study of their socio-economic life (Morris 1982: 79), they do not hunt, but rather gather animals from the forest, in the same way as they collect nuts and yams. An egalitarian ethos pervades their culture, and they do not make a stark contrast between themselves and the animal world. Like other hunter-gatherers, they often keep pets, and I have recorded how one young woman breast-fed and cared very affectionately for a young chevrotain deer, only to put it in the pot later (Morris 1978: 15; cf. Serpell 1986: 156; Katcher & Beck 1991: 265-7). For like other hunter-gatherers, the Hill Pandaram attitude towards animals is both empathetic and pragmatic (cf. Guenther 1988).

This sharing and generally egalitarian attitude towards animals expressed by the Hill Pandaram is consonant with that described elsewhere among hunter-gatherers. Animals are seen essentially as social and spiritual equals, with thoughts and feelings analogous to those of humans. Pet keeping, as Serpell describes (1986: 142), is popular among them, and the hunting of animals is hedged with ritual, and the focus of ambivalent feelings. As James Frazer long ago discussed (1922: 679-98), an attitude of respect towards animal life was characteristic of many tribal people, and a hunter could expose himself to vengeance 'magic' on the part of the animal's spirit, if he did not show proper ritual respect towards the slain animals. (For interesting discussions of hunter-gatherer attitudes towards animals, see Tanner [1979], Morris [1981: 130-1], Nelson [1983], Campbell [1984: 81-122], Serpell [1986: 142-9], and Ingold [1986: 243-73].)

Such beliefs, implying an essential 'kinship' between humans and animals, and an emotional involvement between the hunter and the animal, such that, as Serpell writes (1986: 144), the act of killing has the flavour of homicide, are not confined to hunter-gatherers. They have a resonance throughout the world, and are widespread in Africa, where beliefs relating to the Vengeance' power of the blood of a slain mammal, if the killing is not done with appropriate ritual respect, have been widely documented (Baumann 1950). Nevertheless, it has to be recognized that the advent of farming has had a profound effect on the way humans relate to the natural world, and specifically towards animal life. Goodman (1992: 19) speaks of the change in culture ushered in by the advent of horticulture as being profound, and the working of the soil as representing a 'fundamental break' with hunter-gatherer attitudes, though she has little to say on people's attitudes towards animal life *per se*. In his lucid study of human-animal relationships Serpell (1986: 174-6) is, likewise, equally explicit in contrasting hunter-gatherer attitudes towards animals -predominantly ones of respect and egalitarianism - with those of farming communities. The neolithic revolution is seen as a 'journey of no return' and as a 'fall from grace', for farmers have no choice but to set themselves up 'in opposition to nature': in keeping the fields clear of weeds, in protecting themselves and their crops from wild animals, and in controlling and confining domestic livestock. The entire system, Serpell writes, 'depends on the subjugation of nature' and on the 'domination and manipulation of living creatures' (1986: 175; cf also Kent 1989). The 'ethic of domination' towards animal life, thus, does not begin, it seems, with the rise of mechanistic philosophy in the sixteenth and seventeenth century, but much earlier, with the advent of agriculture.

What is of interest about the Malawian context is that these two attitudes towards the natural world and specifically towards mammals, one – the sacramental egalitarian - associated with hunter-gatherers, the other - implying an ethic of opposition and control — associated with agriculturalists, do in fact co-exist. They form together a pervasive attitude towards mammals in Malawi which may be described as one of dialectical opposition. This 'unity-in-oppo-sition' does, however, have gender implications, for men, as affines, are identified with wild mammals and with the woodland, while women are closely identified with the village environs and thus in opposition to wildlife.

The village/woodland dichotomy

As in many other societies people in Malawi make a fundamental distinction, which has both ecological and symbolic import, between the village *(mudzi)*, the domain of living humans, and the Brachystegia woodland *(thengo)*, the domain of wild animals *(nyamd)* and of the spirits of the dead.

This kind of conceptual distinction has been widely discussed in the literature, largely under the rubric of the opposition between 'culture' and 'nature'. Although this opposition has a deep resonance within European thought and science, given the dominance of the kind of dualistic metaphysic that stems from Cartesian philosophy, it has been subject to a plethora of meanings and interpretations. Long ago Lovejoy (1948) discussed the diversity of meanings of the concept of 'nature' even within the European literary tradition. He described the term as a Verbal jack-of-all-trades', nature being at once the most sacred and the most protean of the concepts used during the Enlightenment period. The Greek distinction between *nomos* (custom) and *physis* (nature) can, however, in no sense be equated with the kind of dualisms that were bequeathed to us by the Enlightenment tradition - culture/nature, society/individual, mind/body - although there are fundamental affinities between Plato and Descartes. For many Greeks, Aristotle in particular, *physis* (nature) was in , an important sense animate, with latent potentialities.

Recent scholars who have discussed the nature/culture dichotomy have emphasized its problematic nature if applied uncritically as a cross-cultural conception (MacCormack & Strathern 1980; Croll & Parkin 1992). The dichotomy, along with its homology with gender categories, is reflected in much European thought (Ortner 1974; Merchant 1980), but the tendency to see this dichotomy as involving a Promethean ethic - the metaphor of 'man against nature', or of human (culture's) dominion over nature - has not been found to jell at all neatly with the cultural categories of pre-literate communities. Among the people of the New Guinea Highlands for example, as Marilyn Strathern (1980) has shown, although the distinction between the 'domestic' and the wild has a crucial significance, it is neither homologous with the gender division, nor can it be equated with the culture/nature division of Western thought. But what crucially emerges from much of the ethnographic literature on small-scale farming communities is that a pervasive symbolic dualism is evident which contrasts settlement or the domestic realm with that of the wild, even though its underlying cultural logic may be distinctive. It may indeed, as in New Guinea, not be seen as a rigid 'dualism' - in the Neoplatonic or Cartesian sense — and may evoke quite different symbolic associations, the 'wild' or forest being associated with men and the spirits rather than with women (as it is in much Western thought) (Gillison 1980).

In the African context the symbolic demarcation between domesticated space and the 'bush' or forest has been widely reported. In her classic and perceptive ethnographic writings on the Lele, Douglas (1954; 1975: 9-46) writes of the importance of what she calls 'religious categories' among the Lele, and how these symbolically, even if implicitly, structure their thought. One fundamental distinction is that between the village and the forest, mediated by the grassland which is associated with women and the cultivation of groundnuts. By contrast the forest is seen as the abode of the spirits and animals, and as the source of many of the necessities of life - maize, fish, meat, water, firewood, fertility. Likewise Jean Comaroff (1985: 54) writes of the distinction between the social or domesticated domain and the 'wild' or bush as the 'most fundamental' of all oppositions in the Tswana cosmos, even though the opposition is seen as being mediated by women and production. Recent ethnographic studies of the Do-gon, Mende and Aouan of West Africa confirm this widespread articulation of an 'opposition' between the 'bush' and the 'village'. For the Dogon of Mali the 'bush' is associated with the spirits and animals, and with danger, yet at the same time it is considered the origin, the 'ultimate source' of everything that makes life possible - knowledge, wisdom, power, fertility, as well as life itself. The bush/village dichotomy thus implies an entropic system (Van Beek & Banga 1992: 67-73). For the Aouan of the Ivory Coast, the forest forms an all-encompassing environment surrounding the village, and contains the spirit beings that bestow life and which rule over animals and plants. It is on the forest that the people depend for physical subsistence, and various taboos and rules exist to maintain the boundary between the two domains (Van der Breemer 1992: 99).

There is, in Malawi, no widely used general category that could be considered equivalent to the English concept of 'environment', nor even to the more abstract category of 'space', although Malawians, like other Bantu speakers, have a highly developed spatial sense which is built into their language. The 'gaps' between things such as garden plants are referred to as *danga,* while the space between rocks and hills are denoted by the term *mpata.* A valley between hills, a mountain pass or a gorge, is thus referred to by the latter term, and the famous gorge on the River Shire is named *mpatamanga (manga,* 'to make', 'bind').

The crucial spatial distinction for people in Malawi, however, is that between the Brachystegia woodland (together with the hill forests) and the villages and their cultivated environs. *Mudzi* means village, and the term has both an ecological and a social connotation, referring in rural areas to a cluster of huts -which may or may not form a discrete geographical unit occupied by the core members of a matrilineal group. When Mitchell spoke of the village as a 'key concept in Yao thought' and as the 'fundamental unit' in their social structure (1956: 2-3), he was not exaggerating, and it is of interest that he entitled his study of the political and social structure of the Yao *The Yao village.* The village head is a key figure in the day-to-day activities of the village and in the organization of rituals, even though his or her political standing in the wider community may be limited. When people refer to their own village or kin group, they commonly use the expression *kwathu,* 'ours', which essentially means 'home' in both a geographical and a social sense, and the term carries connotations of intimacy. Within the village structure there are distinct households focused around a woman and her in-marrying spouse. The village environs include also the cultivated area *(munda)* which produces mainly maize, millet and cassava, together with pumpkins and beans which are planted inter-spaced. In the past, people in Malawi were largely shifting hoe-cultivators, although permanent gardens along the lake shore or in wetlands or valley areas were important.

Beyond the village cultivations are the Brachystegia or *miombo* woodlands which, although they tend to look rather monotonous and uniform to an outsider, are in fact floristically rather complex, their nature and composition depending not only on specific local factors such as altitude, rainfall, drainage and soil type, but also on their past history. Many have stressed that such woodland is a plagio-climax - a plant community which has been formed and is maintained by continuous human agency (Morris 1970: 155). The Malawian attitude to such woodland is essentially positive, and contrasts markedly with that of Europeans. Even wildlife biologists who have spent long periods in Africa 'have little love for *miombo*'. The woodlands are described as a 'flat, monotonous stretch of trees' and as 'unchanging', and to travel through them one has to endure 'numbing boredom' (Adams & McShane 1992: 123-4). Surprisingly, the woodland environment is hardly mentioned in Mandala's (1990) important account of the peasant economy of the Mang'anja of the Lower Shire. This environment, however, is a crucial source of essential subsistence goods - timber, string and thatching grass for building houses and granaries, mushrooms, fruits and wild vegetables, all kinds of medicine and, of course, wild animals, which provide an important source of relish. The woodland is also the primary source of energy in the form of firewood, which is -often gathered by women far from the village.

Malawians refer to the woodland as *thengo* or *tchire*, and although the words are often used interchangeably, discussions with Malawians suggest that *tchire*, in contrast to *thengo*, is often more associated with regenerate Brachystegia woodland, where ample thatching grass and fieldmice are to be found. In Malawi the firing of the woodland at the end of the dry season has both a pragmatic and a symbolic significance; in the past the right to initiate the burning of the woodland was vested in one of the senior chiefs *(mwini mzinda)*, and it was a serious offence for anyone to burn the bush before the allotted time (Rangeley 1948: 51). Formerly this was done late in the season and, as Schoffeleers (1971) has discussed, the burning of the bush had an important significance in the regeneration of the cosmic cycle and the subsequent coming of the rains. Burnt woodland is referred to as *lupsya;* the verb *ku-psya* meaning not only to cook, roast or burn, but also to be ripe.

The village environs are associated with what Fortes (1969) called the 'axiom of amity', with order, moral rectitude, structure and social well-being. But it would be misleading to equate the mudzi/thengo division with either a culture/nature dichotomy or a gender division. Although men as hunters are often associated with the woodland, woodland is not specifically the domain of men *(amuna),* but rather the domain of men as affines. Women too are associated with the woodland as gatherers of firewood and wild foods, while men are also identified with the village domain. Men clear the woodland of trees so that cultivation may be established, they bring in woody material to construct the houses, they gather medicines from the woodland, as well as meat, and most importantly it is from the woodland and from men (as affines/spirits) that fertilizing power is derived for the procreation of children. Semen is called *ubwamuna* — the essence, as it were, of males as affines — and blood is referred to as *mwazi* or *magazi,* which is semantically close to the word for the female gender, *nkazi.* In essence, the procreation of a child consists concretely of the mixing of the semen of a man with the blood of the woman. Analogously, the most satisfying meal consists of a relish *(ndiwo,* meat from the woodland)[3] taken with maize porridge *(nsima,* derived from women's activities in the village), and the most powerful medicines consist of plant substances *(mitengo,* roots, leaves, bark of woody plants) activated by *chizimba* medicines, primarily the skins, tails and horns of animals from the woodland.'* It would be easy to construct a homologous series of complementary symbolic oppositions:

Thengo	Mudzi
woodland	*village*
hunting	*cultivation*
animals	*plants*
men	*women*

However, such a structural analysis tends to over-systematize the cultural reality (cf. Schoffeleers 1968: 231). The complementary opposition between the woodland and the human habitus reflects less the gender division than the opposition between affines and kin, for symbolically it is as affines that men are associated with the woodland and with the animals. Although spirits of the dead/ancestors are also associated with the woodland, it would again be misleading specifically to identify men with these spirits. What essentially is expressed in Malawian culture with respect to the *thengo/mudzi* division is that whereas in the village environs a fundamental - but complementary - opposition is articulated between men and women, kin and affines, humans and wild animals - in the woodland there is a fundamental identity between these categories. In an important sense the spirits of the dead are collective ancestors — both men and women, kin and affines. In the woodland domain there is an essential identity between men and animals, and also between spirits and animals - and this is reflected in rituals. In the village, however, there is an opposition between humans and animals - and this too is reflected in rituals.[5]

The woodland and spirits of the dead

The Brachystegia woodland, in contrast to the village domain, is associated with medicines, wild animals and the spirits of the dead. Given a tradition of slash-and-burn agriculture and the essential nature of Brachystegia woodland itself, with its inherent ability to regenerate vegetatively, many areas of woodland represent old village sites. The site of a former village, or an uninhabited area of woodland, is referred to as *dzinja,* a term which also refers to the rainy season between December and March. Throughout Malawi, even in the heavily populated area of the Shire Highlands, areas of woodland are set aside as burial sites for the dead.[6] They are known as *manda* and the ancestors, or the dead, are collectively referred to as *amanda* (those of the woodland grave). In the Domasi district where I lived, almost every village had its own area of woodland where the dead were buried. These burial sites are in the nature of a sacred grove; no trapping or hunting of animals is allowed in them and the area is protected from fire, for the site has to be kept 'cool'. It is also an offence against the spirits of the dead to collect firewood, medicines and thatching grass from the *manda.* In times of acute pressure on resources due to population increase, people may in fact gather firewood or grass from the *manda* woodlands, but this is not approved of. When I was in Ntcheu in the central region many Chewa people I spoke to were very critical of the recent refugees from Mozambique who had gathered firewood from the nearby hill forests, forests which were particularly associated with the rain deities. Apart from attending funerals and making ritual offerings to their dead, people do not normally enter the *manda* woodlands. It is in these woodlands that the initiation site of the Nyau dancers[7] is to be found. The *manda* woodlands thus essentially form a conservation area, and a refuge for wildlife. Even monkeys, when raiding the village gardens, act as though they feel safe in such environs.

The forests/woodlands associated with the graves of important chiefs, or with the rain deities, are of particular importance as ritual sites, and may be entered only with the special permission of the ritual specialists associated with the spirits. The forest on almost every important hill in Malawi is associated with some particular rain spirit, and many of the lowland forests — because they have been untouched for many generations by either hoe or fire - are important ecological sites. In 1964 I was granted permission to enter the relic forest on the loop of the Litchenya River, Mulanje (which is the graveyard of the ancestors of Chief Mabuka), in order to study the epiphytic orchids still to be found there. The forest is unique in being a remnant patch of the evergreen forest that once clothed the southeastern slopes of Mulanje Mountain, and which was cleared in the early part of the century to make way for the tea plantations (Chapman 1962: 16-17; see also Chapman 1988; Kathamalo 1965; Schoffeleers 1992). Sacred forests associated with spirits of the dead or with territorial rain deities are, however, to be found throughout Malawi.

An important distinction seems to be drawn between the *manda* woodlands associated with the spirits of a particular local community, and the forests to be found on particular hills or mountains, which are associated with various rain deities, or with the original inhabitants of Malawi, the Batwa people. Mountains such as Mchesi, Thyolo, Mulanje and the Nyika seem to be essentially seen as abodes of spirits and many people look upon these mountains with respect, with awe, even with fear. I have elsewhere written on Michesi mountain in southern Malawi, which one Lomwe writer has referred to as *malo otchuka a mizimu* - 'the famous place of spirits' (Soka 1953: 28-9; Morris 1994).

Evidently in the Malawian context the complementary opposition between the woodland and the village is conceived as homologous to that between the spirits of the dead and living people. This latter opposition must, however, be seen in terms of a cyclic conception of life processes. There are specific ceremonies known as *manyumba (nyumba,* house) whereby individuals are seen - or rather witnessed - as undergoing a symbolic rebirth, as the reincarnation of their grandparents. But this process is not a karma-like reincarnation of some immortal 'spirit', but rather a cycle of transformation.[8] It implies a metamorphosis between the living and the dead, a cyclic transmutation. This process may be seen as an exchange of substances, for people make offerings for their dead relatives; on death a person is transmuted into an ancestral spirit. But essentially it is a cyclic process of life and death, or rather a process of life and its continuing renewal, activating agencies coming from the woodland.

Since wild animals are associated with the woodland, they are identified with the spirits, and with affinal males, who are essentially seen as aggressive and sexual. This is why the in-marrying male affine is always conceptualized as a stranger *(mtendo)* and is typified by the cock and the hyena. *Nyau* and *chinyago* rituals among the Chewa, Mang'anja and Yao (see footnote 7) essentially involve the cultural creation of an affinal male, and the theriomorphic figures that are involved in such rites represent the spirits of the dead in animal form. Thus it implies the identity - almost - of spirits, wild animals and affinal males. And such figures dance at the girls' initiation rites in opposition to the women, as a kin-group. Thus a clear distinction is made in Malawian culture between, on the one hand, the personality of a territorial chief and the affinal male (husband), who are conceptualized as outsiders and as hunters, and on the other hand, the village headman, who as a brother is identified with the collectivity of women who constitute the matrilineal core of the village community. Ideally he should be a male mother.

But in certain contexts, the woodland may also be seen as antagonistic to human endeavours, particularly to their endeavours as agriculturalists. Thus a perceptive observer of Malawian culture, Thomas Price, has written that to an ordinary villager, even trees may be seen as an 'enemy'. Price writes that when the trees are cleared away to make room for the gardens 'they sprouted up again, snagging hoes', and that people when travelling between villages invariably carried a machete, which they automatically used to slash back the growing saplings. He contended that the designation of forest reserves by the government was seen by local people as an intolerable interference with their movement and settlement under shifting cultivation (Price cited in Potter 1987: 145). The point, of course, is that while in terms of medicine, energy, building materials, and a supply of relish in the form of animal meat and mushrooms - and equally importantly of human fertility via the spirits of the dead - the woodland is a crucial and indispensable provider of much that is important to human life, for the agriculturalist the woodland, and particularly the animals that are associated with it, are serious threats to livelihood. Hence their ambivalence towards this domain, and towards animals in particular.

Wild mammals (chirombo) of the woodland

It is, I think, difficult for people living in urban areas to realize how precarious life is for subsistence agriculturalists; and it has to be remembered that historically the matrilineal peoples of Malawi were fundamentally subsistence hoe cultivators. Not only is such agriculture highly dependent on rain, but the depredations of wild animals were a constant source of concern and anxiety, as they still are. Such depredations take a toll both of agricultural crops - and baboons, monkeys, elephants, porcupines and wild pigs are the main culprits -and of human life itself.

Thus, although in hunting, or in certain ritual contexts, a close identification is expressed between affinal males, wild mammals and spirits of the dead, in other contexts the opposition between wild mammals and humans (the kin community) is emphasized. Thus a dialectical opposition emerges and this is reflected in the two key concepts that are used to describe mammals - *nyama* and *chirombo* - both of which have a taxonomic and functional usage, and indicate a wide range of referents (Morris 1984). Essentially *nyama* is a polysemic term meaning both meat and prototypically any edible species of mammal, although it can also refer to wild animals generally. Domestic animals *(chiweto)* are typically *nyama,* though the goats, sheep and chickens which form the basic livestock are eaten only on important or ritual occasions. But *nyama* also has a ritual significance, because of its association with hunting, and connotes the mystical power associated with the mammal. In Malawi there is a particular affliction, *chirope,* that affects hunters, and which is associated with the vengeance power of the mammal, especially mammals such as the kudu or eland. Hunting is therefore hedged with ritual. Offerings to the spirits must be made prior to the hunt, protective medicines used, and because the woodland is considered a cool environment, a hunter must enter in a 'cool' condition. He must therefore have no feelings of anger or discord, and must abstain from sexual intercourse prior to the hunt, for sex generates heat. The provision of meat incorporates the wild mammal into the kin group as relish food. Significantly, while 'meat' is food and is associated with nurturance and the kin group, the skins, horns and tails of mammals are associated with activating medicines, with the spirits of the dead, and with the affinal male. The latter animal constituents express the ongoing continuity of life processes, as I have explored elsewhere.[10]

Chirombo, on the other hand, is a category that refers to all organisms that are either useless or harmful to humans. The prototypical *chirombo* are the hyena, lion and leopard. But the term may refer to all mammals associated with the woodland, as 'wild' animals, particularly if they damage crops. Like *nyama,* the term has important symbolic connotations, for it is the term used to describe the masked dancers and the theriomorphic figures in *nyau* and *chinyago* rituals, the male dancers impersonating the spirits of the dead who take animal forms. The *nyau,* as *chirombo,* come from the woodland, and are aggressive, fierce, vital and sexual - as the male affine is expected to be.

Conclusion

In a number of different ways, focusing specifically on wild mammals, I have explored the dialectic that centres around the symbolic opposition - pervasive in Malawian culture — between the woodland and the village. The woodland domain is associated with wild animals, with the spirits of the dead, and is fundamentally a cool place.[11] This is why such a creative act as hunting is profoundly hazardous, and why in the past both iron-smelting and childbirth (among the Yao particularly) took place in the woodland.[12] The woodland is also associated with hunting, and with the male affine, which is why boys' initiation ceremonies always take place in this setting. The village domain, on the other hand, is associated with agriculture, with sexuality and procreation, and is essentially the domain of a kin community, focused around a group of matrilineally related women, under the guardianship of an elder brother. The initiation of girls always takes place in the village, close to the hut of the headman, and the initiation essentially involves the incorporation of the girl into the collectivity of women.

I have attempted also to indicate that the series of complementary oppositions that I have outlined do not imply a static order, nor a karmic process, but essentially reflect a cyclical process in which life, particularly the social life of the kin community, is sustained and regenerated. In seeing the woodland and its mammalian life both as the source of much that is essential to life - meat, building materials, medicines, wild foods and, most importantly, male fertility - and as the harbinger of much that is detrimental to human well-being, above all in the form of the depredations of wild animals, I have also suggested that this underwrites an attitude towards the world that is ambivalent, one of dialectical opposition. Perhaps this attitude is widespread among horticultural people who are still dependent upon a woodland environment that is frequented by wild mammals.

NOTES

I have spent more than ten years in Malawi and have lived for short periods and researched in every part of the country. The present article, however, is based on two extensive periods of research studies in ethnobiology, 1979-80 and 1990-91, supported by the ESRC and the Nuf-field Foundation. I am grateful to these agencies for their support. I should also like to thank the Centre for Social Research, Zomba, for institutional support, and my many friends in Malawi for their help and encouragement. With respect to the present article, I am grateful to Pat Caplan and to the anonymous readers of this journal for helping me to put my rambling thoughts into some kind of order. My indebtedness to the early pioneering studies of Rangeley and Schoffeleers will be self-evident.

[1] My reflections in this article essentially refer to the rural people of central and southern Malawi, for I firmly believe, like Levi Mumba, that the matrilineal peoples of Malawi share a common cultural heritage, although there are, of course, cultural variations between the different ethnic communities. I use Chewa terms in the article for two reasons: 1) this is the language I used in my conversations with Malawians, and 2) Chewa is now regarded as the national language and is spoken and understood throughout Malawi, although one may occasionally encounter an elderly Yao or Lomwe woman who speaks little Chewa. Although I have spent several weeks in the Mua, Dedza, Kasungu, Lilongwe and Ntchisi areas, I have lived most of my time in Malawi among Yao and Lomwe speakers.

[2] Based on hoe agriculture, and with hunting and trade important aspects of their political economy, the people of Malawi historically formed part of what has been described as the 'matrilineal belt'. Since around the sixteenth century they were also organized through a changing pattern of chiefdoms, thus confirming what both Bachofen (1967: 152) and Harris (1993: 64-9) intimate, namely that a close link exists between matriliny and petty chiefdoms based on hunting, trade and warfare, where men are frequently away from a kin community focused around women and agriculture.

3 It is of interest that men - the in-marrying affines - are essentially seen as the providers of meat from wild animals, providing the highly valued ingredients for the relish which goes with the maize porridge. The historian of the Chewa, Samuel Ntara (1973: 119) mentions an exchange of meat for sex, a theme explored by Knight (1991) in his study of the origins of culture.

4 The analogy, of course, refers not to ecological or symbolic domains, but to the distinction between substance and activating agency.

5 A colleague has suggested to me that there are contradictions evident in my analysis. But as Berdyaev and others have suggested, contradictions lie at the very heart of existence, and are there in the empirical world that constitutes Malawian culture whose ethos I attempt to portray (Berdyaev, cited in Seaver 1950: 10). As Malawian thought is diverse, shifting and proces-sual, I have been reluctant to press the analysis into a static symbolic schema. This is why I deliberately eschew the structural analysis of Schoffeieers (1968), which implies a totalizing logic.

6 When I lived in Malawi in the late 1950s, much of the country was a mosaic of woodland and villages, and the graveyards were often on the edge of the woodland. The graveyards thus had a marginal existence between the woodland and the gardens, a focal point, as it were, of the woodland just as the meeting place/court is the centre of the village community. Over the last thirty years much of the Brachystegia woodland has disappeared, leaving the *manda* often as isolated patches: around the major urban centres even these have been cut for firewood.

7 *Nyau* is a secret male fraternity among the Chewa and Manganja, consisting of those who have undertaken the initiations. It performs dances on certain ritual occasions, especially at funerals of important people, commemorative rites, and as a part of the girls' initiation rites. Members of the cult perform at these rituals as masked dancers or theriomorphic figures. The *chinyaga* *(chinambande)* rites among the Yao perform a similar function in relation to the girls' initiation rite.

8 This kind of eschatology seems to be widespread among kin-based communities (cf. Parkin 1992: 203-15 on the Munda of central India for whom the conceptual unity of alternative generations is a fundamental doctrine - as in Malawi - and grandparents are 'reincarnated' in their grandchildren). Parkin stresses its distinction from the karmic doctrine of the transmigration of an immortal indwelling soul.

[9] Although there has been a great reduction in the population of the larger mammals over the past fifty years or so, wild mammals are still fairly plentiful in Malawi. For though Malawi is one of the most densely populated areas of Africa, 33 per cent, of the country is still under 'natural vegetation' and wildlife conservation areas and forest reserves constitute some 20 per cent, of the total land area. Thus leopards and hyenas still roam at night in the Zomba and Blantyre townships, and in rural areas throughout Malawi local people are still engaged during the agricultural season in a constant battle with hippopotamuses, porcupines, monkeys, baboons and wild pigs - not to mention the smaller rodents - in an effort to defend their crops. On the predations of wild animals in the past see Balestra (1962), Carr (1969: 84-99), Dudley (1979), Muldoon (1955), and various papers in the National Archives of Malawi (Zomba, MNA 51/1721A).

[10] In an interesting analysis of Chamba ritual, Fardon (1990: 30-2) suggests that where the matrikin is associated with subsistence, animals, blood, body and sexuality, the patrikin is associated with the spirits, skulls and bones. The spirits of the dead are thus seen as essentially masculine. Although this analysis has resonance with respect to Malawian culture, the spirits of the dead are not seen as specifically masculine - if anything, *makolo* (ancestors) has connotations of grandmothers. Thus a matrilineal emphasis pertains, and it is the skins, horns and tails of animals that have salience in Malawi, and these are specifically associated with spirits of the dead, activating medicines and male affines, as I have explored elsewhere (Morris 1993).

[11] The woodland is also associated with the past, not only with the spirits of the ancestors, but also with the original inhabitants of Malawi, the Batwa hunter-gatherers, who are believed still to frequent many mountain forests in Malawi (Morris 1994).

[12] Hunting, like all creative or transformational activities - cooking, pot-making, iron-smelting, childbirth, initiations - must be undertaken by participants in a cool condition, otherwise misfortunes, or even deaths, might result. Hunting, like menstruation, is hazardous because it involves the shedding of blood: but it is viewed positively by Malawians and is not seen, in gnostic fashion, as the antithesis of childbirth.

REFERENCES

Adams, J.S. & T.O McShane 1992. *The myth of wild Africa*. New York: Norton.

Balestra, F. 1962. The man-eating hyenas of Mulanje.^ *Wildlife* 16, 25-7.

Bachofen, JJ. 1967 [1861]. *Myth, religion and mother right*. Princeton: Univ. Press.

Baumann, H. 1950. Nyama: die Rachemacht iiber einige Vorteilungcn in Afrika. *Paideuma* 4,191-230.

Campbell, J. 1984. *The way of the animal powers*. London: Times Books. Carr, N. 1969. *The white impala*. London: Collins.

Chapman, J.D. 1962. *The vegetation ofMlanje mountains, Nyasaland*. Zomba: Government Press.

———— 1988. Mpita Nkhalango: a lowland forest relic unique to Malawi. *Nyala* 12, 3-26.

Comaroff, J. 1985. Body *of power, spirit of resistance*. Chicago: Univ. of Chicago Press.

Croll, E. & D. Parkin (eds) 1992. *Bush base, forest farm: culture, environment and development*. London: Routledge.

Douglas, M. 1954 The Lele of Kasai. *In African worlds* (ed.) D. Forde. Oxford: Univ. Press.

———— 1975. *Implicit meanings*. London: Routledge & Kegan Paul.

Dudley, C. 1979. History of the decline of the larger mammals of the Lake Chilwa basin. *Soc. Malawi* 32 (2), 27-41.

Fardon, R. 1990. *Between god, the dead and the wild*. Edinburgh: Univ. Press.

Fortes, M. 1969. *Kinship and the social order*. Chicago: Aldine.

Frazer, J.G. 1922. *The golden bough*. London: Macmillan.

Gillison, G. 1980. Images of nature in Gimi thought. In *Nature, culture and gender* (eds) C. MacCormack & M. Strathern. Cambridge: Univ. Press.

Goodman, F. 1992. *Ecstasy, ritual and alternate reality*. Bloomington: Indiana Univ. Press.

Guenther, M. 1988. Animals in Bushman thought, myth and art. In *Hunters and gatherers* (eds) T. Ingold *et al*. Oxford: Berg.

Harris, M. 1993. The evolution of human gender hierarchies. In *Sex and gender hierarchies* (ed.) B.D. Miller. Cambridge: Univ. Press.

Ingold, T. 1986. *The appropriation of nature*. Manchester: Univ. Press.

———— 1988. (ed) *What is an animal?* London: Unwin Hyman.

Jonas, H. 1966. *The phenomenon of life*. Chicago: Univ. of Chicago Press.

Katcher, A.H. & A.M. Beck 1991. Animal campaigns: more companion than animal. In *Man and beast revisited* (eds) M.H. Robinson & L. Tiger. Washington: Smithsonian Institution Press.

Kathamalo, BJ. 1965. Khulubvi: Thicket - Port Herald. Soc. *Malawi J.* 18(2), 53-4.

Kent, S. 1989 (ed.). *Farmers as hunters: the implications of sedentism*. Cambridge: Univ. Press.

Knight, C. 1991. *Blood relations*. New Haven: Yale Univ. Press.

Lovejoy, A. 1948. *Essays in the history of ideas*. New York: Johns Hopkins Press.

MacCormack, C. & M. Strathern (eds) 1980. *Nature, culture and gender*. Cambridge: Univ. Press.

Mandala, E.G. 1990. *Work and control in a peasant society*. Madison: Univ. of Wisconsin Press.

Mayr, E. 1982. *The growth of biological thought*. Cambridge, MA: Harvard Univ. Press.

————— 1988. *Toward a new philosophy of biology*. Cambridge, MA: Harvard Univ. Press. Merchant, C. 1980. *The death of nature*. London: Wildwood House.

————— 1992. *Radical ecology*. London: Routledge. Mitchell, J.C. 1956. *The Yao village*. Manchester: Univ. Press.

Morris, B. 1970. Nature and origins of Brachystegia woodland. *Commonwealth Forestry Rev 49*, 155-8.

————— 1978. Ecology and mysticism. *Freedom* May, 9-16.

————— 1981. Changing views of nature. *The Ecologist* 11, 130-7.

————— 1982. *Forest traders*. London: Athlone Press.

————— 1984. The pragmatics of folk classification./ *Ethnobiol. 4*, 45-60.

————— 1993. Skins, horns and tails: reflections of the use of mammals as medicine in Malawi. Seminar Paper, Univ. of Kent, November 30, 1993.

————— 1994. Michesi: mountain of the spirits. *Malawi Mountain ClubJ*.

Muldoon, G. 1955. *Leopards in the night*. London: Hart-Davies.

Nelson, R.K. 1983. *Making prayers to the raven*. Chicago: Univ. of Chicago Press.

Ntara, SJ. 1973. *The history of the Chewa*. Wiesbaden: F. Steiner.

Ortner, S.B. 1974. Is female to male as nature is to culture? In *Woman, culture and society* (eds) M.Z. Rosaldo & L. Lamphere. Stanford: Univ. Press.

Parkin, R. 1992. *The Munda of central India*. Delhi: Oxford Univ. Press. Potter, J.R. 1987. Mizimu: demarcated forests and contour profiles: conservation in Malawi 1800-1960. Thesis, Williams College, Massachusetts.

Rangeley, W.H.J. 1948. Notes of Chewa tribal law. *NyasalandJ*. 1(3), 5-68.

Ritvo, H. 1987. *The animal estate*. Cambridge, MA: Harvard Univ. Press (Penguin 1990).

Schoffeleers, J.M. 1968. Symbolic and social aspects of spirit worship among the Mang'anja. Thesis, University of Oxford.

————— 1971. The religious significance of bushfires in Malawi. *Cah. Relig. Afr.* 10, 271-87.

————— 1992. *River of blood*. Madison: Univ. of Wisconsin Press.

Seaver, G. 1950. *Nicolas Berdyaev: an introduction to his thought*. London: J. Clarke.

Scrpell, J. 1986. *In the company of animals*. Oxford: Blackwell.

Soka, LJ. 1953. *Mbiri ya Alomwe*. Limbe: Malawi Publishing House.

Strathern, M. 1980. No nature, no culture: the Hagen case. In *Nature, culture and gender* (eds) C. MacCormack & M. Strathern. Cambridge: Univ. Press.

Tanner, A. 1979. *Bringing home animals*. London: C. Hurst.

Van Beek, WE.A. & RM. Banga 1992. The Dogon and their trees. In *Bush base, forest farm: culture, environment and development* (eds) E. Croll & D. Parkin. London: Routledge.

Van der Breemer, J.RM. 1992. Ideas and usage: environment in Aouan society, Ivory Coast. In *Bush base,forestfarm: culture, environment and development* (eds) E. Croll & D. Parkin. London: Routledge.

Willis, R. (ed.) 1990. *Signifying animals*. London: Unwin Hyman.

WILDLIFE CONSERVATION IN MALAWI (2001)

This article discusses the history of wildlife conservation in Malawi from the beginning of the colonial period to the present day. It concludes by suggesting a new approach to wildlife conservation in Africa.

This essay explores the history of wildlife conservation in Malawi, specifically focusing on national politics rather than on the broader issues of local people's relationships with wildlife, which I have explored elsewhere.[1] Wildlife conservation in Malawi has essentially passed through three distinct phases: an initial phase (1895-1930) of 'game preservation' when the hunting of game animals was the preserve of an European sporting 'elite'; a second phase (1930-1964) when the game reserves were established but sport hunting remained an essential concern of government, coupled with a strong emphasis on crop protection and the eradication of the offending mammals; and a final phase when sport hunting declined and viable game sanctuaries were established with a tourist clientele (1964-1990). We are now moving into a fourth phase, with the recognition that wildlife protection geared solely to the generation of foreign exchange and to the aesthetic enjoyment of rich overseas tourists - and to the detriment of the wellbeing of local people - is highly problematic. It is a strategy that is not conducive to the long-term conservation of wildlife, whose survival is ultimately in the hands of African people. I will discuss each of these phases in turn.

1. THE EARLY COLONIAL PERIOD (1895-1930)

Recent historiography has shown that in the early part of the nineteenth century Malawi was a well populated region, particularly along the lake shore and in the Lower Shire valley. The area was the focus of developed trade routes, a complex agricultural system which used dry season cultivation in low-lying areas (dimba) and where there was a flourishing iron industry and cotton production commented on favourably by Livingstone.[2]

By the end of the century, however, the increasing ravages of the slave trade after 1840, the advent of militaristic Ngoni and the incursion of Yao traders into the Shire Highlands, all adversely affected population distribution and disrupted the economy of the area. This led many people to take refuge in such places as high in the mountains of Zomba and Mulanje, or Chisi island in Lake Chilwa. In his travels near Lake Chilwa towards the end of the century the Scottish divine Henry Drummond reported that the region was 'almost uninhabited' and that 'nowhere else in Africa did I see such splendid herds of the larger animals as here'.[3] Zebra were particularly abundant, and he went on to describe central Africa as the 'finest hunting country in the world', where elephant, buffalo, eland, leopard, zebra, hippopotamus, rhinoceros and 'endless species' of antelope were all to be found.[4]

The reason for this abundance of wildlife Elias Mandala puts down to - in the Lower Shire at least - people's loss of control over nature, resulting from the devastation and desolation caused by the slave trade, coupled with the chaos and instability that followed the famine (chaola) of 1862-63, when the rains failed over two seasons.[5] Around the turn of the century, beginning with Johnston's administration of 1891, further disruption of the local economy and to the land was caused by the alienation of vast tracts of land to European settlers and companies. Almost four million acres, representing 15 percent of the land was granted in freehold to Europeans, and this included much of the land of the Shire Highlands.[6]

It was in this context that the colonial government established the first game laws and 'game reserves'. But the term 'conservation mania'[7] to describe these measures is something of a misnomer, for the colonial administration were not concerned with conservation but rather with a much more limited conception -that of game preservation. And for Europeans at the turn of the century 'game' had a more restricted meaning even than the cognate term in Chewa, nyama: it applied only to the larger mammals, the hunting of which was considered 'sport'.

Following, it seems, the perspectives of Kjekshus and Vail, Vaughan's contention that the government had a policy of 'carving out game reserves in populous areas' is misleading.[8] For what early game regulations of British Central Africa (1897) were in essence concerned with, was to restrict the hunting of larger game animals only to Europeans, who alone could afford the game licences. Only two 'game reserves' were in fact specified in the first game ordinance - the Elephant Marsh near Chiromo and Lake Chilwa - both popular duck shooting areas for Europeans - as they still are. Neither of these was initially a 'reserve' in the true sense, for those possessing the appropriate licences could freely hunt there. The animal species specified in the 1897 game schedule were all ungulates - elephant, blue wildebeest, rhinoceroses, zebra, buffalo, eland, warthog, bushpig and around 19 species of antelope.

The game ordinances of 1902,1911 and 1926 all followed a similar pattern, essentially restricting the hunting of larger mammals to Europeans; looking at the lists of those who took out game licences, these included missionaries as well as planters and administrators. There was much controversy focussed around the 1926 game ordinance, which was opposed by many missionaries and planters, though for very different reasons. The opposition to the ordinance centred on the following issues:

i. It was felt that there was a strong association between game and the presence of tsetse fly, which had increased its range during the early decades of colonial rule. This had led to the loss of livestock through the disease nagana and several outbreaks of sleeping sickness.

ii. That the government protection of game, and the restriction on the traditional methods of hunting, had a detrimental effect on the wellbeing of local people, in terms of nutrition and in crop degradation from wild game. The losses of life due to elephants and carnivores were particularly stressed. It must be borne in mind that prior to the introduction of muzzle-loading guns humans and elephants vied with each other for territory. Ecologically, and in terms of social organisation, humans and elephants are very similar. Elephants and many communities in east central Africa have social groupings that are essentially matricentric, and both humans - as shifting cultivators - and elephants are extremely destructive to the woodland habitat. Even the life cycles of human and elephants are similar, for both have protracted childhoods and are exceptionally long-lived species.[9]

iii. It was felt that economic progress of the country was being retarded by the protection of game animals, and some missionaries suggested that it would be better for the protectorate if the larger mammals were exterminated. In spite of the protracted opposition, the 1926 game ordinance became law, mainly supported by the game warden, Rodney Wood.

The main outcome of the 1926 game ordinance was to establish three game sanctuaries - Lengwe, Tangadzi and Kasungu - which offered complete protection for the wildlife within their boundaries, and to make hunting outside these reserves the exclusive right of the Europeans who could afford the game licences. All traditional methods of securing meat, whether by trapping or hunting were proscribed. Subsistence hunting by local people was thus deemed illegal.

Many writers have indicated similarities between the game ordinances implemented by colonial governments and medieval hunting laws in Europe.[10] As in medieval times, the game ordinances devised and enforced by the colonial government of Nyasaland, made all game animals - essentially the larger ungulates - the sole property of the crown, the state. It assumed the 'royal prerogative' to game, and with the system of game licences, the colonial state ensured that hunting was the sole privilege of Europeans - as an aristocratic elite. As Graham, remarked: 'It is a universal feature of game laws that they never favour the unprivileged'." The colonial rulers thus claimed exclusive ownership of wild mammals, and all subsistence hunting, whether by traps, snares, nets, fire or dogs was declared illegal - a crime. As in the European context, subsistence hunting was described as 'poaching' and throughout the colonial period Europeans - the majority of whom engaged in hunting as a recreation - gave subsistence hunting a very bad press. It was described as wasteful, cruel, barbaric and irrational, and as being the primary factor in the decline of the larger mammals.

Even more enlightened Europeans, such as Rodney Wood, expressed strong antipathy towards subsistence hunting, particularly towards the communal hunt *(uzimba)*. Such hunts were in direct contravention of the game ordinance although they were common throughout the colonial period - and in some areas still take place. Wood thought this kind of hunting an 'abominable practice' and made every effort - through pleas and directives to the governor and administrative officers - to get the practice not only proscribed but also eradicated in places. He was particularly concerned because on a visit to the Bua river with the governor, Bowring, they had observed a large-scale hunt taking place. Though indulged in throughout the protectorate, he wrote, this 'barbarous method of hunting' should not be tolerated. Needless to say, Wood did not succeed in putting an end to the traditional *uzimba}2*

2. THE LATER COLONIAL PERIOD (1930-1964)

When Rodney Wood resigned as game warden in 1931 he recommended to the government that the post of game warden be abolished, and that the maintenance of the three main game reserves, together with the duties of crop protection, be undertaken by the district administration. But by the 1930s, with much of the game population depleted in Malawi, there was a shift of opinion in the thinking of many Europeans, and a need was felt to preserve game mammals. Many of these new conservationists were 'penitent butchers', as Rodney Wood described himself. While in the early game period the game laws essentially functioned to preserve game for rituali sed sport hunting - focusing on the collecting of trophies and, to an important degree, serving as a ritual of prestige and domination - the establishment of 'game reserves' had a different motivation. Even so, the motivations behind the establishment of 'reserves' in colonial Nyasaland were many and varied, and largely geared to human problems and needs: with Lengwe, the need to protect declining numbers of nyala; with Kasungu, the need to protect people from the ravages of sleeping sickness; with, later (1938) Nkhotakota game reserve, the need for a refuge for marauding elephants who were causing crop depredation along the lake shore. Whatever the motivations towards the establishment of game reserves, the end of the colonial period went hand-in-hand with crop protection, and a determined effort to control, even to eradicate, all larger mammals outside of the reserves. This signified an implicit acknowledgement by the administration that the presence of larger animals and human populations whose subsistence was based on agriculture, did not easily co-exist. Such crop protection activities are still an important aspect of the present government.

From 1931 until the end of the Second World War, game conservation was thus handled by the district administrations, and was to remain at a virtual standstill. Game guards were employed by these administrations mainly to protect crops, especially against the ravages of hippopotamuses and elephant -often attempting to drive the latter back into the forest reserves or game sanctuaries. The game reserves themselves, like Kasungu and Nkhotakota were largely a 'no-man's land'. They had few staff and there was no serious effort to enforce wildlife legislation. They were frequented only by the occasional subsistence hunter and people travelling across the country.

In June 1946, the report of a commission, especially appointed by the colonial government to look into the whole issue of forest and game reserves, recommended the formation of the Department of Game, Fish and Tsetse Control. The department was finally established in 1949, and flourished - if that is the right word, for it was always under-staffed and under-funded - until 1962. With regard to wildlife, it had essentially a dual function, being concerned with both game conservation and crop protection. Yet it is clear from the beginning that crop protection rather than wildlife conservation was the primary role of the department. As its 1949 report acknowledged: 'since the main reason for the formation of the game side of the organisation was the protection of crops, emphasis has to date been laid on game and vermin control rather than on game conservation'. Indeed, the game rangers were initially described as 'game control officers'. During the 14 years from 1948-1961 the following animals were killed in the protection of crops: elephant 852, hippopotamus 1048, buffalo 562, waterbuck 489, roam, eland and kudu 554, other antelope 1199, as well as more than 300,000 'vermin' - mainly bushpig and baboons. By 1955 buffalo, roan, eland and kudu and the other antelopes had ceased to be a problem, and hippopotamus had been drastically reduced in number. They are now virtually extinct along much of the lake shore, and recent efforts (1995) to curb human-hippo conflict in the Lower Shire have led to their demise from this region as well.

Towards the end of the colonial period, non-hunting areas were established on the Nyika plateau and in an area around Majete hill (1952), and four years later, largely through the initiative of Chief Katumbi, a controlled shooting area was declared around the Vwaza Marsh.[13]

3. THE POST-COLONIAL PERIOD

When the Department of Game, Fish and Tsetse Control was disbanded in 1962, the work of crop protection and game conservation came under the auspices of the Forestry Department - as the Department of Forestry and Game. A decade later, in 1973, the Department of National Parks and Wildlife was established -and a new era of conservation began. At its inception it had around a hundred personnel.[14] Already in 1983 the new government had shown an awareness of the wider aspects of wildlife conservation and had issued a Wildlife Policy Statement which read:

It is the policy of the Malawi government to afford all the protection in its power to game animals and wildlife in general in so far as such protection does not conflict with planned development of other essential national resources. In affording protection to game and wildlife the government has in mind the value of this national resource as a tourist attraction, as a possible source of food and a scientific and educational asset of national importance.

It is the intention of the government to afford protection to wildlife in all existing game reserves and forest reserves by means of enforcing restriction of hunting and the prevention of disturbances of the natural habitat. In other areas it is the intention to control the hunting of animals, birds and other forms of wildlife through restriction' by licence both of hunting and of trade in game meat and trophies through the provisions of the game ordinance.

The government intends to encourage the fullest public support for its wildlife policy through education in wildlife conservation and by general publicity to stimulate the interests of the people of Malawi in the importance of wildlife as a national asset and to obtain the willing co-operation of the people in all wildlife conservation programmes.[15]

Although the statement failed to acknowledge that the wildlife of the country has intrinsic value, nevertheless it recognised the importance of the fauna and flora as national assets. Following suggestions laid down by the NFPS it accepted that the government should play a leading role in environmental education, and seek the active co-operation of the people in its wildlife conservation programmes. The policy was a far cry from the earlier focus on crop protection. Nevertheless, the government still recognised the crucial importance of protecting gardens from the depredations of wild animals, particularly hippopotamus and elephant. This was seen as crucial near the wildlife sanctuaries - Nkhotakota, Kasungu and Liwonde in particular. In 1975 a crop protection unit was established by the Department of National Parks and Wildlife.

By 1973, four important national parks, Nyika, Kasungu, Lengwe and Liwonde had been established, totalling an area of 6,885 square kilometres. This constituted around seven percent of the total land area of the country. By the end of the decade, tourist facilities had been established in each of these parks. Together with the four game reserves - Vwaza was declared a game reserve in 1977, and Majete, Mwabvi and Nkhotakota had long been proclaimed sanctuaries for wildlife - these constituted a further 3,614 square kilometres (4 percent) - Malawi, as G.D. Hayes admitted, probably had as many wildlife sanctuaries as the country could afford. For within just over a decade, since independence, 11 percent of the land area of Malawi had been set aside purely for the conservation of wildlife.

The emphasis was thus put - by both the Department of National Parks and Wildlife and the NFPS - on developing these sanctuaries for a growing tourist clientele and in putting increasing energy and resources into environmental education.

How important wildlife is to the tourist industry is reflected in all the tourist brochures that have been produced by the Malawian government and by other tourist agencies since independence. All highlight the aesthetic enjoyment to be derived from wildlife. Although there have been some setbacks, with the depletion of such larger mammals as the elephant, rhinoceros, zebra and hartebeest within some of the reserves, the establishment of wildlife sanctuaries in Malawi has largely been a success story.[16]

But what also has to be recognised is that these sanctuaries contribute very little to the wellbeing of the local people - on the contrary, by restricting hunting and the utilisation of the woodland for basic subsistence needs and in being a 'reservoir' of wild mammals which cause serious depredations to crops and human life, the sanctuaries cause much harm to local communities living within their vicinity. Small wonder, then, that the majority of rural people in Malawi have an antipathy, even a more actively hostile attitude towards such wildlife sanctuaries.

4. A NEW APPROACH TO WILDLIFE CONSERVATION

A recognition of this state of affairs had led many conservationists to suggest the need for a complete re-thinking of wildlife conservation, even a change of attitude towards the African hunter, who, as a 'poacher' had been maligned and criticised by wildlife conservationists for over half a century. One of the best accounts of this changing attitude towards conservation is Adams and McShane' s *The Myth of Wild Africa* (1992), which is subtitled *Conservation Without Illusion*. It is of particular interest because McShane spent four years undertaking wildlife research in Malawi, mainly at Vwaza Marsh reserve, and the study has a short chapter on poaching within this reserve.[17]

The myth of wild Africa pertains to the idea - depicted in many books and on TV - that Africa is an untouched 'wilderness', an 'unspoilt Eden' (which is how Malawi is described in the tourist brochures). Deep ecologists and people like Laurens Van Der Post have stressed the intrinsic value of such 'untouched' wilderness areas as a source of spiritual renewal, as a means of reaffirming our 'lost harmony' with nature. But of course Africa has never been a pristine wilderness, for humans have long been an integral part of the landscape. And Malawian people neither advocate the control and domination of nature, nor the celebration of the wilderness in its own right, but have always acknowledged the close interdependence of humans and nature, including its wildlife. But what is significant is that when game reserves and national parks were established in Malawi - as elsewhere in Africa - they largely followed the pattern of the United States' national parks, such as Yellowstone and Yosemite. This pattern was later taken up by the International Union for the Conservation of Nature and Natural Resources based in Switzerland, and it is this pattern that has been largely advocated by conservation agencies, and implemented by governments. The result, as one observer put it, has been a 'bizarre situation' in which 'Africans are hired, trained and armed to guard African parks to keep out African people, for the benefit of both the protected animals and the foreigners who come to see them - and of course for the tourist revenue, which goes into the government or hotel bank accounts, not to rural people'.[18]

Adams and McShane echo these sentiments, suggesting that the mode of establishing parks in Africa has resulted in a park 'surrounded by people who were excluded from the planning of the area, do not understand its purpose, receive little or no benefit from the money poured into its creation, and hence do not support its existence'.[19]

They conclude that the notion of wilderness 'does not apply to the African context'. For human and animals have evolved together in the continent's diverse ecosystems. They also maintain that African countries have, historically, successfully coexisted with wild animals, although of course, this has only been the case where human populations have been relatively low and sparsely distributed. But given the current antipathy of local people towards game sanctuaries, in Malawi as elsewhere in Africa, their contention is that such sanctuaries will eventually be overrun by people in their need for land, unless the national parks serve, or at least are not inimical to, the wellbeing of local people.

Conservation and development thus need to go hand in hand, as part of a single process. For 'conservation cannot ignore the needs of human beings, while development that runs roughshod over the environment is doomed'. [20]

Adams and McShane give graphic accounts of the conflict between game scouts and local people living near Lake Kazuni in Vwaza Marsh game reserve, where an angry mob of local villagers killed two game scouts, and the life and times of one local hunter - poacher - Joshua Nyirenda. Armed with an 1844 Tower Musket, a relic of the Swahili slave trade, he was arrested with three other men for hunting elephants in the reserve. As a second offence he was fined $500 or five years' hard labour. Unable to pay the fine - the annual income for a farm worker in Malawi in 1990 was only $176 - Joshua went to prison. What is of interest about their account - quite unique among conservationists and wildlife officers - is that they sympathise with the hunters' predicament and acknowledge the crucial importance of subsistence hunting in the local economy, and to the very livelihood of men like Nyirenda. The 'poacher' is no longer depicted as a 'villain' - the origins of this term is worth reflecting upon in this present context - and Adams and McShane suggest that conservationists are gradually coming to realise the 'futility of waging constant war against poachers'.[21]

These authors therefore conclude that a completely 'new approach' is needed towards wildlife conservation, one which ensures that the benefits derived from conservation are directed more towards the needs and wellbeing of the local rural communities. 'Conservation will either contribute to solving the problems of the rural poor who live day to day with wild animals, or those wild animals will disappear'.[22]

The person who, perhaps, more than anyone else has been responsible for this changing orientation in conservation is Richard Bell. Like McShane, Bell spent many years in Malawi as a wildlife research officer. His essay on 'Conservation with a Human Face' is, in fact, seminal.[23]

Bell stridently challenges two images of Africa that are currently portrayed in the literature and media. The one, emphasised by tourist agencies in particular, depicts Africa as we have noted as a garden of Eden, or wilderness area teeming with wildlife - and suggestions are made to keep parts of Africa in this 'pristine' state for the good of future generations. The wilderness concept was well expressed by Bernard Grzimek and Laurens Van Der Post. Grzimek was an avowed and passionate advocate of African wildlife conservation in the early post-war period, hi his classic *Serengeti Shall Not Die* (1987) - the jacket of the book significantly patterned like a zebra skin - which he co-authored with his son Michael who was tragically killed in a plane crash in 1959, Grzimek portrayed the African plains as a wilderness. It was 'eternal' nature, with great herds of wild animals, untouched by humans. This Africa was 'dying', and so much of Africa he tells us was already dead. But small parts of Africa, such as the Serengeti must be retained in its 'awe-filled past glory'. He argued that a national park, to be effective, must be a 'primordial wildness' and that no humans, certainly not Africans, should be allowed to live within its boundaries. That there were any wild animals at all in the Serengeti was largely because the Maasai people who lived in the area had changed its landscape and co-existed with the larger mammals for several centuries. But this was lost on Grzimek. He was utterly opposed to granting grazing rights to the Maasai, and failed to see the idea of striking a balance between wildlife and human needs was a constructive and creative approach to wildlife conservation.[24]

The other image of Africa is quite different. It depicts Africa as in crisis - both politically and ecologically. The image we thus have of Africa, as portrayed through the media, is one where political violence and repression, famine, civil war and ecological degradation are ubiquitous. And for some political analysts and conservationists, the situation is hopeless. Nowhere on the continent, one commentator wrote, is there a 'flicker of hope'. Although Africa does indeed have its problems - like the rest of the world - Patrick Chabal has countered, as far as politics is concerned, this biased and highly prejudiced image.[25] Richard Bell has attempted to do the same with regards to the alleged ecological crisis.

Africa, according to many commentators, is facing 'environmental bankruptcy'. It is dying through ill-advised attempts to modernise itself, and such development has led to famine, soil erosion, desertification and ecological degradation. Africa is held to be in 'crisis' and on the brink of ecological collapse.[26]

Again, although Africa does have serious ecological problems that need to be addressed, Bell suggests that this scenario is overdrawn and misleading. Bell points out that although the human population in Africa is indeed increasing rapidly, the continent still has not reached ecological carrying capacity, and that surveys have indicated a considerable area of usable land is available. When Europeans encountered Africa at the outset of the colonial period, they encountered a human population probably smaller than it had been since the iron age revolution two millennia earlier - given the slave trade, the introduction of diseases and the rinderpest pandemic which ravaged throughout the continent in the 1890s. As human and livestock populations were reduced to a low ebb, Bell writes, so wildlife and its habitats expanded - a situation that was perpetuated by much of the colonial conservation legislation.[27] As regard to famines, when these are not related to droughts, Bell suggests, they are invariably associated with civil disturbances or are related to political and economic rather than to ecological issues. With respect to the availability of land, Bell points out that although Malawi is the fourth most densely populated country in Africa, some 33 percent of the land is under 'natural vegetation', over and above the national parks and game reserves (11 percent), forest reserves (9 percent), agriculture (36 percent) and urban developments (11 percent). Except on a local basis, such figures suggest that Africa is not facing an immediate shortage of arable land. The figures also indicate a high degree of commitment by the Malawian government to wildlife conservation, and a similar pattern is found in Botswana, Zambia and Tanzania, where over 10 percent of their land area have been allocated to wildlife sanctuaries.

The primary objectives of the World Conservation Strategy outlined by the IUCN in 1980 were as follows:

i. To maintain essential ecological processes and life support systems.

ii. To preserve genetic diversity.

iii. To ensure the sustainable population of species and ecosystems.

Bell argues that there is an inevitable conflict between short-term, individual interests and long-term commercial needs and that the costs and benefits of conservation are not equally shared between different sectors of a society. The administration of conservation programmes, in terms of management and costs, are the concern of national governments, which also enjoy the international prestige, and most of the revenue derived from wildlife resources. The benefits of recreational and aesthetic experience, Bell writes, as well as scientific opportunities, are enjoyed mainly by foreigners. Local communities, however, bear most of the costs of having wildlife sanctuaries, but derive few benefits. Moreover, the World Conservation Strategy and other conservation bodies tend to stress the indirect, utilitarian values than can be gained by conservation - for example, the preservation of genetic diversity on grounds of its potential as a source of useful products. Such stress is probably due to the fact that aesthetic and long-term, ecological values are felt to carry insufficient weight with government and local communities. But, as with the Master Plan For Malawi Wildlife, Bell argues that the emphases on the utilitarian justification of conservation is opportunistic and potentially counter-productive. He writes: 'If conservation is justified on the grounds of utilitarian befits, anything that produces more of those benefits must take precedence over conservation'.[28]

The reality of the conflict between conservation and local interests is also emphasised by Bell who notes that most conservation agencies are paramilitary organisations, with armed and uniformed game guards, and that a good deal of expenditure is devoted to law enforcement and public relations. We have noted the serious conflict that exists on the boundaries of almost all game sanctuaries in Malawi, and Bell remarks that under existing 'game laws', normal, rural existence is impossible without breaking the law. In Malawi, around 500 people a year are charged with breaking wildlife offences, and in many African countries there are serious armed conflicts between poachers and those enforcing wildlife legislation.

In such circumstances, Bell advocates a more flexible and liberal approach to conservation, one that aims to reduce the conflict between short-term interests and long-term community needs and which seriously takes into account the needs of local communities and the unequal benefits and cost of wildlife conservation.[29] It is this more flexible approach that is advocated by Adams and McShane .

Bell recognises that many species of the larger mammals in Africa are incompatible with most forms of agricultural development, even though pastoralists and wildlife can happily co-exist if the human population is not too high. I have noted the depredations to crops and human life in Malawi due to elephant, buffalo, bushpig, hippopotamus, hyena lion, crocodile, baboons and in some situations, the larger antelopes. Bell thus acknowledges that the integration of wildlife conservation - he suggests that the allocation of at least five percent of the land area of a country to conservation in the form of national parks would be sufficient to meet the objectives of the World Conservation Strategy - with other forms of land use, particularly agriculture, has always been a 'chronic problem' in Africa. Its solution would entail two strategies. The first was the protection of people and their cultivation from depredations through controlled hunting, the creation of 'buffer zones' and the development of electric fencing

- all of which have been tried in Malawi with varying degrees of success. The second strategy aiming to reduce the conflict between local communities and wildlife was to ensure that the revenues earned by conservation areas (that is, from tourism, professional hunting or culling) should be explicitly fed back into the communities that largely bear the cost of the conservation area. Such revenue allocation schemes have been tried in Zambia and Zimbabwe. The funds often went, however, to district administrations rather than the local communities near the conservation areas. Moreover, such local communities did not participate in the decision-making. Nor did they derive any aesthetic benefits from conservation. But rather, 'they are being treated as a nuisance that is being bribed to keep quiet'.[30] Thus Bell advocates a more radical proposal; namely, that local communities living in the vicinity of the conservation areas should be allowed concessions allowing them to use wildlife resources in certain areas, and that the conservation agencies should act as marketing agents for the products. Bell noted that in 1981 poachers in Malawi were obtaining about $10 per kilo for ivory,, which at that time was fetching at least $50 on the world market. If, in this situation, he suggests, the conservation agency purchased ivory from the hunter, for, say, $30 per kilo, 'all parties would benefit, while the reward would be targeted precisely to the sector of society paying the cost of lost opportunity' .[31] It would be a mistake, however, to suggest that local peoples' interest in wildlife is only utilitarian, although this is clearly important for subsistence cultivators - and can thus be 'bought off' with development schemes or the allocation of revenues derived from the conservation areas.

Although conservation areas tend to be the 'playgrounds' or 'recreational areas' of rich tourists, there is evidence to suggest that wildlife sanctuaries have an aesthetic appeal to local Malawians, although the cost and difficulties of transport and accommodation can make visits to these sanctuaries impossible for the average Malawian. Both Bell and Adams and McShane emphasise the fact that rural communities will only tend to support wildlife conservation when they not only derive benefit from it - to offset the costs - but also become participants in the process of conservation. They fear that simply protecting wildlife for the benefit of rich tourists will, in the long-term, be disastrous, quite apart from the failure to meet the needs of local communities. Unless local people support conservation projects and areas, by participating in their management and receiving some material benefits from them, it is felt that the African national parks will not long survive. Bell cites the Campfire project in Zimbabwe (Communal Area Management Programme For Indigenous Resources) and the Luangwa Integrated Resource Development Project (LIRDP) as two projects combining conservation and local community development that are worthy of consideration for future wildlife conservation in Africa.[32]

In recent years there have been developments on a number of fronts with regard to wildlife conservation in Malawi. The National Fauna Preservation Society in 1989 changed its name to the Wildlife Society of Malawi, establishing in 1992 its own headquarters in Limbe. Funded by grants from US AID and various other trusts, the Society became a fully independent NGO with a full time executive director and staff, including two environmental education officers. The society thus greatly expanded its activities, and was instrumental in efforts to 're-introduce' the black rhino and the blue wildebeest to the country (Liwonde National Park) and in establishing community forestry projects in the Chiradzulu and Chikwawa districts, as well as working on various projects with regard to rural small-holders and with people living close to wildlife sanctuaries. The emphasis of the Society is now on resolving environmental wildlife concerns through the encouragement of community participation. Working in close cooperation with the Department of National Parks and Wildlife, the Wildlife Society has also devoted considerable efforts to environmental education, in establishing various environmental education centres, and in encouraging the formation of wildlife clubs for young people. At present over five hundred have been established throughout the country, and regular visits are arranged for members to conservation areas, where student hostels have been established.

Alongside these developments there has been a sustained effort to encourage and develop wildlife tourism through private initiatives, especially at Liwonde and Kasungu National Parks. Here expensive tourist lodges continue to cater essentially for a rich overseas clientele, and the extent to which the 'profits' from these tourist enterprises are channelled into local communities seems a debatable issue.[33] But 'poaching' continues to be a problem throughout Malawi, and at Liwonde (for example) antelopes such as kudu, sable, impala and waterbuck are still hunted using muzzle-loaders or trapped with wire snares. In the period September-November 1994, game guards collected around 5000 snares that had been set to capture mammals, as well as apprehending six men in possession of firearms.[34] Regrettably, in Malawi, as elsewhere, the protection of wildlife conservation areas still has an aura of a para-military exercise.

Long ago, Keith Eltringham remarked that in general 'wild animals and agriculture do not mix'.[35] This is no doubt true, but what is surely needed in Malawi is the maintenance of wildlife sanctuaries that benefit not only visiting tourists but also local people, and which will ensure the coexistence of humans and wildlife for the mutual well-being of both.

NOTES

[1] See my study *The Power of Animals: An Ethnography* (1998) 2Livingstone 1865: 536.
[3] Drummond 1889: 30-2.
[4] Ibid.: 106.
[5] Mandela 1990: 74-8.
[6] Pachai 1978: 11-47.
[7] Vaughan 1978.
[8] Vaughan 1978: 9. Cf. Kjekshus 1977, Vail 1977.
[9] Graham 1973: 97-98.
[10] Graham 1973, MacKenzie 1988.
[11] Graham 1973: 40.
[12] MNA/NC 1/10/1.

[13] Although much of the initiative for the establishment of game reserves came from the colonial government, and the newly formed (1947) Nyasaland Fauna Preservation Society (which was largely an expatriate organisation), many Malawians were also instrumental in conservation issues. Chief Katumbi was the 'moving spirit' behind the idea of Vwazu Marsh becoming a controlled hunting area (Report of the Game, Fish and Tsetse Control 1958), and the establishment of Liwonde game reserve was largely due to the initiatives of Chief Liwonde and the game ranger Les Kettle. The idea of the latter reserve was first broached at a council of chiefs held at Kasupe (Machinga) in 1965.

[14] Clarke 1983: 10.

[15] Hayes 1972: 29-30.

[16] This success has to be measured in terms of the conservation of wildlife habitats, and the continuing presence of many species of larger mammals in Malawi - zebra, eland, kudu, sable, inpala and especially the nyala. Compared to East Africa, many of the wildlife sanctuaries in Malawi have not been great tourist attractions and have never been 'profitable'. This was recognised by the Department of National Parks and Wildlife in resisting efforts to turn much of Kasungu National Park over to tobacco farming. This success, however, has to be tempered by the fact that in the recent decades rhinoceros and cheetah have both become extinct in Kasungu National Park, and the elephant has almost been completely eradicated from the Majete Game Reserve, where it was once common.

[17] Adams and McShane 1992: 122-138.

[18] Timber-lake 1985: 160.

[19] Adams and McShane 1992: XV.

[20] Ibid.: XIX.

[21] Ibid.: 130.

[22] Ibid.: XIX.

[23] Bell 1987.

[24] Adams and McShane 1992: XVI, 50-53; Collett 1987.

[25] Chabal 1992.

[26] Timberlake 1985.

[27] Bell 1987: 89.

[28] Ibid.: 81.

[29] Ibid.: 90.

[30] Ibid.: 93.

[31] Ibid.: 93.
[32] For these projects see Martin 1986, Adams and McShane 1992:105-107,178-183:for earlier discussion on the conservation of mammals in Africa see Eltringham 1979: 207-46; Delany and Happold 1979: 364-95.
[33] Research studies undertaken at Kasungu National Park and Vwaza Game Reserve in 1991 indicated that very few Malawians visit the wildlife sanctuaries (11 and 14 per cent respectively) and that most of these tended to be government officials.
[34] WSM Newsletter, February 1995.
[35] Eltringham 1979: 213.

REFERENCES

Adams, J.S. and McShane, T.S. 1992. *The Myth of Wild Africa*. New York: Norton. Anderson, D. and Grove, R. (eds) 1987. *Conservation in Africa*. Cambridge University

Press. Bell, R.C.V. 1987. 'Conservation with a Human Face', in Anderson and Grove, op. cit.,

pp. 79-101.

Chabal, P. 1992. *Power in Africa*. London: Macmillan. Clarke, J.E. 1983. Principal Master Plan for National Parks and Wildlife Management.

Lilongwe: Dept. Nat. Parks and Wildlife. Collett, P. 1987. 'Pastoralists and Wildlife: Image and Reality in Kenya Maasailand', in

Anderson and Grove, op. cit., pp. 129^8.

Delaney, M.J. and Happold, D.C.D. 1979. *Ecology of African Mammals*. London:

Longman.

Drummond, H. 1889. *Tropical Africa*. London: Hodder and Stoughton.

Eltringham, S.K. 1979. *The Ecology and Conservation of Large African Mammals*.

London: Macmillan.

Graham, A.A. 1973. *The Gardeners of Eden*. London: Alien and Unwin. Hayes, G.D. 1972. 'Wildlife Conservation in Malawi'. *SocMal. J.* 25(2): 22-31.

Kjekshus, H. 1977. *Ecology, Control and Economic Development in East African*

History. London: Heinemann.

Livingstone, D. and C. 1865. *Narrative of an Expedition to the Zambezi and its Tributaries 1858-1864.* London: John Murray.

MacKenzie, J.M. 1988. *The Empire of Nature.* Manchester University Press.

Mandala, B.C. 1990. *Work and Control in a Peasant Economy.* Madison: University of Wisconsin Press.

Martin, R.B. 1989. 'Communal Area Management Plan for Indigenous Resources', in R.H. Bell and E. McShane Caluzi (eds) *Conservation and Wildlife Management in Africa.* Washington: Peace Corps.

Morris, B. 1998. *The Power of Animals: An Ethnography.* Oxford: Berg.

Pachai, B. 1978. *Land and Politics in Malawi 1875-1975.* Kingston, Ont: Limestone Press.

Timberlake, L. 1985. *Africa in Crisis.* London: Earthscan.

Vail, H.L. 1977. 'Ecology and History: the Case of East Zambia'. *J. Southern Africa Studies* 3(2): 129-56.

Vaughan, M. 1978. 'Uncontrolled Animal and Aliens: Colonial Conservation Mania in Malawi'. Chancellor College, University of Malawi, history seminar paper.

THE POWERS OF NATURE (1998)

The aim of this paper is to explore Malawi culture *by* looking at their conceptions of medicine, particularly as this relates to their herbalist tradition, and to the use of mammals as medicine. Surprisingly, in a recent encyclopedia of anthropology (Ingold, 1994) which aims to provide a conspectus of contemporary anthropological knowledge there is no mention at all of herbalism— which just so happens to be the earliest, the most important, and the most widespread form of therapy. And what I want to emphasise is that rural Malawians—like Aristotle—do not make a radical distinction between the spiritual (unseen) and the material aspects of life, and that the natural world, specifically plants and animals, are seen as real entities, not simply pegs for symbolic forms or hierophanies of the spirit, and that they are thus believed to have inherent powers and causal agency.

The paper is in three parts. In the first section, I attempt two things. Firstly, I offer some critical reflections on the widespread tendency, particularly exemplified in John Janzen's text *Ngoma* (1992), to identify traditional healing in Africa with 'spirit healing' (and 'rites of affliction'), and thus to see medical herbalism simply as an adjunct to spirit healing. Secondly, I briefly outline Malawian conceptions of being *(-ntu)*, emphasising that Malawians do not see the world as consisting of inert matter to be activated by spiritual agencies, but rather as constituted of things: mushrooms, plants, animals, that are held to possess inherent powers or potentialities.

In the second section, I outline medical herbalism in Malawi, suggesting that this represents a domain of empirical therapy that is largely independent of spirit healing. I thus emphasise the importance of medicine *(mankhwala)* in Malawi social life. I argue, making reference to comparative material on the Bemba, Ndembu and Zulu, that in Malawi medicinal substances (both plants and animals) are seen as possessing intrinsic power *(mphamvu)* and efficacy *(nchito)*.

In the third section I discuss the role of mammals as medicine in Malawi, specifically outlining their use as 'activating' medicines *(chizimba)*.

I conclude the paper by suggesting that Malawians have essentially a vitalistic or pantheistic attitude towards the world, rather than a 'spiritualist' one, and that this is reflected in their conception of medicines, which are seen as substances that have intrinsic powers or capacities.

Malawian conceptions of being

I begin this section by recalling a little incident.

In June 1991 the then national newspaper of Malawi, the *Daily Times,* carried a news item with the heading 'Scramble for Hyena's Brain'. It reported on the "pandemonium" that had broken out at the Nthalire trading centre. Apparently a hyena had been killed by the Karonga/Chitipa bus near Changoloma Hill. The driver had picked up the animal and had taken it to the trading centre for viewing. When the news got around of the hyena's demise, crowds of people soon rushed to the scene, brandishing knives and axes. Within minutes, one eyewitness reported, "People started hacking the hyena's head for its brain while others jostled for the tail and its other parts". The Malawi news agency concluded this article with the words: "The brain and the tail of the hyena are believed to be potent magical medicines".

This report indicates the passion many Malawians have to acquire certain animals for medicinal purposes—and the hyena is not alone in this regard. Yet, rather surprisingly, animals hardly get a mention in John Janzen's important study of "cults of affliction" in central and southern Africa (Janzen, 1992). He notes that the sacrifice of chickens and goats is one of the core features of these rituals, but he sees such sacrifices simply in terms of atonement and exchange and has nothing to say on animals as medicine or even on the close relationship, evident in a worldwide context, but particularly in Malawi, that seems to exist between animals and spirits of the dead. Indeed, he has a rather theological approach to African therapeutic systems, seeing all medical traditions and practices as essentially focused around spirit healing, around "rituals of affliction", which he sees as a pan-Bantu institution. He titles this institution *ngoma,* a word that throughout much of Africa prototypically means 'drum'. But like the cognate term 'dance', it may come to have a wider meaning, covering not only communal rituals of affliction, but also initiations and secular entertainment. While, in his early study, Janzen was concerned to emphasise the diverse and pluralistic nature of the "quest for therapy" in Lower Zaire, the institution *ngoma*, focused as it is on 'spirit rituals', has a rather totalising quality, subsuming all other 'medical' beliefs and practices. Janzen (1978) makes some important criticisms of the tendency of scholars to connate what he calls the spirit hypothesis" with spirit possession per se, and recognises that there is an important practical and empirical dimension to the rituals, but his essential thesis is that the "spirit" rituals provide the major framework that sets up and legitimizes as an "institution" "many kinds of perspectives and theories" (p. 176). It is hardly surprising, then, that witches and spirits of the dead tend to be virtually equated, all part of the same world view, and the herbalist and the 'secular cosmological" traditions—the latter tradition relating to conceptions of colour, of blood and to a 'balance' between hot and cold in the maintenance of health—becomes completely marginalised, or is seen simply as an adjunct to a ritual process that is essentially 'spiritual'. Bewailing the fact that other anthropologists have been preoccupied and fixated on exotic trance and possession, Janzen himself seems equally obsessed with the 'spirit hypothesis' and its associated 'performance ritual' and discourse—although he is alive to the need to situate such 'rituals of affliction' in a social and historical context. My misgivings about Janzen's study are thus not with the content of the study itself, focused as it is on 'cults of affliction'. This study is exemplary. They are rather on what is left out—the material dimension to African thought. Herbalism, used in its widest sense to include animal substances, which is how people in Malawi use the concept of medicine *mankhwala*, is as much a pan-Bantu 'institution', with its own theories and practices, as are 'cults of affliction', and both, of course, have wide cross-cultural reference that extends well beyond the Bantu context.[c]

Having broken down, as Janzen puts it (1992, p. 4), the division between religion and healing, the latter is now verily equated with religion, with spirit healing. It is indeed described as the "classical" healing system of central and southern Africa (p. 9). Some time ago Kwasi Wiredu (1981) remarked that one of the ways in which African culture was continuously being misunderstood was through the 'exaggeration' of the role of religion in African life—to the neglect of its empirical aspects. Contrary to the ethos that Janzen portrays, Malawian culture, it seems to me, is less concerned with 'spirit' than with 'life';

it is pantheistic or biocentric rather than theocentric. Although Janzen has a central focus on 'health', especially on its 'social reproduction', he nowhere examines the indigenous concepts of life—although the book is essentially concerned with a lexical exploration of proto-Bantu concepts. In Malawi *moyo* (life) is not only the principle of animate life but also the generally recognised term for health and well being in its widest meaning. In an important sense, therefore, Malawian thought is closer to that of Aristotle than to that of Plato and the Judeo-Christian tradition, with its dualistic emphasis—'god' being seen as outside the world and material existence as being in essence 'unreal', 'inert' or 'lifeless'— plant and animal substances only having efficacy or being efficacious if 'activated' by cultural metaphors, eidos or by spirit. For Janzen (1992) "metaphors" have "active agency", "power" and "efficacy" because of their association with the "spirits", but seemingly plants and animals do not, they are, it seems, "lifeless", without intrinsic efficacy or power. Medicines only become powerful, he writes, if the ancestors are invoked (p. 67). This neo-Platonic kind of interpretation[d] is similar to that of Maurice Bloch, who, in a recent analysis of ritual, sees the "spirits" as the antithesis of life and vitality. Becoming a spirit is to become dry, bone-like, lifeless. But as Eliade (1960., p. 83) long ago recognised, the bones and skins of animals—and animal life is intrinsically connected with spirits of the dead—do not represent the antithesis of life, but rather its essence, life that does not die. This belief in 'life' as an ongoing process via immaterial spirits is, however, by no means restricted to the Bantu context, and it represents an episteme or world view quite different from that of Plato and the Judeo-Christian tradition, with its radical dualism of spirit and vital matter, a dualism that was inherited and developed by the mechanistic philosophers of the 17th century. Carlo Ginzberg (1991), attempting to unearth the folkloric roots of Indo-European culture, has stressed its shamanistic origins, involving the close identity between spirits and animal life reflected in the use of animal bones and skins. He writes of the "profound identification" of animals with the dead (p. 262), and the same may be said of the Malawian context. 'Spirit', for Malawians, is the essence of life, not its negation or antithesis. And so are skins and horns and tails—that is why they have medicinal value.

It is of interest that, while many contemporary scholars give a very theological or neo-Platonic interpretation of African culture (Gyekye, 1987; Idowu, 1973) the founders of African ethnophilosophy were much more inclined towards Aristotle via, of course, Aquinas and the Catholic Church (Thomism). Thus Tempels (1959) in his famous text, argues that the key to Bantu thought was the idea of "vital force". He writes:

'In the minds of Bantus, all beings in the universe possess a vital force of their own: human, animal, vegetable or inanimate. Each being has been endowed by God with a certain force, capable of strengthening the vital energy of the strongest beings of all creation ... (the) Bantu speak, act, live, as if, for them, beings were forces' (p. 32-5).

He thus argues that there is a fundamental difference between Western thought, which has allegedly a static conception of being (he evidently has Plato in mind)[e] and that of the Bantu, who have a dynamic conception of being. There has been a welter of criticism levelled at Tempels' thesis, but his general approach has affinities with that of Alexis Kagame (1956), who continually evokes Aristotle and has I think some substance[f]. For the central concept 'ntu' does not mean [as Janzen (1992) suggests (p. 58)] 'person', but is a much wider category, meaning, in Malawi at least, 'being' or 'substance'.

It is clearly unhelpful to make sweeping generalisations about the ontology of so-called Western and pan-African thought, and clearly Tempels' concept of 'vital force' is problematic, implying as it does some form of animism (which in the Malawian context is quite misleading) (Tempels, 1959). But neverthe-less Tempels' reflections have a ring of truth in that they suggest that African people are realists [as the term is currently used in philosophy (Collier, 1994; Devitt, 1984) and thus that the world for them does not consist of inert mat-ter, but of things that have inherent powers and agency.

To turn now to Malawian conceptions of being. 'Chinthu' in Chichewa refers to 'things', 'kanthu' colloquially to 'anything', and 'munthu' to a person (pi. anthu), 'Nthawi', which is derived from the same root, means 'time', and by extension 'space'. Although Malawians do not explicitly articulate the kind of ontological categories suggested by writers like Kagame (1956), the root 'nthu' certainly has close affinities with Aristotle's concept of substance (ou-sia). For, like Aristotle and the pre-Socratics, and in contrast to the neo-Pla-tonists, Malawians have a dynamic conception of being. The material world is conceived as an active substance with potentiality and god (Mulungu) is not a being outside the world but is a shaper, the nourisher and the ultimate source of life within the world and is intimately associated with thunder, lightning and rain. Malawians make a clear distinction, again like Aristotle, between those aspects of the natural world that have life *(moyo)* and those things that do not *(zinthu zopanda moyo)*. In conversations with people regarding what existents have life *(zili ndi moyo)*, it is generally regarded that the following have life: *mtengo* (tree), *mbalame* (birds), *nyama,* (animal), *njoka* (snakes), *bowa* (edible mushrooms) and spirit entities such as *napolo* (a serpent-spirit associated with the mountain) and *mizimu* (spirits or souls of the dead). There is ambiguity as to whether or not soil *(thaka)* and water *(madzi)* have life, but both *phiri* (mountains) and rocks *(mwala)* are not considered to have life. It is thus clearly evident that in Malawi people recognise a category of living things *(zamoyo)*. It is important to note that for Malawians, ancestral spirits *(mizimu}* are a part of the world and have life, they are created beings, and it is thus misleading to see the dead *(amanda,* those of the grave, almost always addressed in plural form) as somehow in opposition or as the negation of life. In a sense life is an ongoing process that includes the living and the dead. Skins, horns and claws of the dead mammal are thus like the spirit; they are not dead but represent the essence of life as an ongoing process and, with regard to certain mammals, they have intrinsic efficacy as medicine. John Mbiti (1969) was, therefore, essentially correct when he referred to the spirits of the dead as the "living dead" (p. 25).

Although Malawians conceive of the spirits of the ancestors *(mzimu ya makolo)* as being associated symbolically with certain animals and trees or even in certain circumstances taking the form of animals, it would be quite misleading to describe their world view as spiritual or animistic. They do not conceive of the whole world as animate (any more than did Aristotle), only certain aspects of it, and although they make a distinction between *moyo* (life) and *mzimu* (spirit of the dead), and specifically associate the latter with humans only, the two notions are closely identified as life, human life in particular, is nourished and regenerated by the spirits of dead (Morris, 1995). Because mammals more than any other aspect of the material world embody life and power, and because the essence of life is essentially conceived as residing in the outer coverings, as it were, of the mammal—substances such as skins, horns, teeth, bones and tails of mammals are believed to have intrinsic power and efficacy, power that may be used, of course, for diverse ends.

Medical herbalism in Malawi

In my studies of comparative medical systems (Morris, 1986a, 1989a, b) I tried to indicate that a clear distinction could be drawn between three medical traditions that co-existed throughout the world. These were: an empirical herbalist tradition, based on a belief in the intrinsic efficacy of certain plant and animal substances; a cosmological tradition, which saw the human subject as a microcosm of the world and in which health was seen as restoring a balance or mix between certain vital 'humours' or principles; and a tradition that was focused on 'communal rituals of affliction', and involved spirit healing. Although these traditions often overlapped and the use of herbal medicine was often, but not always, a component of all three traditions, they were, I felt, nevertheless, distinct.

Until recently, therapeutic systems in Africa have been essentially part of a folk tradition but, as I have tried to show in my studies of herbalism in Malawi (Morris, 1996a), this tradition is pluralistic and diverse and, as elsewhere, consists of several distinct systems, each with its own etiological emphasis and medical practitioner, the herbalist, diviner and spirit medium having distinctive therapeutic roles and strategies. That there is a secular medical tradition with its own cultural logic, separate from both herbalism and spirit healing, has also to be recognised. It revolves around what Audrey Richards (1956) described as "blood, sex and fire" (p. 30) (Laguerre, 1987), and is concerned fundamentally with 'balance'. In Africa 'medicine' underpins all the different folk traditions. In a sense 'herbalism', not spirit healing, is the classical therapeutic tradition of Africa. In a perceptive essay written many years ago, Mary Douglas (1954) stressed the importance of medicines in the Lele context, noting how the idiom of medicine so dominated their religious ritual that it was often hard to distinguish the two spheres of action. In Malawi the use of medicine permeates cultural life and it is highly misleading to see it as simply an adjunct to spirit healing.

In Malawi there is a close and intimate relationship between plants and medicine, as elsewhere in Africa, where such concepts as *nguo* and *muti* are polysemic, meaning both woody plant and medicine. In Yao *ntera* has this polysemy. But in Malawi generally, a distinction is made between woody plants *(mtenga)*, grasses *(maudzu)* and mushrooms *(bowa)* and medicine. The term for medicine is *mankhwala,* which is allied to the widespread term *bwanga,* and is used to cover a variety of substances believed to possess an inherent potency and efficacy. The term *bwanga* in fact essentially refers to the vital power within the medicinal substance. *Mankhwala* thus covers various charms, amulets and protective medicines, as well as medicines in the normal sense. Western phar-maceuticals and agricultural fertilisers are also called by the same term. The general term for the traditional healer in Malawi, *sing'anga,* is derived from the term for medicine (as potency) and essentially means 'medicine person'. The prototypical *sing'anga* is the herbalist [g], but the term is extended to also cover healers such as diviners and spirit mediums. It is worth emphasising that, although anthropologists have a strong proclivity to work with famous spirit mediums, the majority of healers to be found in Malawi are ordinary folk herbalists of both sexes (Morris, 1986b, 1996a). The majority of substances used for *mankhwala* are plant materials—the roots, leaves, bark, fruit and seeds of various plant species. This seems to be a common pattern among many other African communities, for as Krige and Krige (1943) wrote with regard to the Lovedu, "Fully 80 per cent are of vegetable origin. There is hardly a plant in that rich lowveld vegetation that is not used in the pharmacopoeia of some herbalist or doctor" (p. 215).

I would put this figure even higher for Malawi and suggest that the vast majority of medicines used by Malawians are of plant origin. In my studies of the medicinal plants of Malawi I have recorded and described over 500 species used as medicine (Morris, 1996a). Such medicines may be used for a wide variety of purposes, extending far beyond the therapeutic context. Thus, medicines may be used for good luck charms, for assistance in a variety of activities and concerns (hunting, friendship, employment, marriage, agriculture, court cases), as protective medicine against witches, at all important initiations (especially funerals and maturity rites), for potency and reproductive purposes, and to counter the ill effects of illicit intercourse, as well as herbal remedies for a wide variety of ailments. Equally, medicines may be used by people of evil intent *(anthu wa chipongwe,* insolent people) or by witches *(afiti).* They are then described as bad medicines *(mankhwala woipa),* or if more powerful through the utilisation of *chizimba* (see later), as sorcery medicine, *nyanga (nyanga),* animal horn, which is also used as a divining instrument, the prefix *nya*—may allude to its negative connotations).

In rural areas most people have a wide knowledge of herbalism and folk and market herbalists are found throughout Malawi. The stalls of the market herbalists contain a fascinating array of just about every conceivable part of any animal or plant used for medicinal purposes. Typically on the counter one may find rows of bottles containing the infusions of various roots and barks, all coloured differently, owl pellets and the beaks of small birds, various animal horns, porcupine quills, pieces of hedgehog spines, pangolin scales, hyena dung, snake skins [particularly that of the python *(nsato)},* various tins or gourds containing resin, oil, ashes or powders, animal skins (serval is a favourite) as well as great quantities of plant material—freshly gathered leaves and fruits, seeds, pieces of bark, and the roots from a wide variety of different plants. Given the esoteric impression that these stalls conjure up for many Europeans, and for some Malawians, it is I think worth stressing that the bulk of the saleable items on these stalls, and what is offered by the ordinary village herbalist, consists of plant materials which are believed to have therapeutic value. The stalls of some market herbalists consist essentially of bottles containing bark and root infusions, together with medicinal herbs, while one herbalist I knew at Migowi only had two bottles, the remainder of the commodities were roots, of which he had an enormous pile for sale. What esoteric impression these market stalls can invoke may be gleaned from Landeg White's (1987) description of one 'native doctor' selling medicines at Chimwalira. Medicines were offered to White to bring him good luck, sexual potency and to prevent thieves from ambushing him in his car. But the herbalist also had "wrinkled pods and seeds and dried herbs for headaches, diarrhoea, constipation and barrenness". White eventually brought some good luck medicine—a lion's tooth (actually the tusk of a warthog) for K15. This, then, was almost a month's wage for an agricultural worker in Malawi. The herbalist lives, White (1987) writes, "by imagination and wit, and what he sells are metaphors" (p. 250-1). His metaphors seem to have worked on White! It is, however, highly misleading and one-sided to see the herbalist in Malawi as simply dispensing 'metaphors', for he is concerned crucially with selling medicines—animal and plant substances that are believed to have intrinsic efficacy and power. Like Janzen, and most academics it would seem, White frequents a cultural space that is largely divorced from the material world of plants and animals. He frequents a world where language and symbol have primacy. Thus for White, like Janzen, ideas and metaphors seemingly have more reality than the plants and animals themselves. And the latter constitute part of a life-world whose essential ethos and meaning is lost, if it is equated, and it usually is, simply with the economic or the pragmatic. Analogical thought, of course, permeates Malawian cultural life, and I remember vividly on one occasion questioning one of my herbalist friends why the herb *nyambata (Desmodium velutinum)* was so widely used as a medicine for friendship and love *(mankhwala achikonkd)*. He immediately picked a leaf from the plant, slapped it with gusto on my shirt, to which it adhered, remarking *sagwirizana* 'doesn't it hold?'. The homoeopathic element to medicines is well known to local herbalists, but this is no reason to presume, with V. Turner, that "sympathetic magic" accounts for the employment of the majority of 'medicines', even in the ritual context (1967, p. 343). But the important symbolic dimension to life, given free play in the ritual context, and the fact that animals and plants are widely used metaphorically in Malawi, should not oblate or lead us to ignore or devalue (as with Plato) the 'natural' powers that are believed to inhere in plants and animals, conceptualised by Aristotle as 'necessity'.

It is therefore important to stress that for Malawians the plants (and even more so the animals) used as medicine, are seen to have intrinsic powers, and thus to have inherent curing properties. Apart from writers like Idowu (1973, p. 199) and Janzen (1992, p. 149) who seem to think that medicines only have efficacy if 'spirits' are invoked, or if they become 'metaphors' through song and rite, most anthropologists writing on African cultures have stressed the widespread belief that plant medicines have intrinsic powers. Audrey Richards, for example, writes of *bwanga* (which like many early anthropologists she translates as "magic", though 'vital power' would perhaps be more appropriate) as being for the Bemba the force "contained in the leaves, roots or bark of various trees and shrubs and a number of activating agencies *(afishimba)*, such as parts of animals and human beings" which are used by the Nganga for a variety of purposes (1956, p. 29). V. Turner (1967) likewise, although acknowledging that the distinction between medicine as a 'drug' and as a 'ritual symbol' is not easily drawn (the distinction betrays a dualism that is quite contrary to Ndembu thought) suggests that for these people "All things are felt to be charged with powers of various kinds and it is the job of the herbalist and ritual specialist to manipulate these for the benefit of society" (p. 335). Writers on Zulu medicine have also stressed the powers inherent in medicinal substances *(imithi)*. Harriet Ngubane (1977) notes that many medicines are believed to contain potency in themselves, independent of any ritual context (p. 109) while Berglund (1976) in his detailed ethnographic text emphasises that practically all the various species of vegetation, collectively known as *imithi* (medicine) are believed to contain intrinsic power *(amanda)*, embedded in the material substances. The power is, he writes, "embedded in the species itself and may be manipulated by humans for both good and evil purposes (p. 156-7). It is equivalent to the Malawian concept of *mankhwala,* which is distinct from such ethnobiological categories as *nyama* (edible quadruped), *bowa* (fungi) and *mtengo* (woody plant) and which is used both as a rubric for medicinal substances, and to refer to the intrinsic power *(bwanga)* that these substances contain. To interpret this vital power in theological terms as 'spirit' (in opposition to the material world) would not I think be appropriate, for Malawians do not make a categorical distinction between the natural and the spiritual realms (cf. V. Turner, 1967, p. 302 on the Ndembu).

The use of mammals as medicine

What is equally important, however, in the Malawian context is that an important distinction is drawn between general medicines that are used for a variety of purposes, which may or may not have symbolic import, and a special group of medicines called *chizimba*. These are seen as essentially 'activating' medicine. They give additional power to the other medicines. In my paper on herbalism and divination in Malawi (Morris, 1986b) I stressed that with respect to the more serious and chronic ailments that came before the diviner, the medicines have to work, as it were, on two levels. At the empirical level of symptoms, medicines are thus given with the purpose of healing *(kuchira)* the body ailment; at the level of causation the body is protected *(kutsirika)* from further harm by medicines which ward off witches *(afiti)*. As far as the diviners are concerned, both kinds of substances are medicine *(mankhwala)* though their effects are different: both are considered necessary for treatment. Importantly, however, medicines used to counter sorcery or witchcraft, or to influence the spirits, also tend to include animal substances, whereas purely empirical treatment of diseases, or the treatment of minor ailments tend invariably to involve only herbal remedies. The tendency to focus on the 'sorcery' or etiological aspect of therapy has led many writers to undervalue the empirical dimension of disease treatment. For this reason to translate *mankhwala* as "magical substances" as does Marwick (1965, p. 256) with reference to the Chewa of *Zambia,* seems to me somewhat misleading. There is nothing particularly 'magical' or 'mysterious' about the majority of medicines used in Malawi.

The recognition of a special class of medicines that have 'activating' properties has been reported widely in the literature, although given his focus on 'spirit' healing, it is not mentioned by Janzen (1992). In Zambia, for example, a special class of activating medicines associated with animals is recognised. With the Bemba, as Richards records, animals are thought to have magical attributes and parts of their skin and bones "are used as activating principles *(ifishimbo)* in many charms and medicines" (1939, p. 343). With the Ndembu likewise, there is a special class of medicines *(mpelu)* which is distinct from general medicine, the latter consisting primarily of plant material *(yitumbu).* *Mpelu* medicines it would seem, consist essentially of parts of animals—and V. Turner (1967) mentions antbear, wild pig, leopard, hyrax and rabid dog, as well as humans (p. 304-5, 318-9). He sees this as "symbolic" and as operating by "contagious magic"—a suggestion that presupposes that these animals embody and transmit intrinsic power. In her recent study Edith Turner et al. (1992) describes *mpelu* as "vital medicine" or as "magical substances". Turner notes that the category *mpelu* also includes the famous *ihamba,* the subject not only of her own book but also of Victor Turner's early studies (1967, 1968). *Ihamba* is a healing cult associated with hunting, the term referring to the upper incisor tooth of a dead hunter, which embeds itself in the body of the inflicted person. The tooth is therefore identified with the spirit *(mukishi)* of the dead hunter, who is said to 'bite' its/his victim for being neglected. The tooth is also an object of 'contagious magic' *(mpelu)* and has the character of a hunting charm or amulet. Edith Turner's study is concerned centrally with her own spiritual experience and how the *ihamba* spirit was made visible. But essentially what the book portrays is the strong pantheistic ethos that pervades Ndembu culture, where through a close pre-occupation with life processes, the spiritual (i.e. immaterial) and material aspects of being are closely identified. It is not pantheistic in Spinozian terms, involving the notion that god is identical with the world, but pantheistic in the sense that there is a close identity between spirits of the dead and the animal world, which includes humans. Ali Mazrui (1986, pp. 50-1) has indeed described the indigenous African world view as "Afro-pantheism".

BRIAN MORRIS

In his classical study of sorcery among the Chewa of Eastern Zambia, Max Marwick writes that Chewa medicines are made from roots, leaves and other parts of woody plants, but that, to be effective, they require the addition of 'activating agents' *(chizimba,* pi. *vizimba)* of human or animal origin. The *chizimba* gives the medicines potency and they can then be used for a variety of "magical" purposes (1965, p. 70). Given his focus on sorcery, Marwick tends to see *chizimba* as essentially activating otherwise "inert" root concoctions (p. 300), but as we have seen in Malawi and elsewhere, plants themselves have efficacy and power. What animal substances do is to give additional power *(mphamvu)* in dealing with more complex issues, concerns that have a more immaterial quality—such as success in employment or hunting, stable and fulfiling relationships, good crops and protection from the ill effects of sorcery, which itself involves the harmful use of powerful medicines. Steven Friedson, in his study of *Vimbuza* rituals among the Tumbuka, describes *chizimba* as the "witchcraft base" (1996, p. 55) which gives the *nyanga* (sorcery medicine) its efficacy. But this is quite misleading, for *chizimba* is an essential component of all powerful medicines, especially those which protect *(ku-tsirika)* people from the proclivities of witches. In Malawi *chizimba* is thus often associated specifically with those diviners *(asing'anga)* who are thought to possess and to have knowledge of the respective medicines, invariably the skins, bones, teeth and horns of animals or humans. As protective medicine *(ku-tsirika)* they relate to the body *(thupi),* garden *(mundd)* or household *(nyumba).* The *chizimba* medicine is always only one ingredient in a remedy which contains several herbs; and it is seen as 'strengthening' the medicine. In contrast, ordinary herbal remedies are 'simples', given by 'empirics'. There is a contrast too in the administration of the medicines. Ordinary herbal medicines, lacking *chizimba,* are usually drunk as an infusion, taken with thin porridge *(phala),* or inhaled as a vapour. Although herbal medicine may be used as a wash, essentially it is taken internally. In contrast, medicines containing activating substances *(chizimba)* are administered externally, at the boundaries of the garden, house, or the body. The medicines are thus ground and reduced to ashes *(kuocha)* and the ashes rubbed into body incisions *(ku-temererd)* or used as a wash, the medicinal waters being sprinkled by means of a medicine tail. Alternatively the ingredients, including the *chizimba,* may be put in groundnut or castor oil, and the oil used to anoint the body *(ku-dzold)* after bathing. More serious ailments often entail

265

the used of *chizimba*. The strong association between these 'activating' substances and animals has to be stressed, along with the association of animal substances (horns, skins, teeth) with the spirits of the dead. *Chizimba* is a cognate of *uzimba* which is a general term for the communal hunt and in the past *Zimba* referred to an 'ethnic' group of professional elephant hunters who made incursions into Malawi from the Zambezi region (Alpers, 1975; Mandala, 1990; Morris, 1996b).

To give the local sense of *chizimba* I give the words below of a Blantyre herbalist, Heronimo Kanjanga, whom I have known for more than a decade.

Chizimba is a kind of medicine *(gulula mankhwald)*. Its work is to strengthen *(kulimbikiza)* the medicine, so that it has power *(ndimphamvu)*. Medicine without *chizimba* lacks power, it is the animal substance *(chizimba cha nyamd)* that gives the medicine its power, and with it the medicine works on many ailments *(ntchito kwa mathenda onse)*. For example, in the treatment of rheumatism *(nyamakazi)*, we take several horns *(nyanga)* together with a scorpion *(nankalizi)* and burn them *(kuocha)* and the ashes are applied to incisions on the person *(kuntemera munthu)* to cure the ailment *(imatha)*. If a person is sick with large head *(mutuwaukulu)* we cut various herbs into small pieces, and these we cook *(tikaphikd)*, together with the blood *(magazi)* of a chicken *(mkhuku)*, which is the *chizimba*. For other ailments like stomach ache and *kanyera* (wasting disease affecting men) we do not use activating substances. For epilepsy *(chifufu)* we take various woody plants *(mitengo)* and as *chizimba* we use the teeth *(mano)* of the warthog *(njiri)*. Thus, here is a difference between some diseases where we use activating substances and other diseases where no *chizimba* is used to protect the body *(pteteza thupi)*.

Activating medicines involving animals are thus used to strengthen or 'give power' to herbal remedies and they may be used for both positive ends (for healing, as good luck charms, for success in hunting, employment and court cases and as a love potion) or for destructive purposes associated with sorcery *(matsenga)*. Because of the latter associations many famous spirit healers in Malawi such as Chikanga and Bwanali profess not to have any dealings with *vizimba* medicines.

Mammals, or course, are used widely in Malawi as medicine in other contexts, in rituals of affliction such as *vimbuza, malombo* and *nantongwe,* and in initiation rites *(chinamwali, jando, chiputu)*. They also play a crucial role in the *nyau* and *chinambande* rituals of the Chewa and Yao, respectively, when the spirits of the dead make their appearance at initiations in the form of mammals (hare, elephant, lion, hippo and various antelopes), humans essentially forming the flesh, the substance, of the *mzimu,* the horns, skins and tail of the animal structures constituting their forms. Mammals *(zirombo)* and spirits of the dead *(mizimu)* are thus intrinsically identified in these rites, for, in essence, the spirits of the dead take the form of animals. It is commonly believed in Malawi that the spirits of ancestors, particularly of chiefs, are able to take the form of animals—a snake such as the python or puff-adder, a leopard, lion or hyena, or even a creature as humble as a locust *(dzombe)*. But importantly this relationship is not expressed in dualistic terms, as if the spirit of the dead 'incarnates' the animals [still less do they believe that animals themselves have spirits *(mizimu)]* but rather it is expressed in terms of a transformation, a metamorphosis. The verb used is *ku-sanduka,* to change or transform, as a tadpole transforms into a frog. The spirit is transformed into and takes the form of a material being.

It is worth noting that all circumcisors in the boy initiation rites of the Yao *(jando)* and many diviners and spirit healers drape themselves with the skins, tails and claws of the animals that are considered to invoke power, leopard, lion, serval, genet, crocodile, snake. The circumcisor is referred to in Yao as a *mmichila,* which essentially means 'person of the tail' *(mchira,* tail), and the horns of antelope and the skins of animals such as the sun squirrel and genet, are frequently used in divination rites. In a sense these ritual specialists by draping themselves in the skins of animals invoke the spirits of the dead, who take the form of animals (cf. the photographs in Chavunduka, 1978); and the spirits get their power not simply because they are spirits; but because they are intrinsically associated with animals, which themselves express and embody the inherent powers of nature. Recent studies of the Dogon (1992) have indicated that for these people the 'bush' is the ultimate source of power, knowledge and life energy. This is true also of Malawi, but Malawians conceive of such powers more in terms of substances, that is as being derived from specific plants and animals.

Tables I and II indicate the medicinal uses of mammals in Malawi. They are based on my own personal observations of the animal substances used as medicine by several herbalist and diviners whom I know well. Potentially, of course all mammals may be used as an activating substance *(chizimba)*, and I have no doubt that many other mammals not recorded by me may be used by herbalists in Malawi for medicinal purposes. It is worth noting too that many of the larger mammal species have a restricted distribution, or are confined to wildlife sanctuaries.

In this paper I can hardly discuss all the mammal species that are utilised as medicine, but I will briefly mention two species—the pangolin and hyena. As with hedgehog spines and porcupine quills, the scales *(liwamba)* of the pangolin *(ngakd)* are widely used in Malawi as medicine.[h] They are used in a variety of ways to give protection against sorcery and as a good luck charm, assisting in court cases, friendship, employment and family concerns. They may be used like hedgehog spines, as an ingredient in a medicine bag or bottle, or may be reduced to ashes with other herbs, the ashes then being rubbed into skin incisions *(kutemera muthupi)*, in order to protect the body. The pangolin of course is widely used as medicine throughout Africa, and has been the subject of much anthropological discussion (Douglas, 1966, 1990; Lewis, 1991). Among the Lele it is the focus of a specific religious cult, the 'Pangolin men', who are the leading religious experts in the village and who alone are allowed to eat the flesh of the pangolin (Douglas, 1954). In Malawi few people eat the pangolin, although in early times its meat was considered a delicacy and could be eaten only by the chiefs *(afumu)*.

But the important point which Douglas's rich ethnography of the Lele makes clear is that the pangolin was not the only animal that was subject to dietary restrictions or given ritual salience. It was only one of many of animal species that were associated with the spirits and the forested streams. There was in fact a close and intimate relationship between animals and spirits of the dead in the Lele context. Douglas (1975) writes that the "spirit animals" *(hut a ngehe)* were "in some contexts ... spoken of as if they were spirits. In others they are animals, closely associated with spirits" (p. 130). As "the fertility of humans is thought to be controlled by the spirits inhabiting the deepest, dampest parts of the forest" (p. 33) there is thus an intimate and intrinsic relationship between the forest animals, spirits and fertility. Men as affines in this matrilineal context, are symbolically associated with this domain. All this has resonances in the Malaw-ian context,[21] and throughout Africa. But why is the pangolin given such prominence? Probably because the pangolin, unique among African mammals, has scales, hundreds of them. These are easily detachable and they represent, like the spirits, the permanency of life. A pangolin scale, like the horns and skins that once decorated many huts in Malawi, symbolises in a sense not 'eternal life' (which has a neo-Platonic ring about it) but immortal life (Arendt, 1978). Needless to say, in Malawi a little piece of pangolin scale does wonders for

Table I. Animals as medicine

	Status as food*	Protection against sorcery	Strengthening medicine	Good luck medicine	Spirit illnesses	Medicine for subsistence activities	Medicine for general ailments	Association with witchcraft
Wild dog *mbulu*	x	✓						✓
Side-striped jackal *nkhandwe*	x	✓	✓					✓
Otter *katumbu*	o	✓					✓	
Ratel *chuli*	x	✓	✓					
Zorilla *kanyimbi*	x	✓			✓	✓		
Civet *chombwe*	✓	✓	x	✓		✓		✓
Genet *mwili*	✓	✓		✓		✓		
Mongoose sp. *nyenga*	✓			✓				
Marsh mongoose *khakhakha*	x		✓		✓	✓		
Banded mongoose *msulu*	x		✓					
Spotted hyena *fisi*	x	✓	✓	✓	✓	✓		✓
Leopard *nyalugwe*	x	✓	✓			✓		
Lion *mkango*	x	✓	✓	✓		✓		
Serval *njuzi*	✓	✓		✓				
Wild cat *bvumbve*	x	✓						
Elephant *njobvu*	✓	✓	✓			✓		
Black rhino *chipembere*	✓		✓					
Burchell's zebra *mbidzi*	✓		✓					
Warthog *njiri*	✓	✓						
Bushpig *ngulwe*	✓							
Hippopotamus *mvuu*	✓	✓	✓				✓	✓
Hartebeest *ngondo*	✓							
Blue duiker *kadumba*	✓	✓	✓					
Grey duiker *gwapi*	✓		✓		✓			

Table I. Continued

Species							
Klipspringer *chinkhoma*	✓						
Sharpe's grysbok *kasenye*	✓						
Impala *nswala*	✓						
Roan *chilembwe*	✓						
Sable *mphalapala*	✓						
Buffalo *njati*	✓	✓					
Kudu *ngoma*	✓						
Nyala *boo*	✓						
Bushbuck *mbawala*	✓						
Eland *ntchefu*	✓						
Reedbuck *mphoyo*	✓						
Waterbuck *nakodzwe*	✓						
Elephant shrew *sakhwi*	✓		✓				
Musk shrew *sunche*	x		✓		✓	✓	
Cane rat *nchenzi*	✓						
Mole rate *namfuko*	✓						
Angoni vlei rat *thiri*	✓						
Bushveld gerbil *phanya*	✓		✓		✓		
Giant rat *bwampini*	✓						
Pouched rat *jugu*	✓						
Fat mouse *kapeta*	✓						
Spiny mouse *nyerere*	✓						
Creek rat *mende*	✓						
Striped mouse *mphera*	✓		✓		✓	✓	✓
Long-tailed forest mouse *sonthe*	✓						
Pygmy mouse *pinji*	✓						
Brush furred rat *chitwa*	✓						

Table I. Continued

	Status as food*	Protection against sorcery	Strengthening medicine	Good luck medicine	Spirit illnesses	Medicine for subsistence activities	Medicine for general ailments	Association with witchcraft
Multimammate mouse *mpuku*	✓							
Red veld rat *mphakadzi*	✓							
Black rat *khoswe*	x							
Dormouse *kadyamlamu*	x							✓
Hedgehog *chisomi*	x	✓		✓				
Fruit bat *mleme*	x	✓	✓				✓	
Insectivorous bat *nanthuthu*	x		✓				✓	
Bushbaby *changa*	O	✓					✓	
Night ape *kamundi*	O		✓		✓		✓	
Yellow baboon *nyani*	O		✓			✓		
Vervet money *pusi*	O		✓			✓		
Blue monkey *nchima*	O	✓				✓		
Rock hyrax *zumba*	✓				✓	✓	✓	
Yellow-spotted hyrax *mbira*	✓		✓		✓	✓		
Antbear *nsele*	✓	✓	✓	✓		✓		
Pangolin *ngaka*	x	✓						
Sun squirrel *gologolo*	O							
Bush squirrel *gologolo*	O							
Porcupine *nungu*	O	✓						
Hare *kalulu*	✓							✓

*Status as food: ✓ Used widely O Ambiguous status X Not usually eaten

Table II. Animal medicines sold by market herbalists.

	Adoniyo Visendi	Mary Jemusi	Jafali Dzomba	Robert Mkorongo	William Pakani	Heronimo Kanjanga	Muzimu Shumba	Edwin Kamwendo	Januario Wede
Shrew *sunche*	X								
Hedgehog *chisomi*	X	X	X	X	X	X	X	X	
Porcupine *nungu*	X	X	X	X	X		X		X
Mole rat *namfuko*	X								
Pangolin *ngaka*	X			X	X	X	X	X	
Bushbaby *changa*	X		X						
Hyena *fisi*	X	X	X	X					
Elephant *njobvu*	X						X	X	
Lion *mkango*	X								
Fruit bat *mleme*	X								
Civet *chombwe*		X		X					
Monitor *gondwe*		X					X		
Otter *katumbu*				X					X
Baboon *nyani*				X					X
Python *nsato*							X		X
Warthong *njiri*				X	X				
Vervet monkey *pusi*									
Crocodile *ng'ona*					X		X	X	
Serval *njuzi*					X			X	
Leopard *nyalugwe*					X			X	
Ratel *chiuli*					X				
Hippopotamus *mvuu*				X			X		
Tortoise *kamba*									

fertility. And the hyena too, more so than all the mammals of Malawi, represents male fertility, or rather the fertility that comes from the affinal aspect of the ancestral spirits.

The hyena, as one of my Malawian friends put it, is greatly enjoyed *(tima-mukonda kwambiri)* as medicine. The skin *(chikopa)*, brain *(ubonga)*, tail *(mchira)* and excrement *(matuzt)* are all used, and for a variety of purposes. It is particularly important as a strengthening medicine, the hyena is credited with the ability to run long distances without tiring, and as a medicine that induces dreaming *(kulotd)*. Throughout Malawi parts of the hyena are thought to offer both protection against theft, whether by ordinary people or witches *(afiti)*, and to enable a person to steal without being detected. It is widely used as a protective medicine *(kutsirika)* against sorcery and is used in a variety of ways, being particularly associated with the protection of goat or cattle pens *(kutsirika khola la ziweto)*. The hyena has a prominent place in Malawian folklore and is identified closely with the potency and fertility of the male affine among matrilineal communities in Malawi. Thus in both Chewa and Yao rituals the surrogate male who performs the act of ritual coitus is referred to as *fisi* (Y., *litunu)*. The hyena in fact is the *chizimba* medicine par excellence, whether for protective or malevolent purposes.

Conclusions

In one of his many studies of Ndembu ritual, Victor Turner stressed the need to overcome the dualism inherent in the Western philosophical traditions, and he wrote that African thought "embeds itself from the outset in materiality, but demonstrates that materiality is not inert but vital" (1975, p. 21)—thus echoing the thoughts of Aristotle and the pre-Socratics. But given his proclivity to emphasise a radical dichotomy between a cultural "structure" and an existential "communitas" and to equate the latter with the "flow of experience", "reality", the "sacred" and the "godhead"—thus completely inverting the thoughts of Plato and Eliade, Turner ends up by 'spiritualising' what he refers to as the urgrund of social structure, the primal ground of experience, thought and social actions. But the 'ground' of Malawian thought like that of the Ndembu, is neither 'spiritual' nor 'mystical' nor does it entail a radical dualism between two modalities of experience however conceptualised, but rather entails a fundamental emphasis on a 'life-world', on *moyo*, that is, in a sense, ontologically prior to the spirit/matter dichotomy. Essentially Malawians have a vitalistic and pantheistic attitude towards the world, and their conception of therapy or salvation, if one wishes to use such a term is like that of the Taoists (Girardot, 1983) it is medicinal rather than religious or spiritual, in both intention and structure. The world that surrounds the rural Malawian is a world that is 'alive' and 'vital', and as Hans Jonas (1966) has perceptively written on pre-literate people more generally, life is to that extent accepted as the primary state of being. Thus the medicinal use of mammals in Malawi can only be understood if this 'panvital-ism' is taken into account—and thus that medicine is not seen simply as an inert adjunct to spirit rituals. In a recent text Peter Dickens (1992) advocated a dialectical way of thinking and a realist ontology in which entities, humans, other organisms and those of inorganic nature, are envisaged as having "latent powers or capacities" (p. xv). This surely is Aristotle's conception of the world, suggested more than 2000 years ago. It is also the viewpoint of rural Malawians in their conception of animal medicine. [j]

Acknowledgements

I have spent more than 10 years of my life living and working in Malawi, and the present paper is based on two periods of field research 1979-80, 1990-91, supported by the E.S.R.C. and the Nuffield Foundation. I am grateful for their support. I should also like to thank the Centre for Social Research for institutional support, and my many friends in Malawi for their help and encouragement. My indebtedness to the early pioneering ethnographic studies of Rangeley and Schoffeleers will be self evident. The paper originally formed the substance of my Monroe lecture at the University of Edinburgh given in November 1995. I am grateful to members of the Anthropological Department for the invitation, and for their helpful feedback, and especially appreciated the critical reflections of Roy Willis and Judith Okely.

Notes

(a) I am aware, of course, of Malawi's ethnic diversity. And I am aware, too, that I speak of Malawians, while essentially referring to Chewa examples and to the Chewa language. This is I think admissible for two reasons.

One is that Chewa is regarded as the national language and is now spoken and understood throughout Malawi, although one may occasionally encounter an elderly Yao or Lomwe woman who speaks little Chewa. Secondly, as I have worked and researched mainly among Lomwe and Yao, and have spent time in every locality in Malawi (apart from the Chitipa district) I thus have a strong sense of a cultural unity existing among matrilineal people who nominally belong to diverse ethnic groups (Chewa, Yao, Mang'anja, Nyanja, Chipeta, Lomwe). This cultural unity was mentioned by almost all the early ethnographers, Cullen Young, Levi Mumba, Mitchell *et al.*

(b)   I cite Aristotle for comparative purposes. I'm not in the least suggesting an equation between Aristotle's philosophy and Malawian thought, although his thoughts on folk classifications, on 'nature' as having inherent powers, and on human procreation certainly have resonances in African ethnographic literature. Aristotle was a Greek philosopher.

(c)   I am aware that many earlier scholars have emphasised the importance of herbalism in African therapeutics, and the material dimension to African thought. I have reviewed some of this literature in my *Chewa Medical Botany* (Morris, 1996a). But it is of interest that a recent reader on the social basis of healing in Africa[5] has very little discussion on either medicinal plants or on the herbalist traditions in Africa.

(d)   I am aware, of course, that the work of all scholars is complex and diverse. In my *Anthropological Studies of Religion* I tried to indicate and emphasise the diverse theoretical orientation of scholars like Weber, Evans-Pritchard and Geertz. Bloch is no different and the neo-Platonic ahistoric ring of *Prey to Hunter* contrasts fundamentally with his earlier Marxist approach. I am not, of course, using the term 'neo-Platonic' as if it was a term of abuse.

(e)   A colleague has posed the question 'which Plato?'. In my recent study *Anthropology of the Self* (Morris, 1994), I have discussed Plato's varying conceptions of the psyche that are found in his writings. But the mature Plato has always been interpreted as a radical dualist. This is how his pupil and colleague Aristotle understood him, and how he has been interpreted in a long philosophical tradition stretching from Aquinas through to Cassirer, right up to a present day scholar like Deane Curtin. I have simply followed this tradition. Like Heidegger, Tempels equates Western thought with Platonism, in suggesting that it implies a static conception of being.

(f)   The mention of Tempels seems to cause intellectual apoplexy among many anthropologists. Useful discussions of Tempel's work, and African ethnophilosophy more generally, are to be found in the writings of Mbiti (1969), Hountondji (1983), Mudimbe (1988) and Masolo (1994).

(g)   This statement has been questioned by a colleague. Famous spirit healers, of course are only too keen to emphasise that the only real *(kweni kweni) sing'anga* are themselves, and thus, like biomedical practitioners, come to emphasise the power, the esoteric quality, and even the prophetic nature of their healing practices. But the fact is that the majority of traditional healers in Malawi are herbalists/diviners who do not conduct public spirit rituals, nor are they the focus of any cult fraternity or church. Anthropologists seem only too prone to emphasise the esoteric nature of other cultures (see Olivier de Sardan, 1992), and thus to ignore, or dismiss as of little interest to scholars, the more mundane aspects of social life, such as herbalism or the trappings of mice for food.

(h)   In Malawi only one species of pangolin is found, *Manis temminckii.*

(i)   See Arendt (1978) (p. 134) on the Greek distinction between 'immortal' and 'eternal'.

(j)   For studies that emphasise the non-religious aspects of illness in Africa see Fassin (1992), Jaffre (1996) and Olivier de Sardan (1994).

References

Alpers, E. A. 1975. *Ivory and Slaves in East Central Africa.* London: Heinemann, pp. 46-50.

Arendt, H. 1978. *The Life of the Mind.* New York: Harcourt Brace.

Berglund, A.-I. 1976. *Zulu Thought Patterns and Symbolism.* London: Hurst.

Block, M. 1992. *Prey Into Hunter.* Cambridge: Cambridge University Press.

Chavunduka, G. L. 1978. *Traditional Healers and the Shona Patient.* Gwelo: Mambo Press.

Collier, A. 1994. *Critical Realism.* London: Verso.

Devttt, M. 1984. *Realism and Truth.* Oxford: Blackwell.

Dickens, P. 1992. *Society and Nature.* Hemel Hempstead: Harvester.

Douglas, M. The pangolin re-visited: a new approach to animal symbolism. In R. G. Willis (ed.) *Signifying Animals.* London: Unwin Hyman, pp. 25-36

Douglas,M. 1954. The Lele of Kasai. In Forded, ed. *African Worlds,* pp. 1-26. Oxford: Oxford University Press.

Douglas, M. 1966. *Purity and Danger.* Harmondsworth: Penguin.

Douglas, M. 1975. *Implicit Meanings.* London: Routledge & Kegan Paul.

Eliade, M. 1960. *Myths, Dreams and Mysteries.* London: Collins.

Fassin, D. 1992. Pouvoir et maladie en Afrique. *Anthropologie sociale dans la banlieue de Dakar.* Paris: PUF.

Feierman, S. & Janzen, J. M. ed. 1992. *The Social Basis of Health and Healing in Africa.* Berkeley: University of California Press.

Friedson, S. M. 1986. *Dancing Prophets: Musical Experience in Tumbuka Healing.* Chicago, IL: University of Chicago Press.

Ginzberg, C. 1991. *Ecstasies.* London: Hutchinson.

GIRARDOT, N. J. 1983. *Myth and meaning in early Taoism.* Berkeley: University of California Press, p. 42.

Gyekye, K. 1987. *An Essay in African Philosophical Thought.* Cambridge: Cambridge University Press.

Hountondji, P. J. 1983. *African Philosophy: Myth and Reality.* London: Hutchinson.

IDOWU, E. B. 1973. *African Traditional Religion.* London: SCM Press.

Ingold, T. ed. 1994. *Companion Encyclopedia of Anthropology.* London: Routledge.

Jaffre, Y. 1996. Dissonances entre les representations sociales et medicales de la malnutrition dans un service de pediatrie au Niger. *Sciences Sociales et Sante,* 14(1), 41-72.

Janzen, J. M. 1978. *The Quest for Therapy in Lower Zaire.* Berkeley: University of California Press.

Janzen, J. M. 1992. *Ngoma.* Berkeley: University of California Press.

Jonas, H. 1966. *The Phenomenon of Life.* Chicago, IL: University of Chicago Press, p. 8. Kagame, A. 1956. *La Philosophie Bantu-Rwandaise De L'Etre,* Brussels: Academic Royale de Sciences Coloniales.

Krige, J. D. & Krige, E. J. 1943. *The Realm of a Rain Queen.* Oxford: Oxford University Press. Laguerre, M. 1987. *Afro-Caribbean Folk Medicine.* South Hadley MA: Bergin & Carey, pp. 64- 72.

Lewis, I. M. 1991. The spider and the pangolin. *Man, 26,* 513-25.

Mandala, E. C. 1990. *Work and Control in a Peasant Economy.* Madison: University of

Wisconsin Press, p. 89.

Marwick, M. G. 1965. *Sorcery in its Social Setting.* Manchester, Manchester University Press.

Masolo, D. A. 1994. *African Philosophy in Search of Identity.* Bloomington: Indiana University Press.

MAZRUI, A. A. 1986. *The Africans: A Triple Heritage.* London: BBC Publications.

Mbiti, J. S. 1969. *African Religions and Philosophy.* London: Heinemann. morris, B. 1989a. Many ways of healing. Unpublished manuscript.

Morris, B. 1986b. Herbalism and divination in southern Malawi. *Soc. Sci. Med. 23,* 367-77.

MORRIS, B. 1989a. Ayurveda and the myth of Indian spirituality. *Man & Life,* 15, 103-21. morris, B. 1989b. Thoughts on Chinese medicine. *Eastern Anthrop.* 42, 1-33.

MORRIS, B. 1994. *Anthropology of the Self.* London: Pluto.

Morris, B. 1995. Woodland and village: reflections on the "animal estate" in rural Malawi. J. R. Anthrop *Inst.* (NS) 301-15.

Morris, B. 1996a. *Chewa Medical Botany: A Study of Herbalism in Southern Malawi.* Intern. African Inst., Hamburg: Lit Verlag.

Morris, B. 1996b. Hunting and the gnostic vision. *J. Human & Environ. Sci.* 1; 13-39.

Mudimbe, V. Y. 1988. *The Invention of Africa.* Bloomington: Indiana University Press.

Ngubane, H. 1977. *Body and Mind in Zulu Medicine.* London: Academic Press.

Oljvier de Sardan, J. P. 1994. La logique de la nomination. Les representations fluides et prosa'iques de deux maladies au Niger. *Sciences Sociales et Sante,* 12(3), 15—45.

Olivier de Sardan, J. P. 1992. Occultism and the ethnographic "I". *Critique of Anthrop* 12, 5-25.

RICHARDS, A. I. 1939. *Land, labour and diet in Northern Rhodesia.* Oxford: Oxford University Press. Richards, A. I. 1956. *Chisungu,* London: Tavistock.

Tempels, P. 1959. In *Bantu Philosophy,* trans. M. Read. Paris: Presence Africaine.

Turner, E., Blodgett, W. Kahona S. & Benwa, F. 1992. *Experiencing Ritual.* Philadelphia: University of Pennsylvania Press.

Turner, V. W. 1967. *The Forest of Symbols.* Ithaca, NY: Cornell University Press.

Turner, V. W. 1968. *The Drums of Affliction.* Oxford: Clarendon Press.

TURNER, V. W. 1975. *Revelation and Divination in Ndembu Ritual.* Ithaca, NY: Cornell University Press.

Van beek, W. E. A. & Banga, P. M. 1992. The Dogon and their trees. In Crolle, Parkin D, ed. Bush Base: *Forest Form,* pp. 57-75. London: Routledge.

White, L. 1987. *Magomera: Portrait of an African Village,* Cambridge: Cambridge University Press.

Wiredu, K. 1981. Morality and religion in Akan thought. In *Philosophy and Culture,* ed. H. O. Oruka, D. A. Masolo Nairobi: Bookwise.

HUNTING AND THE
GNOSTIC VISION (1995)

Hunting, according to Matt Cartmill, is the "violent killing" of wild animals, and represents a "war waged by humanity against the wilderness" (1933: 30). In a similar fashion Marilyn French has suggested that the advent of hunting marked a profound change in human's relationship with nature, and was implicated in the emergence of 'patriarchy' — it heralded the 'fall' from an early state where humans were peaceful, gentle and humorous folk (1986: 17). Symbolic anthropologists have been equally negative towards hunting, and in gnostic fashion, have portrayed it as the antithesis of life-giving procreation and sexuality. Hunting has, indeed, had a very bad press, particularly from feminists scholars. I want in this paper to counter this negative portrait, both by offering some reflection on this literature and by briefly examining the ritual aspects of hunting in Malawi.

The paper thus has two sections. In the first part, I discuss hunting with special reference to hunter-gatherers; and in the second I focus on the communal hunt in Malawi and on its ritual aspects — aiming to counter the suggestion that hunting is always perceived anti-life, and expressive of both a gender hierarchy and a Promethean attitude towards nature.

1. Hunting — Historical Perspectives

The essence of hunting, wrote Andree Collard, is that it is "an exercise of power on the part of one who feels overwhelmed, fragmented and frightened and it explains the pathetic urge to kill anything bold enough to be alive". (1988: 47). Hunting is thus seen as the Modus *Operandi* of patriarchal societies, and those who engage in it — males — are seen as motivated purely sadomasochistic fantasies. That plants have life seems tobe lost on this self-proclaimed biophilic writer. Thus among many feminist scholars hunting has come to be seen universally as a 'blood sport' that is intrinsically linked with war and violence, and with the power of aristocrats and men. It has even been linked to slavery and racism, although, importantly, Marjorie Spiegel made a crucial distinction between hunting as an "exercise of power" and hunting for subsistence by such people as the native Americans. They are seen as hunting out of necessity, with respect for and in harmony with the balance of nature. (1988: 58). This distinction has, I think, to be kept in mind.

Other scholars, however, seem to take a more monolithic view. Carol Adams (1990) thus argues in her history of vegetarianism that hunting is specifically linked with male dominance while Nick Fiddes (1991) suggests that hunting (along with meat eating) is symbolic of human domination over nature.

Adams has little to say on hunting *per se,* focusing a few pages only on aristocratic blood sports. Yet she suggests, like French, that with hunting 'incremental violence' "(81) is introduced into human communities, and implies that it is intrinsically related to the oppression of women — meat being a symbol of male dominance and patriarchy(1990;33). As the hunting of animals goes back into antiquity or at least to the origins of human culture around forty thousand years ago, this would suggest the universality of male dominance — something that has been challenged by many feminist anthropologists (Leacock 1981: Poewe 1981). Fiddes, on the other hand, couples hunting with meat eating, and suggests that they both symbolize and authenticate human control over the natural world. Hunting is thus seen as implying the 'subjugation' of 'wild' nature by humans, and 'meat' as a potent symbol of environmental control. (1991: 6). Although noting that killing animals for 'sport' is rare among clan-based societies, and is largely an elitist pursuit in western culture, Fiddes, nonetheless, emphasises throughout his study that hunting implies mastery, aggression, control, masculinity and the domination of humans over nature.

He virtually denies — by omission — that hunting may coexist with an attitude to nature that is ecological and biocentric rather that Promethean (cf. Speck 1938, Brown 1992).

It is of interest that while among writers like Adams and Fiddes hunting is taken as a metaphor for violence and domination — and thus seen in essentially negative terms — less than three decades ago hunting was viewed as wholly positive. Hun ting, although it involved our estrangement from nature, was seen by many anthropologists and ethnologists as the key factor in the development of the human species. Our bipedality, use of tools, intelligence, language and sociality and culture — what makes us human — were ail seen as the essential product of the 'hunting' way of life. Hunting, and the addition of meat to the human diet 'created', according to many scholars, the human species. As Serge Moscovici put it — though in androcentric terms — "man made himself into man when he set himself up as a hunter" (1976: 30). Earlier, at the same conferemce that was to affirm the fundamental importance of 'woman the gatherer' among hunter-gathering societies, Washburn and Lancaster were to suggest that the way of life of our earliest ancestors was akin to that of carnivores like wolves, rather than to that of primates, and that "In a very real sense our intellect, interests, emotions and basic social life - all are evolutionary products of the success of the hunting adaptation" (1968: 298).

This thesis was given popular circulation in Robert Ardrey's evocative book, *"The Hunting Hypothesis* (1976) which suggested that we became uniquely human because we "killed for a living". He dismissed the importance of gathering and scavenging, and argued that the essence of our humanity was the outcome of the fact that early humans were 'social predators'; they were, he suggested, 'killer apes' who, during a crucial period of human evolution derived most of their calories from meat.

There have been numerous critiques of the hunting hypothesis. When Ardrey's book first came out I offered my own critical reflections on it, stressing its androcentric bias (Morris 1979). But the thesis still has its supporters. Robert Foley, for example, in giving a useful survey of the debates around the role of hunting and meat-eating in human evolution, seems to suggest, following Glyn Isaac, that the development of the gender division, of a home base, and food sharing is intrinsically linked to the incorporation of meat into the diet of early humans (1987: 44-45). Even more stridently Matt Cartmill has recently implied that the 'killer ape myth' is "essentially true" (1993: 18-27).

What is of interest, however, is that the advocates of the hunting hypothesis thesis like Ardrey and feminist critics of hunting such as Adams and Coilard — and in a more guarded way, French — share fundamentally the same viewpoint, even if their attitude towards hunting is totally dissimilar. For both groups of scholars see hunting as destroying the "peaceful relationship' that formerly existed between proto-humans and animals and as involving violence, aggression, the creation of a gender hierarchy and the estrangement of humans from the natural world. Whereas Ardrey sees these features as inherent in the human condition, Adams views them negatively as social correlates of the hunting way of life. What both scholars tend to ignore is the wealth of anthropological data on hunter-gathering communities. What this data suggests is that hunting is widespread among such communities, meat accounting for up to 20 per cent of their daily intake of calories (Hill 1982). More importantly, it also suggests that subsistence hunting co-exists with social attitudes that are very different from those portrayed by Ardrey, Adams and Fiddes. Among earliest humans communities, and most contemporary hunter-gatherers, a pervasive egalitarian ethos is evident, and there is no pronounced gender hierarchy, nor an attitude of dominance towards nature. Hunting is not carried about in an aggressive spirit at all, and is certainly not motivated by sadomasochistic tendencies. As Frank Speck long ago remarked (1938: 77), hunting is not a war upon animals, but rather is almost a sacred occupation. Hunter-gatherers' social attitudes towards the natural world express neither an attitude of dominance over nature, nor a passivity or abject submissiveness towards overpowering natural forces, but rather stress the need to maintain a sense of harmony with the world. Hunting therefore invariably involves a sense of kinship between the hunter and the animals word. As Mathias Guenther writes with reference to the "bushmen" of the Kalahari, each hunt is a renewed encounter with a fellow creature. He writes: "Activated in each hunt is a feeling of sympathy and an implicit recognition that the animal is a moral and sentient kindred being". (1988: 198). Among hunter-gatherers, therefore, an attitude of respect towards animals is a pervasive idiom. Ritual power is seen as manifested in the game animals that they hunt, and typically hunter-gatherers view animals as spiritual equals who, in an important sense-allow themselves to be killed if the hunter is in the right mental and spiritual condition. Among many North American Indian communities, animals are ultimately seen as under the control of spiritual guardians. Given this sense of kinship and empathy between themselves and the animals they kill, hunting is invariably hedged with religious ritual and approached in a manner of regret. This empathy and identification with the mammal is built into the act of hunting itself, which requires that a hunter to be successful may ask himself what he would do if he were an animal. And, as Louis Liebenberg writes, "In the process of projecting himself into the position of the animal, he actually feels like the animal". (1990: ix) The subsistence hunter therefore invariably develops a sympathetic relationship with the hunted animal. Thus hunter-gatherers are not motivated by destructive or warlike impulses, nor by pleasure in the killing — it is not a sport — but rather their attitude towards the hunted animal is one of compassion, even of regret of having to kill the animal in order to subsist. This attitude in many communities is not restricted to mammals but relates to all organic life. (Speck 1938: 77). They thus express an awareness of economic conservation and the need to sustain the balance of nature. (For sympathetic accounts of hunting peoples in the Americas see Nelson 1983, Brown 1992).

Many years ago James Frazer noted the 'apparent contradiction' in the lives of many hunter-gatherers who venerate and almost deify the animals that they habitually hunt, kill and eat. He noted also that such people regarded all living creatures as practically on an equal footing to themselves (1922: 678-680) and that with regard to many of the larger mammals rituals of atonement are conducted to show respect to the animal that is killed for food and clothing (698). Given the sense of kinship that exists between the hunter and the animals they hunt among hunter-gatherers, it is not surprising that some kind of atonement for killing the animal is enacted. Serpell (1986: 145) has written perceptively of the 'undercurrent of guilt' that is found among many hunter-gatherers, and has discussed its cross-cultural variability.

Importantly, however, among hunter-gatherers, it is only certain species of the larger mammals that are the focus of rites of atonement; those noted in the literature include caribou, eland, buffalo, elk, deer, elephant and gemsbok.

Although hunting has, fundamentally, a religious dimension to it, this does not deny that is not also an empirical or pragmatic activity in being focussed not on sport or prestige but on subsistence. Just as hunting does not necessarily imply a feeling of human supremacy over nature, so it does not necessarily entail a gender hierarchy. A gender division of labour seems to be found among all known hunter-gathering societies, and from the evidence, it probably goes back to the origin of the human species. But some feminist scholars seems unable to conceive of such a gender division of labour without this implying a universal male dominance (eg, Ortner 1974, Collard 1988: 36). Yet there seems plenty of evidence that among many hunter-gathering societies and small scale agricultural societies, while there may be a gender division of labour with men basically the hunters and honey-gatherers and women the collectors of vegetable food and undertaking the prime responsibilities of childcare and cooking, this division was neither a rigid one nor did it necessarily imply a gender hierarchy (Kent 1993). There are, moreover, many examples in the ethnographic record of women hunting and killing wild animals. The gathering of small mammals reptiles and fish by women is widespread among hunter-gatherers, but in some societies even the hunting of larger mammals is practised by some women at certain stages of their lives. (Leacock 1981: 146, Sanday 1981: 125-126, Ingold 1986: 87).

Acknowledging this fact in discussing women's participation in whale hunting among the Nootka people of the North West Coast, Andree Collard suggests that this is not hunting but merely "the capture of an animal for economic survival" (1988: 15). To equate 'hunting' with blood sports of aristocratic elites (in which both men and women participate), whether the hunting is for sport, pleasure or trophies, is hardly conducive to understanding. Hunting for food, and basic necessities such as clothing and medicine, is still hunting. It also has to be said that hunting, among hunter-gatherers, though may be linked with the gender identity of males, and often implies prestige for a successful hunter, is not necessarily an activity that promotes hierarchy or status differences. To the contrary, hunters are expected to show gentleness, humility and to minimise the tendency towards self aggrandizement. Any show of arrogance is strongly discouraged, and the 'theme of modesty' and 'egalitarianism', permeates the social life of hunter-gatherers like the IKung of the Kalahari (Lee 1979: 243-46, Liebenberg 1990: 55). Equally important is the fundamental importance attached to the sharing of the meat. The meat obtained from the hunt is rarely under the control of the hunter himself, and Chris Knight has described in detail what he has termed the hunters' 'own kill' rule. This is the rule, widely found among clan-based societies, which prohibits the hunters from appropriating or eating their own kills. Knight highlights too, how there is a a strong identification between the hunter and the animal he hunts, that the animal is in a sense kin, of 'one's own flesh' and therefore analogous to a sister (1991; 97-121) .The importance of meat sharing has been equally emphasised by Susan Kent (1993), who stresses that such sharing is not simply an economic strategy, but rather is an "institutionalised mechanism to maintain and enforce an egalitarian milieu", sharing nullifying the variations in hunting skill and success. Meatsharing is therefore fundamentally important in fostering social networks among egalitarian hunter-gatherers.

What is important, however, in the ethnographies on hunter-gatherers is that although men may be the primary hunters of the larger mammals both men and women eat the meat. Moreover meat seems to be highly esteemed as food in these communities. Besides adding.to the quality of the diet in terms of protein and calories, and as a relish dish, many people see meat as 'the real food'. James Woodburn has noted that the Hadza speak of themselves as suffering from 'hunger' when they merely have less meat that they would like (1968: 52, see also Tanaka 1976; 113, Kent 1993; 491).

From the ethnographic record on hunter-gatherers one must therefore conclude that subsistence hunting is neither motivated by sadomasochistic tendencies, nor perceived as anti-life, nor does it symbolize a 'war' against nature, or an ethic of environmental control, nor does it imply a gender hierarchy.

In turning now to hunting in Malawi, I shall suggest that even in a context where hierarchical relationships have long been pervasive, the ethos of subsistence hunting still carries similar cultural associations to those of hunter-gatherers.

2. Subsistence Hunting in Malawi

Hunting plays an important role of the subsistence economies of horticultural societies throughout the world and, as Susan Kent (1989:12) remarks, its significance relates as much to its cultural and symbolic value as to its economic importance. In the truly pioneering ethnographic studies by Audrey Richards on the Bemba, by Mary Douglas on the Lele, and by Victor Turner on the Ndembu — all central Bantu people where matrilineal kinship plays a salient role — the cultural significance of hunting is highlighted. All three scholars emphasise that while hunting is important as an economic activity, and such people may exhibit a 'craving for meat', its social and ritual aspects are often given primacy. Communal hunting therefore often has social significance, and to an important degree hunting is given cultural emphasis. "Every Bemba," Richards writes, perhaps with some exaggeration, "is a hunter, by desire and enthusiasm"(1939: 342). Douglas describes the Lele village community as ultimately a political and ritual unit because it is single hunting unit and that the Lele think of themselves as first and. foremost a 'hunting culture' (1954: 16). Turner, likewise, describes the Ndembu social system as, "pivoted on the importance of hunting". (1957: 25).

Hunting in Malawi follows a similar pattern. Historically, the' peoples of Malawi — Tumbuka, Chewa, Mang'anja, Yao, Lomwe — had a dual economic system that combined shifting hoe cultivation focused around a group of matrilineally related women, with subsistence hunting. As uxorilocal residence was the norm, such hunting was symbolically centred on the male affine perceived as an outsider *(mlendo)*. As with other Central Bantu people, although hunting was important in the local subsistence economy, it actually contributed little to the food intake, and its importance was as much symbolic and social as it was economic although the importance of mammals in the provision of meat, skins and medicines, and as items of trade must not be undervalued. For the purpose of this paper, I will focus only on two aspects of the Malawian hunting tradition, the communal hunt, and the rituals associated with hunting.

Uzimba — the Communal Hunt

The hunting of larger mammals in Malawi is essentially the prerogative of men, and consists of two basic types. The first is the kind of hunting undertaken by a solitary man, sometimes accompanied by a younger male, and usually by a dog. The second type is that of a communal hunt, which in the past was often arranged by a local chief or headman, and involved the ritual beating of the bush. Although not as elaborate as in the past, communal hunting, either with nets and dogs is still commonly practiced in rural areas.

Uzimba is a general Chewa term for the collective hunt, although it may also be referred to as *ulenje, liwamba, kaum or buwit*. During the colonial period the communal hunt was an important and widespread method of capturing mammals. G.D.Haves was to describe it as an "abominably cruel method of hunting. "(1978:50), echoing sentiments that had long been expressed by colonial administrators, many of whom made serious efforts to have this form of hunting proscribed.

Communal hunts are still widely practised in Malawi, although there are wide variations as to their nature, with respect as to whether they are organised through the local chief *(mfumu)*, whether they use fire or nets, and with regard to the number of participants. From my own experience a hunting

BRIAN MORRIS

party usually consisted of between five and sixteen men and boys accompanied by around three or four dogs.

A large-scale communal hunt, however, is initiated by either a local chief or village headman, or by a local hunter who takes it upon himself to organise a hunt. He is then known as *mwini luauzimba*, the owner of the hunt. As in the organisation of initiation rites, a group of men with whistles *(pintu)* or reed pipes *(khweru)* will go around the village attempting to drum up support, indicating the time and place of the hunt. Often men of neighbouring villages will be invited along. The area where the hunt is to take place will be associated with a particular kin group, and one of the senior males will be considered to be the *mwini watchire*. This person is often also the leader of the hunt.

At the appointed time, the men gather at the gardens and in a large communal hunt as many as two hundred men and boys may join the hunt, armed with spears, bows and arrows, and knobkernes, and accompanied by several dogs. The hunts I have experienced, however, were on a much smaller scale, although I have been informed of large-scale communal hunts, near Phirilongwe Mountain especially. Only men and dogs participate in the hunt, it being suggested that women lack strength *(alibe mphamvu)* to climb the wooded hills (although to collect mushrooms and firewood they regularly do so), and are also unable to throw the spears and knobkerries *(satha kupomja zibonga)*.

On entering the woodland, the hunting groups will divide into several parties, forming lines of beaters *(liphondo)* on each side of the woodland. They will be referred to as *asmbaliya ku mlmawa* (side of the early morning) and *mbali ya ku madzulo* (side of the evening) — the east and west flanks respectively. If fire is used, all the surrounding woodland will already have been fired, leaving a large 'island' of untouched woodland where the larger mammals will tend to congregate, as the grass undergrowth will afford protective cover for the animals. The burning of woodland by the hunters is seen in positive terms. While ecologists and foresters, and Europeans generally, see the burning of the woodland *(kiioclm tchire)* as a destructive activity, hunters see this as having a quasi-religious significance, and not simply as a pragmatic activity. It is described as warming the place *(kufunda malo)*, and is seen as essential to the regeneration of the woodland with the coming of the rains in late November and December. The optimal time then for the communal hunt is at the end of the dry season in September or October. In symbolic terms the firing of the bush is analogous to sexual intercourse, both of which generate heat and are

289

creative acts. At the end of the mourning period, at the completion of the initiation rites and at the ceremony associated with childbirth *(ku-tenga mwana,* to bring forth the child) ritual intercourse is also described as 'warming the place' *(kufimda malo).*

Driven by the fire and the beaters — young boys playing a prominent part of the hunt, and usually armed with sticks or knobkerries — the animals are driven out of an area of woodland. They are then set upon by the dogs, who often hold them at bay while they are beaten or speared by the hunters. All varieties of mammals mav be taken this way, but the principal mammals sought in the communal hunt — depending on the location — are the duiker *(gwape),* hare *(kalulu),* bushbuck *(nibaiuala),* sable *(inplmlapaia},* porcupine *(nungu),* Sharpe's grysbok *(kasenye),* the vervet monkey *(pusi)* and bushpig *(nguluwe).* Although the communal hunt generates much excitement, and seems to be enjoyed by all the participants — at least this was my impression from talking to the participants — such hunts are organised and under the direction of the hunt leader, usually a senior man *(mwini wauzimba).*

Communal hunts may also utilise nets *(nkonde),* which are staked out in a line, and the game animals driven into it. Entering the nets *(kulowa mlukonde),* they are killed *(kupha)* by spears and knobkerries. The line of nets may extend a hundred metres or more.

At the end of a communal hunt there is a formal sharing of the meat.The sharing is described in terms of a division *(kit gnwanu)* of the game animals. Small mammals, like the hare and elephant shrew, are usually taken by the person(s) who captured it, but the larger mammals — like the sable, duiker and bushbuck — are formally cut up by the 'owner' of the hunt *(mwini zuauzititba).* According to custom, the village chief (mfumu) and the owner of the woodland *(mwiniwatachire)* are given a foreleg of the larger antelopes *(rnwendo wamwambo),* while the owner of the hunt himself gets a hindleg *(mwendo wathako}.* The person who first hits *(kumwemja)* a mammal is entitled to a leg; so too is the man who dealt the fatal stroke *(msomoii).* All the rest of the game meat is shared out by the 'owner' of the hunt, and all participants receive a portion, varying in amount according to their involvement and status.

Although there us no formal rule forbidding the hunter from eating his 'own kill', there is a strong emphasis that meat obtained from hunting has to be shared. There is a general consensus among hunters I knew that the meat from large game animals, ranging from the duiker *(gtuape)* to the buffalo *(nja-*

ti), should be allocated as follows — and this refers also to meat obtained on solitary hunts: a foreleg of the animal should go to the village chief and a mark of respect *(ku-lemekeza);* the back *(msana)* and neck *(khosi)* should be given to the mother's brother *(malume);* flesh without bones *(mnofii yopanda fupa)* should be given to the man's spouse *(mkazi)',* and the rest of the meat, like the intestines *(matumbo),* should be given to the hunter's kin *(abale).* With a communal hunt, it is the 'owner' of the hunt *(mwini wauzimba)* who directs the sharing of the meat; with a small hunting party i t is the man whose spear has killed the mammal, or who is considered the senior hunter *(mkulii waulenji).* An early historian of the Chewa Samuel Ntara spoke of an exchange of meat for sex (1973: 119), but generally speaking the sharing of meat does not simply reflect affinal ties between the man and his spouse, but political — relations with the territorial chief — as well as kinship relationships. In the past the rights of *mzinda,* associated with territorial chiefs, not only included rights over land and over initiation ceremonies *(chinarnwali),* but also rights over the larger game animals. Especially important were the skins of lions, leopards and serval — which only chiefs might wear — and the rights over elephant tusks, the ground tusk being deemed to belong to the chief. As owner of the country, *muini dziko,* the territorial chief was also entitled to a hind leg of all larger mammals taken on hunting expeditions, whether by solitary hunters or during village-wide communal hunts (Rangeley 1948;24-25)

Ritual Aspects of Hunting

The woodland in Malawi is considered to be a cool *(ozizira)* environment, and it is therefore imperative for anyone entering the woodland for hunting to be and remain in a cool condition. Hunting is not viewed negatively, or seen in oppositional terms to that of reproduction, but must, like all vital productive activities — child bearing, the firing of pots, beer-brewing, initiation, iron-smelting — be undertaken in a cool condition. Fire, sexual activity, and contact with blood, all make a person "hot" *(othenta);* it is important then that a man whose wife is menstruating *(asambamo)* should not go hunting. It is equally important that men, prior to the hunt, should not have sexual intercourse with a women, nor must his wife have sexual relations with any other man whilst he is on a hunting expedition. Such illicit sex *(chigololo)* is viewed as extremely dangerous. Equally important, social relations within the village must be peaceful and tranquil *(ntenderc);* there must be no conflict, and the hunter must thus have no anger *(kwnja)* in his heart. His disposition must be calm and gentle, and as the heart is the seat of the emotions, it is decribed as *kitfatsa mtima,* to have a gentle heart. Blood, sex, anger, are contrary to the disposition that is required of the hunter, who must be in a cool *(ozizira)* state. As one hunter said to me: a person who is cool will kill animals well *(akhala ozizira akitplwbwino).*

Any contravention of these rules is seen as having dire consequences. The hunters may not find any game, or misfortunes may befall them. Accidents may occur, and a hunter may be seriously injured, or even killed by a wild animal. If game is not encountered during a hunt, for it is said that the larger mammals are able to smell semen, men may suspect that one of their party is "hot", having had sexual relations prior to the hunt. Or — and this has often been said to me when accompanying hunters — a man's wife is having sexual relations with another man during his absence, and this is the reason he has been unlucky, and has not encountered or killed any game animal. This idea seems to be widespread in Southern Africa (cf. Junod *1927;61).* Some men will not even carry metal coins when on a hunting expedition — for metal is associated with "heat".

There is then, in Malawi, a pronounced antithesis between sex and hunting, but it would be highly misleading to interpret this, in gnostic fashion, as implying a symbolic dualism between men and women, hunting and cultivation, such that hunting is seen as a "life-taking" activity, and sex and reproduction as a "life-giving" one (Rosaldo and Atkinson 1975). This kind of analysis tends to see both

hunting and menstruation in negative terms, and to conceptualize "heat" (and blood) likewise — as the negative side of a symbolic polarity that is associated with red, menstrual blood, fire, witches, sickness and sterility, as opposed to "coolness" — which is associated with white, semen, water, ancestral spirits, health and fertility — as Adam Kuper (1982;20) interprets the symbolism of the Southern African Bantu. But both these accounts imply a radical gnostic schema of good and evil, that is quite foreign to Malawian conceptions, which imply a complementary polarity between men and women, hunting and cultivation, and seeks a symbolic balance between "hot" and "cool". Hotness is a condition, not a disease *(nthenda).* It is associated with blood, fire and sex. But these are not viewed negatively, for they are essential aspects of both human life, and ecological well-being. Thus hunting, like childbirth, beer-brewing, menstruation, pot-making, iron-smelting, and initiation, is not viewed negatively: however, being a creative activity involving "heat" (blood, fire), it must be undertaken in a "cool" condition. A hunter, a smelter, a pregnant or menstruating woman, an initiate undergoing a transition ceremony, all have affinities with each other: they are in a vulnerable state, and must not come into contact with anything that generates "heat". They must remain "cool".

Like an initiate, a pregnant woman, an iron-smelter, a beer-brewer— for hunting is viewed essentially as a rite of transformation (Herbert 1993) — a hunter must observe certain ritual precautions. It is essential then that he places his hunting equipment — especially spears, guns, bows and arrows where they will remain "cool". Some hunters insist that hunting equipment must never be placed near the kitchen fire, or even in the kitchen *(malokuplnka,* the cooking place). Others feel it must not be placed in the sleeping room *(malo wagona),* where sexual relations take place, as there is a fear that this may "cut" the spear or gun *(kuopa imatsemphedwa).*Equally important, a menstruating woman must never step across a bow or spear — for it will then lose its vitality.

When a man goes hunting he must therefore enter the woodland in the correct ritual condition. He must be "cool". This is because hunting is thought to be a highly dangerous and risky enterprise, one dependent on luck, and open to spiritual influences, not only of the spirits of the dead *(mizimu),* but of the mammals themselves. For a successful hunt, the hunter, or the owner of the successful hunt *(mwini wauzimba)* not only needs skill and good luck, but protection also from dangerous mammals for even mammals like the male bushbuck or porcupine can be damgerous in certain circumstances — and against the negative influences that stem from killing certain of the larger mammals. This is associated with the possibility of contracting the highly dangerous condition that is describes as *chirope,* derived from one of the terms for blood, *mlopa,* the other more common term being *mwazi, magazi.*

When going hunting it is important initially to make offering *(nsembc)* to the spirits of the ancestors, who are usually addressed as *ambmje* (grandparents). These spirits of the ancestors *(mizimu l/arnakolo)* are respectfully asked *(kupempha)* for help and support, so that a man may travel through the bush without difficulty, and find game animals *(kitpeza mjama).* Ideally, offerings are made by placing millet flour *(ufa)* at the foot of a tree, the *msolo (Pseudola-clinostylis maprouneifolia)* and the *mposa (Annona sencgalensis)* being favourites, as these two trees are associated with the spirits of the dead, but any tree will suffice. If offerings are not made then this will adversely effect the hunt, and it will be without luck *(mwayi)*.

As I have discussed elsewhere, the use of medicines *(mankliwala)* permeates Malawian cultural life, and medicines — the roots, bark, fruit and leaves of plants — are widely and extensively used, not only for therapeutic purposes, but for all aspects of social life. It is hardly surprising then that medicines play an important and crucial role in hunting. Almost all hunters carry with them a small medicine bag *(chitumwa)*, worn around the neck or carried in the pocket. This holds such ingredients as the dried leaves of *chisoni* (meaning "compassion") (*Myrothamnus flabcllifolius)*, the dried root of *palibekanthit* ("it does not ma *tter")(Dicomaanomala)*, hedgehog spines, the leaves of*nyambata (Desmodium vetutinum)* and some pieces of the stem of the small herb *muitana* ("you call") *(Caliurn bussei)*. This medicine bag is believed to bring the person "good luck" *(mwayi)*, as well as to protect the hunter from accidents and dangers, and the

potential evil influences *(ivoipa)* of witchcraft *(ufiti)*. But medicine is also put on the muzzle of the dog so that it smells well, on the guns, spears and arrows so that they hit their mark, on traps and nets so that they capture the mammals, and on the hunter's body to protect them from the possible detrimental effects of killing the mammal *(chirope)*.

Although men clearly enjoy hunting, and meat is a highly esteemed as food by both men and women, hunting is nevertheless felt to be a highly precarious and dangerous enterprise. It is thus hedged with ritual. This is not simply because it is potentially dangerous and life-threatening. Nor because chance and luck play an important part in determining whether or not the hunt is successful - for even a skilled hunter may spend a whole day in the woodland without obtaining a single game animal. It is rather because the killing of mammals — particularly the large and more "potent" mammals such as the kudu, bushbuck, eland, hippopotamus, elephant, impala, sable, roan, buffalo, and, in the past, the blue wildebeest—may, without proper ritual precaution, have an adverse effect on the physical and mental condition of the hunter. For it is believed in Malawi that the act of killing a game mammal is akin to that of homicide, and that the "blood" *(chirope)* of the mammal may enact a kind of vengeance. It will enter the body of the hunter, bringing punishment *(kubwezera chilango)* in the form of a serious condition. As one person said to me: a person who kills a close relative *(wapha mzake)* through conflict *(ndewa)*, or a game animal *(nyama)*, the eyes of this person will become very red *(wofiira)* If not treated the person will become blind (khungu) or become mad *(misala)*. The redness of the eyes and the hot condition of the man is due to the blood of the mammal *(magazi wanyama)*. A man in this condition, described *aschirope* (blood) easily becomes angry *(sachedwa kupsya mtima,* heat/burn the heart) and fierce *(amaopa)*. He is therefore liable to engage in further killing — especially of his own kin. After killing one of the large "potent" animals medicines have therefore to be taken to counteract the "heat" and the power of the blood. These medicines are called "medicines of the blood" *(mankhwala achirope)*.

All hunters speak of *chirope* as a kind of disease *(nthenda)* that causes the red inflammation of the eyes, and leads to a condition like madness *(ngati misala)*, with a spinning head *(kuzitngiilira mutu)*. It is explicitly seen however as distinct from both true madness and from rabies *(clmueiue)*. It is particularly associated with the hunting of large game animals, especially the larger antelopes, the hunting of which is surrounded with a good deal of "mystique". To hunt such animals as the buffalo, eland or kudu, without first preparing protective medicine is seen as courting disaster, leading to madness or misfortune *(zobvutika)*. Essentially the condition is expressed in terms of the blood entering the head/body of the hunter *(magazi imalowa mutu nnuache)*. Although some hunters may indeed speak of the spirit of the thing *(mzimu diachinthu)* as entering or coming upon the body of the hunter *(chanyama chinabwera kutlmpi laclie)*, normally hunters do not speak of the animal as having a spirit,or that it is the spirit of the mammal that causes the hunter's madness. But rather it is the "blood" of the mammal entering the body of the hunter that makes him prone to violence and madness.

Because of these beliefs the young hunter's first kill and the cutting up *(kutumbula)* of a large mammal is usually accompanied by a good deal of ritual, particularly in the form of a medicinal wash *(kusamba)* to ward off the "blood" of the slain animal. The wanton killing of game animals, or the killing of animals who have not reached maturity *(msinkhu)* is said to lead to *chirope,* or to the angering of the ancestral spirits, one hunter remarked to me that the killing of even a dog was similiar *(chimodzimodzi)* to homocide, and thus could lead to *chirope.*

But although the blood of the mammal has the power to "inflame" the heart of the hunter, and thus without "cooling" medicines may lead to violence and madness, blood, like hunting itself, is not viewed negatively. For it is also seen as the epitome of life and vitality, and the partaking of blood is an important aspect of many spirit rituals, such as those of *nantongwe* and *vimbuza* (Boeder 1984; 47-9, Peltzer 1987, 180-90)

Conclusion

I have suggested that hunting, like fire and menstruation, must

not be viewed negatively, as if it was the antithesis of life-giving human reproduction. But because it involves the use of metal implements, and the spilling of blood, as well as, in the past, the use of "hot" arrow poison" hunting inevitably generates "heat", which, in excess, is extremely dangerous and contrary to human well-being. Moreover, the larger mammals, such as the kudu, roan and eland, are symbolically associated with the woodland and with the spirits of the ancestors *(mizimu yamakolo),* such that the killing of these mammals is akin to homicide. It is then imperative the the hunter, like the menstruating woman, remains in a "cool" condition, that the spirits of the dead are harnessed for support (there must be peace in the village and the killing must not be wanton or violent), and that medicines are used to protect the hunter not only against witchcraft and ill-luck, but also from the ill-effects of the "heat" — expressed as chirope. Heat—— generated by fire, blood and sex (and transmitted via the media of salt, meat and metal) — is abolutely essential to procreative processes, and to human well-being: only in excess, uncontrolled, does it lead to sterility, sickness and misfortune. Thus, rather than seeing sexuality/childbearing (women) and hunting (men) in gnostic fashion as antithetical activities, in the Malawian context human procreation and hunting are viewed analogously as similinr positive social processes. Whereas the semen of the male affine activates the blood of the woman to produce a child — as rain activates the burnt woodland to produce new plant growth — so the hunter uses "heat" — fire, poison, spears and arrow heads — to produce meat *(nyama).* Hunting is therefore viewed not as the negation of life and procreation, but rather as a ritual of transformation. It is a social proces that is analogous to cooking, beer-brewing, initiation, pot-making, iron-smelting, as well as to human procreation itself. It is an expression of what Eugenia Herbert (1993) has described as the "procreative paradigm", which is seen as underlying the cosmologies of Sub-Saharan African cultures. Equally important, although hunting in Malawi is associated with masculinity, at least its hegemonic form, hunting is not in any simple sense an expression of male dominance. Nor does it symbolize either a "war" against the wilderness, or "control" over the biotic universe.

Hunting is not life-negating: it is a social process, a rite of transformation, that is deemed by Malawians to be essential for human well-being — at least in the rural context.

Acknowledgements

I have spent more than ten years in Malawi and have lived for short periods and researched in every part of the country. The present article is based on research studies in ethnobiology (1990-91) supported by the Nuffield Foundation. I am grateful for this support. I should also like to thank the Centre for Social Research, Zomba, for institutional support, and my many friends in Malawi for their help and encouragement. With respect to the present article I should particularly like to thank Ganda Makalani, Davison Potani, Wyson Bowa and Martin William.

References

Adams, C. 1990 *The Sexual Politics of Meat.* Cambridge : Polity Press.

Ardrey, R. 1976 *The Hunting Hypothesis* London: Fontana/Collins

Boeder, R.B. 1984 *Silent Majority; A History of the Lomwe in Malawi* Pretoria: Inst. S.Africa

Brown, J.E. 1992 *Animals of the Soul* Rockport,Mass.:Element

Cartmill, M. 1993 *A View to a Death in the Morning* Cambridge, Mass : Harvard University Press

Collard, A. 1988 *Rape of the Wild* London: Women's Press '

Douglas, M. 1954 The Lele of the Kasai in D. FORDE (Ed.) *African Worlds* IAT Oxford University Press pp 1-26

Fiddes, N. 1991 *Meat; A Natural Symbol* London: Routledge

Foley, R. 1987 *Another Unique Species* Harlow: Longman

Frazer, J. G. 1922 *The Golden Bough* London: MacMillan

Frnch, M. 1986 *Beyond Poiver* London: Sphere Books

Guenther, M. 1988 Animals in Bushmen Thought, Myth and Art in T.Ingold et al *Hunters and Gatherers* Vol 2 Oxford: Berg pp 192- 202

Hayes, G.D. 1978 *A Guide to Malawi's National Parks and Game Reserves* Limbe: Montford Press

Herbert, E.W. 1993 *Iron, Gender and Power* Bloomington : Indiana University Press

Hill, K. 1982 *Hunting and Human Evolution }.* Human Evolution 11; 527-44

Ingold, T.1986 *The Appropriation of Nature* Manchester University Press

Junod, H. 1927 *The Life of a South African Tribe* London Kent, S. 1989 (Ed) *Farmers as Hunters* Cambridge University Press 1993 *Sharing in an Egalitarian Kalahari community* MAN 28/3; 479-514

Knight, C. 1991 *Blood Relations* New Haven : Yale Univ. Press Kuper, A. 1982 *Wives for Cattle* London, Routledge Leacock, E. 1981 *Myths of Male Dominance* New York : Monthly Rev. Press

Lee, R.B. 1979 *The IKung San* Cambridge University Press Liebenberg, L. 1990 *The Art of Tracking* Claremont: D. Philip Morris, B.1979 *Scientific Myths: Man the Mighty Hunter* NEW HUMANIST Feb. 129-130

Moscovici, S.1976 *Society against Nature* London: Harvester Nelson, R. 1993Mate *Prayers to the Raven* Chicago University Press Ntara, S. 1973 The History of the Chewa Ed. B. Heintz Wiebaden: F. Steiner

Ortner, S.B. 1974 Is Female to Male as Nature is to Culture in M.Z. Rosaldo and L.Lamphere (Ed.) *Woman, Culture and Society* Stanford University Press pp 67-88 Peltzer, K. 1987 Some *Contributions of Traditional Healing towards Psychosocial Health Care in Malaiui* Eschborn: Fachbuchhandling fur Psychologic

Poewe, K. 1981 *Matnlineal Ideology* London: Academic Press Rangeley,W.H.J.1948 *Notes on Chcwa Tribal Law* Nyasaland J. 1/3;4-68

Richards. A. 1939 *Land, Labour and Diet in Northern Rhodesia* IAI Oxford University Press

Rosaldo, M.z. and J.Atkinson 1975 Man the Hunter and Women in R. G. Willis (Ed.) *The Interpretation of Symbols* London: Malaby Press pp 43-75

Sanday, P.R. 1981 *Female Power and Male Dominance* Cambridge University Press

Serpell, J. 1986 *In the Company of Animals* Oxford: Blackwell

Speck, F.G. 1938 Aboriginal Conservators in R.NASH (Ed.) *Environment and Americans* New York: Holt, Rinehart pp 74-78

Spiegel, M. 1988 *The Dreaded Comparison: Human and Animal Slavery* London: Heretie Books

Tanaka, J. 1976 Subsistence Ecology of the Central Kalahari San in R.B.Lee and I. Devore (Ed.) *Kalahari Hunter-Gatherers* Cambridge Mass.: Harvard University Press

Turner, V.W. 1957 *Schism and Continuity in an African Society* Manchester University Press Washburn, S.L. and C.S.Lancaster 1968 The Evolution of Hunting

in R. B. Lee and I. Devore (Ed.) *Man the Hunter* Chicago: Aldine pp293-33

Woodburn, J.C. 1968 An Introduction to Hadza Ecology in Lee and Devore *op. cit.* pp 49-55

WILDLIFE DEPREDATION IN MALAWI: THE HISTORICAL DIMENSION (1995)

It is, I think, difficult for people living in urban areas to realise how precarious life is for subsistence agriculturalists. It has to be remembered that historically the matrilineal peoples of Malawi were fundamentally subsistence hoe-cultivators. Not only is such agriculture highly dependent on rain, but the depredations of wild animals is a constant source of concern and anxiety. Thus, although in hunting or in certain ritual contexts a close, interdependent relationship is often expressed between humans and animals in Malawi, in an agricultural context the larger mammals are seen as a constant source of threat to people's well-being and livelihood, as indeed they are. This present paper offers some reflections, from an historical perspective, on such wildlife depredations in Malawi.

The depredations of wild animals in Malawi focused around two distinct groups of mammals: the carnivores (lion, leopard and hyena) who in certain circumstances were a serious menace to human life, and those mammals who raided village gardens for crops. The most important of these were the elephant, baboon, monkey, hippo, porcupine, bush pig, and in certain situations, some antelope species.

We shall discuss each of these categories in turn. In the past Malawi had a reputation for its man-eating lions. The memoirs of all the early missionaries and administrators in Malawi invariably contain a short section on the attacks inflicted on people by lions. Thus, W.P. Livingstone in his biography of Robert Laws, an early missionary at Livingstonia, has a section entitled "Nature's Cruelty". He notes that Christ's work and "civilized conditions" entail the subjugation of the wilderness, making it less ruthless and cruel. And the lion is seen as the epitome of Nature's cruelty. Very many of the patients brought to the Livingstonia mission station, he noted "suffered from mauling by wild animals" and he recalls one night when five women and a child were attacked by a lion who sprang upon the roof and broke through the thatch of the hut. It killed two women and the child. Not long afterwards the same lion killed two other women and a girl, as well as killing another woman who had left her hut to find what the commotion in the night had been about. After failing to poison the lion with strychnine it was later shot by one of the missionaries (Livingstone 1921; 388-9). Laws himself noted in his memoirs that eight people were killed by lions in his first year at Livingstonia (1934; 224). An early administrator Hans Coudenhove, who lived in the Chikala Hills, also wrote of a man-eating lion near Lake Chirwa who for several months spread "terror" among the villagers by its periodic appearance. The lion killed fourteen and wounded six people before its career was ended by chief Chikwewo and a group of men, armed with a rifle and spears (1925;107-8). When some decades later the well-known geographer Frank Debenham wrote his survey of Nyasaland for the colonial office, it was hardly surprising that one chapter was devoted to lions. It was entitled "The Man-eaters of Kasungu" and it reported that one administrative officer at Kasungu had shot a lion which "had taken at least 60 Africans and was known far and wide". Debenham noted the fact that local people tended not to report such man-eating lions as it was "widely believed that a lion may be a reincarnation of a former chief (1955; 186).

It would be tedious to recount all the reports of man-eating lions in Malawi during the past decades, but two particular incidents are worth noting. The first is the case of the man-eating lion which caused havoc in the Mchinji District around 1929-30. In May 1930 the Provincial Commissioner of the Central Province sent a telegram to the Government Chief Secretary in Zomba which read:

"Man-eating lion causing serious trouble in the Fort Manning (Mchinji) District. Stop. Five victims within the past two weeks. Stop. Owing the long grass unable to deal with the matter single-handed. Stop. Consider that the services of two Europeans needed urgently. Stop. Can you assist".

Apparently for some months a lion had been creating havoc and despair in the district and had caused at least 36 deaths in twenty four villages. It attacked people during the daytime while they were working in the fields or fetching water and in one village had been responsible for three deaths in one day. Many deaths, however, were not reported to the administration as people were always quick to remove the body of their dead relative. The majority of the lion's victims were women. The commissioner R.H. Murray, a month earlier, had toured the Mchinji area and had found it in a "state of terror". He reported that half the villages had planted no maize and the inhabitants of the others were afraid to sleep in their gardens. The result, he wrote, is that practically the whole of the crop has been destroyed by wild animals, especially by monkeys. Several villages had been abandoned. The lion he continued, was operating over a wide area, as it never returned to its kill, and generally moved 15-20 miles (24-32 Km) before attacking another victim. The lion was thus covering a territory of around 400 sq miles (lOOOKm²). To deal with the problem 50 police were brought in from Lilongwe, Dedza and Dowa, practically the whole police force from the Central Region. The only game warden for the territory, Rodney Wood, thought the local people themselves were largely to blame for the details - as the men were working away on tobacco estates and would not organize a communal hunt, as the women did not take full precautions and often worked or fetched water alone, and because the relatives removed the victims immediately after the killing not allowing the administration to poison the body. But this was not a unique outbreak. In 1925 the Rev. J. van Heerden of Mchinji mission had reported that people in ten villages in the district had not planted their gardens owing to the danger from lions, and wrote that during his eight years in the district "I do not remember a single year in which there were no man eating lions". One administrator estimated that in most districts throughout the country an average of 50 people were killed annually by lions. In the Ngara District all villages were stockaded as a protection against these beasts of prey. Eventually the Mchinji lion was killed in September 1930 by three well-armed Europeans, assisted by a host of trackers. One of the Europeans was the young E.G. Peterkins, who later became an important political figure in Malawi prior to independence (MNA 51/1721A/23).

The second incident is the case of the "Namwera man-eaters", the title of a chapter in the memoirs of the well known game ranger Norman Carr. Born at Chinde in 1912, Carr spent his early years in Malawi, where his parents were tobacco farmers during the colonial period. Carr worked for the colonial government as a crop protection officer, and records in his memoirs how proud he was on shooting his 50th elephant near Liwonde in 1932 - on his twentieth birthday (1969;20). During the war years he was stationed in the Namwera Hills, near Mangochi. As the area was well-populated, game was scarce, apart from baboons and bush pig. As lions frequently crossed the border from Mozambique, and found it difficult to secure their normal prey, they sometimes turned, Carr wrote, "to the only other available food: man". Thus outbreaks of man-eating lions used to occur from time to time in the Namweras "spreading terror" among local people. While staying in the Namweras Carr received a message from Chief Kawinga about man-eating lions, two lions having been responsible for eleven victims in two weeks. His memoirs give a graphic account of the hunting of the two lions (1969:84-99), both lions proving to be in prime condition. This, he felt, disproved the theory that only lions which are too old or too feeble to catch wild game will eat human flesh. The pioneer conservationist, G.D. Hayes, has more recently, in recalling his own experiences of "man eaters", suggested that a conservative estimate of death attributed to the Namwera lions was "some fifty in a period of a little over three months" (1979;7).

Although at the present time lions are largely confined to conservation areas, occasional lions are still to be noted in the Zomba and Mulanje districts, and in other well-populated areas throughout Malawi-for lions appear to be great travellers. And deaths from lions are still occasionally recorded. George Welsh, who was a forest officer on the Vipya in the 1970s, reported to me the death of one forest worker, who was killed whilst riding his bicycle near the forestry compound. During the colonial period it was considered unsafe to travel on foot at night on the Liwonde road, as well as on the Zomba to Blantyre road. More recently, a game ranger was killed travelling by motorbike on the escarpment road through Nkhotakota Game Reserve.

Unlike lions, neither leopards and hyenas are widely known as "man-eaters", but the records show that they too frequently take a toll of human life, particularly of young children. A missionary of Ekwendeni wrote to Alexander Hetherwick of a woman who put down her child at the edge of the field while she hoed, and on turning round found it gone. Only the footmarks of a leopard were there in evidence. Two man-eating leopards were noted in the Chikwawa District in the 1920s: one had killed four children and mauled many more; the other had killed at least nine youths between nine and thirteen years. Debenham (1955;184) records a leopard in the Kasungu District which had killed 37 people and was so renowned for its fury and cunning that the local chief was not allowed to participate in the final hunt. Though secretive, leopards are still plentiful in Malawi, many still taking their toll of young children, although their presence is usually known by the dogs and goats that regularly disappear from villages, or even from residences within towns. Hyenas, too, may kill or inflict serious injuries to humans.

Throughout Malawi, the spotted hyena is widely feared, as it attacks people at night especially during the hot season, when people sleep outside on the veranda (khonde). Hector Duff at the turn of the century wrote:

"Cowardly as it is, the hyena is a good deal feared by (people) owing to its unpleasant habit of sneaking up to them while they lie asleep, and biting their faces. I was assured in northern Angoniland (Mzimba District) that hyenas there would often lie in wait outside the huts at dawn, and make a sudden rush at the inmates directly they put their heads out of doors" (1903; 107). The Rev. Charles Long at Chididi recorded several cases of human beings attacked while sleeping out of doors on hot evenings (1973;66).

But the region most well-known in Malawi for attacks on people by hyenas is the Phalombe Plain, to the north of Michesi Mountain. In the late 1950s a number of deaths of people were reported from this area. The first to be recorded was in September, 1955, and was reported to Fred Balestra, a local planter, who farmed near Fort Lister. Balestra had lived in the area for over thirty years and was a keen hunter. He was called to a village in which a man, who was reputed to be mad *(misala)* had been killed and eaten by hyenas on a path near the village. Whether he was asleep at the time Balestra could not discover: all he found was patches of blood and a few shreds of cloth.. Seven days later, and some eight miles away, an old lady was dragged from her hut, the flimsy grass door being broken down. She was dragged thirty yards, lost an arm and was badly mauled before her cries for help brought relief. Refusing to go to hospital, she died the next day. There was one more killing that year, a child of six. Thus, that year there were three deaths. Then, Balestra records, the toll really began - five deaths in 1956, five in 1957, six in 1958. This pattern continued until 1961, when eight people were killed by hyenas, the killings always began in September, a time when people started sleeping outside on the veranda, and when bush fires were begun. The latter had the effect of making the normal hunting of game difficult for the hyenas. By January, when people began sleeping indoors again, the killings had ceased.

Balestra wrote his article on the "Man-eating Hyenas of Mulanje" in 1962.

Some three decades later, the hyenas are still plentiful in the area, even moving through the middle of Migowi trading centre at night. But although there are still many reports of people being badly mauled by hyenas, actual deaths are now less frequent - though many people still sleep outdoors during the dry season.

In the above paragraphs I have detailed the toll on human life exacted by three of the larger carnivores: but these same beasts of prey - as well as smaller carnivores like the zorilla, serval, and mongoose - also prey on livestock. The matrilineal peoples of Malawi do not have a developed pastoral economy: nevertheless the carnivores exact a heavy toll on the livestock that they do keep - cattle, goats, pigs and chickens: Records from the colonial period suggest the following depredations.

In a twelve month period 102 goats, 22 sheep, 12 pigs and 20 cattle were taken by carnivores from fourteen villages in the Ntcheu District. In the same district 21 pigs were taken by lions from just three villages in two days - lions being especially fond of pigs. In the same year (1926) it was recorded that twelve villages near Neno Mission lost 6 pigs and 14 cattle to lions, and 32 goats, 5 pigs and 2 dogs to leopards (MNA 51/1721A/23). Wherever leopards and hyenas are still to be found - and hyenas are still common on Soche Mountain overlooking Blantyre Township - they take an enormous toll of domestic livestock. A group of hyena who lived in a cave above my house in the Domasi Valley, became so troublesome in the number of sheep and goats they took from the nearby villages, that a group of men expended a great deal of effort over a number of days smoking out their cave. The popular travel book, *Leopards in the Night* (1955) by Guy Muldoon, has six chapters devoted to lions and leopards. Muldoon in the 1940s was an agricultural officer stationed at Mwera Hill, and one of the main tasks he took upon himself was to shoot the leopards and lions that were molesting local livestock. The Dowa Hills at that period were "infested" with these carnivores, and the lions, which followed a circular route in their travels between Dowa and Ntchisi Mountain in the north, had seemingly lost all fear of humans. They found the sheep and cattle in the villages far easier pickings than wild game - and usually stampeded the animals from the kraal. Like Carr, he noted that the lions he shot, or which became "man-eaters", were neither old or decrepit, but rather young and virile and Muldoon wrote "the most likely explanation for the (lions) acquiring a taste for human flesh is the contempt they develop for man after extensive raids on villages". He noted that one notorious "man eater" of recent years was a lion that killed fourteen persons in one month near Mzimba (1955;38).

Given this background it is not surprising that Malawian attitudes towards the larger carnivores is one of apprehension and fear. They speak of being afraid of animals *(kuopa)* or of expressing fear *(kuchita mantha)*. How deep such feelings may be, can be gleamed from recent experience in Norway, where the presence of a single wild wolf near the vicinity of habitations apparently caused a near-hysterical "frenzy" among the Norwegian public (Rowan 1991;282). Some writers suggest that the fear of the wolf and its subsequent persecution is based primarily on "misrepresentation" and inaccurate epithets and myths (cf Serpell 1986; 159-160) - but the fear and the hostility towards wolves, and, as we have noted, towards also the hyena, is, however, based on substantive experiences of people living in rural environments.

But the carnivores are not the only mammals that subsistence agriculturalists have to contend with. Malawians also have to face the depredations to their crops caused by a variety of animal species. Historically the most important of these was the elephants. Nowadays elephants are largely confined -to conservation areas and forest reserves, but in the past they were widely distributed throughout Malawi, and in many areas they created havoc during the harvest season. Apart from tsetse control, the main function of the Game Department throughout the colonial period was not the conservation of wild animals, but rather crop protection. Guy Muldoon, when he later became Game Control Officer at Nkhotokota, was nominally in charge of the game reserve. But besides dealing with lions and leopards his main duties appear to have been the destruction of baboons and wild pigs which raided local gardens and the control of the elephants that left the reserve (1955;61). The elephants of the Nkhotakota District were particularly troublesome, coming down to the lakeshore from the wooded escarpment, and causing devastation in the local gardens. Other places in Malawi which were particularly known for their marauding elephants were the vicinity of the Tangazi stream in the Lower Shire, the Kasungu District and the southern lakeshore near Monkey Bay and Liwonde. As guns were strictly controlled during the colonial period, although a few men owned old muzzle loaders, local people had very little protection against the elephants. Herds of elephants seemed to be a rule unto themselves, not only raiding the gardens and destroying crops over a wide area, but also raiding the maize granaries. Even with a gun it was a brave man, as one administrator put it, who attempted to drive elephants away, knowing that about one in every three cartridges misfires. Elephants are described in government reports as "wrecking" gardens, as reducing villages to "famine" and as becoming so bold as to ignore flares and drumming and as "terrorizing" villages. The assistant resident at Ngara wrote "complaints come in every week of elephants entering villages during the night, destroying grain stores, while the unfortunate owners are powerless to do anything to protect their stores or to drive away the elephants".

There is the pathetic story of one old lady who went into the night with a lighted torch in an attempt to drive away an elephant who was raiding her granary *(nkhokwe)* - her whole livelihood - and was trampled to death as a consequence.

A.G.O. Hodgson estimated that in some parts of the Dowa District 50 per cent of the maize crop was destroyed by the elephant each year.

One of the most famous, or rather infamous, of the marauding herds was the Mpimbi herd which numbered about a hundred elephant. This herd wandered along the Shire River between Liwonde and Lirande during the 1920s and created havoc and despair wherever it went. It not only destroyed gardens, but the elephants helped themselves - emptied people's grain bins. The herd took not the slightest notice of the flares and the beating of drums, and the people were quite helpless to counter their marauding. Many who did, like the old lady, lost their lives. Many elephants were shot by local hunters working for the game department - as they still are - but this did not offset the damage done to crops by the elephants. Many local European administrators wrote to the government in Zomba in exasperation, suggesting that the best solution to the problem would be the extermination of the elephant population in such areas as Liwonde and Monkey Bay. But as some of the herds, like the Mpimbi herd, consisted mainly of females and carried few tuskers, European hunters were little interested in the herds. One administrator's answer to the problem was to suggest that elephants be used as field target practice for the machine gun section of the KAR (MNA 51/1398/19).

Importantly, however, it has to be recognized that, as subsistence agriculturalists, for Malawians elephants were - and still are - a constant menace, a continual threat to their livelihood and well-being. Yet, in many respects, the most serious depredations to cultivations were done not by elephants - or even by the hippo along the Shire River or lakeshore (though these too can be a menace) - but rather by four mammals still ubiquitous in Malawi - baboons, porcupines, monkeys and bush pigs. All four species in fact are widespread and common, found wherever there are rocky hillsides or woodlands giving them refuge. Essentially the baboons and monkeys raid the garden by day, the other two species by night. There is a saying in Malawi - which is common throughout Central Africa - that in planting maize you need to put three seeds in the hole - one for yourself, one for the guinea fowl, and one for the bush pig. The vast majority of damage to crops by wild animals in Malawi can be attributed to these four species.

During the 1920s when a new game ordinance was being implemented by the colonial government, missionaries, who felt themselves t» be representing the interests of local people, strongly voiced their opposition to the ordinance. And their crucial argument was that the presence of game animals, they suggested, meant not only the presence of carnivores (which took considerable toll of human life in the country) but also the devastation of their crops. One missionary at Neno wrote:

"As for the losses suffered by the depredations of wild pigs and baboons they are very heavy indeed. We may say that there is not a single garden left intact in the whole district. At this season (March 1927) day and night the (people) stay in their gardens. In several villages we find not a soul; everybody is watching maize".

Other missionaries stressed the enormous damage to cultivations suffered from wild animals, particular from the baboons and wild pigs, noting that several villages were short of food on account of such depredations. This was the pattern found throughout Malawi - widespread depredations to gardens by monkeys, bush pigs, porcupine and baboons: local people spending much of their time during the planting season protecting their crops. Although eland, kudu and bushbuck occasionally damaged crops - kudu were renowned for the damage they did to cotton -antelopes generally were not a serious problem, though many species were plentiful. The main culprits were the four species aforementioned. Although these four species were not specifically protected by the game ordinance, the ordinance did, in fact, forbid traditional methods of hunting, viz, the game pit, spring traps, nets and communal hunting with fire and dogs. As firearms were also strictly controlled - all this seemed to many missionaries a great injustice. As one missionary put it; game animals prey upon people's crops, but the ordinance means that local people must simply content themselves with scaring the animals away. Another suggested that what was needed was not a game protection ordinance but a people's protection ordinance.

The adverse conditions under which subsistence cultivators in Malawi laboured was not only recognized by the missionaries in their polemics against the game ordinance: it was also transparent to the administration. Thus, one administrative officer G.W. Kenyon-Slaney, who ironically was later to become a Nyau figure in Chewa rituals, when stationed at Nkhotakota, wrote to the Chief Secretary regarding a tour of the district in April 1927. He wrote how amazed he was at the amount of foodstuffs that were lost to the owners due to the depredations of baboons, bush pig and other wild animals. He speaks of the hardships they have to undergo to save their crops; in some villages men, women and children were living, both day and night, in the gardens, (MNA 51/172A/23).

In a later decade Guy Muldoon continued to detail the crop depredations by wild animals and his memoirs significantly has chapters entitled the "Baboon War" and "Pigs, Wild and Tusky". On the baboons he writes:

"Those who have never lived...in Central Africa...can have little conception of the tremendous damage that baboons cause year in and year out in cultivated fields and gardens. In Nyasaland these creatures destroy thousands of pounds' worth of foodstuffs annually and threaten the very survival of thousands of Africans" (1955; 145).

He speaks of villages and baboons being in a "state of war" during the planting season, and describes in detail the concentrated campaign he launched with the local people, who assisted with nets. Over a two year period in the Dowa and Nkhotakota Districts Muldoon and his assistants destroyed 13 thousand baboons. Similar net-drives were organized against bush pig.

In Malawi during the past decades there has been a tremendous increase in the human population. Less than 2 million in 1930, it now stands at nearly 9 million. As an inevitable consequence there has been a great reduction in the number of the larger mammals over the past 50 years or so. Zebra, Oribi and Blue Wildebeest, for example, are no longer to be found on the Phalombe

Plain (Dudley 1979). Nevertheless, wild mammals are still fairly plentiful for although Malawi is one of the most densely populated areas of Africa, 33 per cent of the country is still under "natural vegetation" and wildlife conservation areas and forest reserves constitute some 20 per cent of the total land area. Thus, leopards and hyenas still roam at night in the Zomba and Blantyre townships, and in rural areas throughout Malawi, local people are still engaged during the agricultural season in a constant battle with hippos, porcupines, monkeys, baboons and wild pigs - not to mention the smaller rodents - in an effort to defend their crops. We therefore find, as in the past, much time and energy devoted during the planting season to warding off crop predators. Wherever gardens border woodland areas special shelters *(chirindo)* are built, often on raised platforms, and people may eat and sleep in these shelters for several weeks - especially to guard against baboons. The importance and severity of what is now described as "wildlife pest impacts" has been of special concern to the Department of National Parks and Wildlife, especially in relation to those village communities lying immediately outside wildlife conservation ares. Buffalo and elephant are particularly important as "pests" in these areas. An FAO funded project in 1989 was specially focused on "Wildlife Management and Crop Protection" and one of its central aims was to seek ways in which to resolve the "conflict" between wildlife and the local communities (Rogers & Jamusana 1989).

In the above paragraphs I have outlined the serious conflicts that exist between wildlife and rural communities in Malawi, communities whose livelihood is centrally focused around subsistence agriculture. Such conflict inevitably give rise to a pervasive cultural opposition between humans and animals, to an ethos of antagonism and opposition which, as Serpell writes (1986; 175) can be specifically related to animals and plant husbandry. This opposition in Malawi is expressed in their eth-nobotanical classifications, in the symbolic demarcation between the woodland and the village domains, and in many rituals. But this ethos of fear and dread *(ku-opsya)*, which is semantically akin to the verb *ku-psya*, to fire, or cook) and of opposition, though pervasive in Malawian social life and culture, reflects only one social attitude that exists between humans and animals. For as in other cultures, Malawians express diverse and often contradictory attitudes towards animals. It has, however, been the "ethic of antagonism" between humans and animals which it has been my purpose to highlight in this essay, an ethic that is fundamentally linked to their life as substance horticulturalists.

REFERENCES

BALESTRA, F. (1962) The Man-Eating Hyenas of Mulanje. *African wildlife.* 16:25-27

CARR, N. (1969) *The white impala.* London, Collins.

COUDENHOVE, H. (1925) *My African neighbours.* London, Cape.

DEBENHAM, F. (1955) *Nyasaland: The land of the lake,* London, HMSO

DUDLEY, C (1979) History of the decline of the larger mammals of the Lake Chilwa Basin. *Soc. Malawi J.* 32(2): 27-41.

DUFF, H.C. (1903) *Nyasaland under the Foreign Office.* London, Bell.

HAYES, G.D. (1979) Lions - man-eaters and others. *Nyala* 5:6-11.

LAWS, R. (1934) *Reminiscences of Livingstonia.* London, Hodder & Stoughton.

LIVINGSTONE, W.P. (1921) *Laws of Livingstonia.* London, Hodder & Stoughton.

LONG, R.C. (1973) *A list with notes of the mammals of the Nsanje District.* Soc. *Malawi J.* 26(l):60-77..

MULDOON, G. (1955) *Leopards in the night.* London, Hart-Davies.

ROGERS, P. & H. S. JAMUSANA (1989) *Wildlife pest impacts and wildlife management in Malawi.* Department of National Parks and Wildlife, Lilongwe.

ROWAN, A.N. (1991) The human - animal interface. *In :* M.H. Robinson & L. Tiger (Eds) *Man and beast revisited.* Washington, Smithsonian Inst. Press, pp 265-278.

SERPELL, J (1986) *In the company of animals.* Oxford, Blackwell.

INSECTS AND MEDICINE IN MALAWI
(2003)

Insects: the dominant life-form

Insects, of course, are the most abundant terrestrial life-form, yet anthropologists on the whole have been little interested in insect life, although in the recent decades with the emergence of ethnobiology and cultural entomology as sub-disciplines, a growing interest has developed in insect-human interactions. Thus scholars have been studying not only the practical uses of insects as food or medicine, but the role that insects have played in the cultural life of human societies - with, regard to literature, mythology, music, art, religion, folklore and recreation (Bodenheimer 1951, Clausen 1954, Hogue 1987, Van Huis 1996). In this paper I shall focus on the role of insects as medicine among the matrilineal peoples of Malawi.

Humans have often tended to see themselves as the ultimate form of life on earth, as either the "apogee of evolution" or as created in the "image" of god, and thus having "dominion" or "stewardship" over the planet. But as (some) humans seem bent on self-destruction, and as insects, are, it appears, several times more resistant to radiation than humans, then humans can hardly claim to being the dominant species (Evans 1970). Indeed, one could well argue that it is the insects that are the truly dominant life-form, for their numbers on earth are quite staggering, and the total number of known (described) insect species in the world is thought to be around one million. It is, however, estimated that there may be at least nine million species of insects in the world, mostly unknown and undescribed. When one compares these numbers with the known number of species of animals and higher plants, the abundance of insect species becomes evident.

	Number of Species Worldwide	Malawi
Mammals	4,327	195
Birds	9,672	630
Reptiles	6,550	124
Fish	22,000	338
Flowering Plants	262,000	3,600

Cornell Dudley has thus recently calculated that there are probably well over two hundred thousand species of insects to be found in Malawi, many of which are still undescribed, although only around four thousand species have been collected (Dudley 1996). It must be emphasized, therefore, that the 140 species of insects that ,nr named and given cultural recognition in Malawi, are only a tiny fraction of the thousands of species that are to be found in Malawi.

Insects as the enemy

"What sort of insects do you rejoice in, where *you* come from?", the Gnat inquired.

"I don't *rejoice* in insects at all", Alice explained, "because I'm rather afraid of them"

Lewis Carroll, *Through the Looking Class* (1872)

In recent years two excellent films have been produced on insect life, reflecting very contrasting attitudes towards the natural world. The first is entitled *"Microcosmos"*, made by Claude Nuridsany and Marie Perennou (1996). Inspired by the writings of Jean-Henri Fabre, it depicts the insect life in the alpine meadows of the French Pyrenees. Without any commentary, the film begins at daybreak and is exquisitely made - simply depicting the sights and sounds of the meadow, time measures in moments - ants drinking from a dewdrop, ladybird beetles feeding on aphids, a swallowtail butterfly emerging from its chrysalis, damsel flies mating, flies held in a sundew trap, rhinoceros beetles fighting on a log, bees feeding on salvia flowers, a small grasshopper caught in a spider's web. As with the deep ecologists, it emphasizes ecological relationships, and expresses a detached, aesthetic attitude towards the natural world, focusing specifically on insect life. No humans are depicted in the film;

it simply takes the viewer on a journey into another world, pristine, intricate, fascinating - the miniature world of another life-form.

The film *Alien Empire,* produced in the same year (1996) specifically for the BBC, is very different. Equally well-made and with a haunting sound track by Martin Kiszko, it is based on the premise that since the dawn of time insects and humans have been in conflict with each other, and that humans are slowly losing the "war" against these ultimate "aliens". Significantly although insects evolved on earth some 350 million years ago, long, long before humans, it is they who are portrayed in the film as the "aliens", and are depicted as invading our houses, damaging our crops, destroying our buildings, and as engaged in a continual warfare against humans. Insects themselves are described in mechanistic terms as alien "monsters", as machines with elegant "hardware" and sophisticated "software", and insect ecology itself is described in terms of conflict - a "battlezone". As insects have invaded every corner of the human world, and are beyond the ultimate control of humans, the future for *Homo sapiens* is bleak indeed! In this rather one-sided portrait of insect life, the importance of mutual aid and symbiotic relationships, long ago stressed by Kropotkin (1902), are ignored; the positive aspects of insects in regard to human life are bypassed; and the crucial ecological role that insects play in almost all biotic communities is barely mentioned. Indeed, rather than being "aliens", engaged in constant conflict with humans, insects, as the dominant terrestrial life-forms, provide crucial ecological support for the very existence of human life.

Both our phenomenal recognition of insect life, expressed in the film *Microcosmos* and our aversion and hostility towards insects suggest but two contrasting attitudes towards insects. But as I have emphasized in my other writings people's social attitudes and relationship to the natural world - including insects - are always diverse, complex, multifaceted, and often contradictory, and cannot be reduced to a single paradigm, let alone to a single metaphor. The common tendency of anthropologists to describe other people's conceptions of nature in monadic terms -usually with a spiritualist bias - and to contrast this, in Gnostic fashion, with a crude and simplistic account of Western attitudes (usually equated with the mechanistic philosophy of the 1 7th century) seems to me quite unhelpful, if not misleading. In my studies of the role of mammals in the social and cultural life of the matrilineal people of Malawi I thus attempted to show the **multiple** ways in which they relate to animals -

pragmatic, intellectual, realist, practical, aesthetic, symbolic and sacramental (Morris 1998). The same pluralism applies equally to their relationship to the various forms of insect life, as people relate, or inter-act, with insects in many different ways. But here I shall focus on the pragmatic dimension, and the use of insects as medicine.

Insects as medicine

Throughout the world insects are reputed to possess medicinal properties, and are widely used in the treatment of many ailments. Honey is almost universally recognized as having healing powers, and is used to cure coughs, stomach problems and a variety of diseases throughout Africa, especially in Islamic communities. Beetles, of many different species, have been widely used as medicine. In Europe in the past fireflies "drunk in wine" were used as an aphrodisiac and blister beetles *(Meloidae)* are commonly noted as medicine. *Cantharidin,* a blistering agent, has been extracted from these beetles, and employed in the treatment of urinary ailments. In large doses it can be a corrosive poison and was well known to the Greeks, *"Cantharos"* being the Greek term for "beetle" (Frost 1942). Many other beetles have been used in folk medicine - stag beetle, dung beetle, weevil, and the larvae of three beetles play a crucial role in the production of arrow poison for hunting. Throughout many parts of South Central Africa, the small *Pheidoie* ants, which commonly invade houses, are consumed as they are believed to cure stomach problems (Van Huis 1996)..Throughout Africa, too, pregnant women eat the clay from termite mounds, which clearly provide them with an essential source of minerals. Fly maggots, particularly of the genus *Wohl fahrtia,* have been used to clean up decaying tissue in wounds, and, as bacteria are now proving resistant to antibiotics, fly maggots are "returning to service", as Lauck puts it (Lauck 1998).

Let me now turn to Malawi.

As I have described in detail in my earlier studies (Morris 1996, 1998) medicines play a crucial and significant role in the social and cultural life of Malawian people, although they tend to be ignored by visiting scholars who are generally more interested in the more esoteric or political aspects of Malawi culture. The term for medicine is *Mankhwala,* which is a cognate of the widespread term Bwanga, and is lo cover a variety of substances believed to possess ilnherent potency and efficacy. In fact, the term essentially refers to this vital power, it thus covers various charms, amulets, and protective medicines, as well as medicines in the normal sense. Western pharmaceuticals, agricultural fertilizers and pesticides are also called by the same term. The general term for the traditional healer in Malawi sing'anga is derived from the term for medicine and essentially means "medicine person". The prototypical sing'anga is the herbalist, but the term is extended to cover other healers such as diviners and spirit mediums.

The majority of substances used for Mankhwala are plant materials: the roots, leaves, bark, fruit and seeds of various plant species. In my earlier studies I recorded over 500 species of plants used as medicine in some way, and it was estimated that around 120 herbs were widely used by herbalists in the treatment of various ailments (Morris 1 996). But importantly such medicines may be used for a variety of purposes, extending far beyond the therapeutic context, as good luck charms, for assistance in a variety of activities and concerns (hunting, friendship, employment, marrjage, agriculture, court cases) as protective medicine against witches, for potency and reproductive purposes, life-cycle rituals, as well as being herbal remedies for a wide variety of ailments (mathenda). Equally important, animal substances are utilized - especially in countering sorcery or witchcraft, or the influence of malevolent spirits - as ^"activating" medicines (chizimba) which give additional power to the plant substances (Morris 1 998).

In the past I studied as an "apprentice" to two local asing'ahga, herbalist-diviners (Useni lifa and Samson Waiti), although I have never felt the need to describe my personal encounters with them, or pretend to my friends that I myself believed in the reality of the ancestral spirits or witches. But as far as I can recall insects were never employed, or even mentioned, as a medicine, or utilized in their divinatory rites. More recent studies seem to confirm this, for insects are not widely used as medicine. But from my observations and my discussions with several herbalists, there are a number of insects that seem to be widely recognized as Mankhwala, and these include the following:

SNOUTED BEETLE, Kafadala, *Brachycerus nr labrusca*

This is a distinctive dark grey beetle, covered in warty tubercles, which has the habit when touched of feigning death. Hence its common names Kafadala or

Mndaferamwendo (-fa, to die). It is thus used as an amulet Worm (-zobvala) on a strong around the neck, to stop fainting or fits (-komoka), especially with regard to someone suffering from epilepsy (khunyu). Other herbalists suggest reducing the beetle to ashes (-wocha), and then rubbing the ashes into incisions made on the sides of the head (-temera mutu) as a cure for the same ailment, or for someone losing consciousness. Among the Yao, in the past, the beetle was used as "gun medicine" to help in the killing of game, and as an item in a divining gourd (ndumba). Its Yao name is Chiwamsagaja (Sanderson 1954).

BAGWORM Mtemankhuni, *Eumeta cervina*

The bagworm is universally recognized as a "poison" or *as* "bad medicine" (Mankhwala Woipa), and it is believed that any person or livestock animal eating the insect will die. Its Chewa name Lipepedwa (-pha, to kill) suggests this. There is, however, little empirical evidence to support this assertion, and Sweeney notes (Sweeney 1970) that the Medje of the Ituri forest regard the bagworm larvae as a delicacy. However, the bagworm is widely used as medicine. The insect, including the silken "bag" of twigs, is mixed (-sanganiza) with various plant medicines usually roots, and then reduced to ashes. These are then rubbed into incisions made on the temple as a cure for various head ailments associated with sorcery (matsenga). It thus may be described as mankhwala amutu, head medicine. More often the insect/twigs are reduced to ashes and rubbed into incisions made on the legs of a young child who is slow or unable to walk (saenda). It is also used as a cure for swollen legs. The ashes of this insect, together with that of various herbs, is usually kept in a small calabash (nsupa). Many suggest that people are afraid (-opa) of the bagworm, and that unlike other caterpillars it is always found alone. Interestingly, this is the only insect noted as medicine in Ken Kalonde's little booklet on medicinal plants "Mankhwala a Zitsamba" (2000). It suggests charring (-psya) the insect (Kachirombo) and turning it into ashes (charcoal) (kusanduka makala), and the ashes rubbed into incisions -mphini (tattoo marks) - made on the legs and around the knees. This is the cure for a child or elderly person (kholo) who has difficulties in walking. The booklet suggests, in a concluding note, that if the medicine does not work after several attempts, then *a* person should run to the hospital immediately (thamangirani ku chipatala msanga}! (Kalonde 2000). Also of interest is that the bagworm

(Psychidae) is the only insect used as medicine by the Kalahari San (Nonaka 1996). But besides being widely recognized as a medicine to assist children to walk, or for rheumatism (Nyamakazi) the ashes of the bagworm has also been noted as a cure for headaches, as a strengthening medicine, and for stomach ailments. It is thus usually the only insect to be found on the stalls of market herbalists.

LAKEFLY, Nkhungu, *Chaobora edulis*

Although the lakefly is an important source of relish, it is also used in the northern region as a medicine. The well-known "African doctor" of Mzuzu market, J Chiwanda Uka Lyoka, informed me that the lakefly has many medicinal uses (nchito kwambiri), and is utilized as a cure for heart problems, pneumonia (chibayo), drowsiness, as well as to assist in difficult court cases (mlandu). The lakefly cake is usually ground-up, made into an infusion and drunk, or it may be rubbed into incisions. He also suggested that if the infusion is poured (-thira) on a termite mound, it will encourage the flying termites to emerge in abundance.

BLISTER BEETLE, Dzodzwe, *Mylabris didncta*

This beetle is often associated by local people with the red-banded longicorn beetle *(Ceroplesis orientalis)* as both are conspicuous red and black beetles, although the longicorn beetle belongs to a different family and has very long antennae. The local name Ligombera is also used for both insects. The blister beetle is used as a medicine to treat venereal diseases such as gonorrhoea (chisonono) and syphilis (chindoko) -known by men as "diseases of women" (mathencla yaakazi). The beetle is pounded in a mortar with various plant medicines, such as mdima *(Diospyros spp.)* and an infusion made of the pounded material is drunk as a remedy. It is also used as a medicine for swollen necks (khosi wotupa), the insect being charred, ground (-pera) into powder, which is then rubbed into incisions made in the neck. The complaint is known as chotupa (swelling). Hugh Stannus noted that his beetle, which contains Cantharidin, is a recognized poison among the Yao and may be used with intent to murder, as well as for suicidal purposes. The symptoms, as described by local people, include constipation, followed by high fever and death around eight hours later (Stannus 1922).

WATER BEETLE, Chinsambisambi, *Cibister vulneratus*

This shiny black beetle is recorded as an ingredient in the preparation of a medicine to protect (-tsirika) a house against the malevolent influences of witches (afiti), spirits (ziwanda) and human thieves (Van Breugel, 2001).

GROUND BEETLE, Chikodzera, *Tefflus cypholoba*

This common, black, solitary beetle has a characteristic habit of squirting fluid if provoked, which can be painful if it comes into contact with tender skin or the eyes. It is recognized as a "poison". Its common name refers to its mode of defense (-kodza, to urinate). The insect is charred on the fire, together with (-phatikiza) several plant medicines, and rubbed into incisions as a cure for headaches and urinary problems.

TOAD GRASSHOPPER, Tsokonombwe, *Lobosceliana haploscelis*

This conspicuous, fat, wingless grasshopper is widely used as a medicine to encourage plant growth, particularly of pumpkin. The insect, whose call is an harbinger of the rainy season, is roasted and then mixed with pumpkin seeds on planting. It is said to make the pumpkins very sweet. The ashes of the insect was also noted as a cure for asthma and chest complaints (chifuwa).

MUTELLID WASP, Nthumbathumba, *Mutilla dasya*

Often described as the "velvet ant" this insect is widely associated throughout Malawi with luck, and is often described as Mankhwala wamwayi - good luck medicine. Its ashes are used either to anoint the body (-dzola) or rubbed into incisions (-temera) to bring good fortune - in marriage, friendship, work, and other undertakings.

I have brief notes on the occasional use of other insects as medicine for various ailments - the king cricket, Chiboli *(Henicus sp.)* as a cure for swollen lymph glands (mabomu) and headaches; the dragonfly Tombolombo *(Philonomon luminans)* mixed with other plant medicines, is used as a wash to bring good luck (Mankhwala amwayi); the tree locust, Chiwala/Mphangali *(Acanthacris ruficornis)* is noted as a medicine for urinary problems and bilharzias (likodzo); and finally, the irritating fluid of the armoured ground cricket, Mvimvi *(Enyaliopsis* peters//) is used as a cure tor sores and abscesses (kanjinji).

It is of interest that many of the herbalists I met in urban areas had little knowledge of insects generally, and apart from the use of bagworm as a cure for rheumatism knew little about the medicinal uses of insects. It seems that much indigenous knowledge of insects is being lost with urbanization.

But generally speaking insects play a minor role as a medicine - which contrasts with their role as vectors of disease, for both the mosquito and the tsetse fly have played a fundamental role in the social history of Malawi - in relation specifically to malaria and sleeping sickness. This history, however, is beyond the scope of the present paper.

References

Bodenheimer, F.S. 1951. *Insects as Human Food,* Junk, The Hague.

Clausen, L.N. 1954. *Insect Facts and Folklore.* MacMillan, New York.

Dudley, C. 1996. How Many Insects Does Malawi Have? *Nyala* **19,** 13-16.

Evans, H.E. 1970. *Life on a Little Known Planet.* Deutsch, London.

Frost, S.W. 1 942. *Insect Life and Insect Natural History.* Dover, New York.

Hogue, C.L. 1987. Cultural Entomology. *Ann. Rev. Entomology* 32, 181-99.

Hott, E. & T. Schultz,1999. *Insect Lives.* Mainstream Publ., Edinburgh.

Kalonde, K.2000. *Mankhwala A Zitsamba.* Sunshine Publ. Lilongwe.

Kropotkin, P. 1902. *Mutual Aid.* Penguin Books, Harmondsworth.

Lauck, J.E. 1998. *The Voice of the Infinite in the Small.* Swan Raven, Mill Spring.

Morris, B. 1996. *Chewa Medical Botany.* Hamburg: Lit. IAI

Morris, B. 1998. *The Power of Animals.* Berg, Oxford.

Nonaka, K. 1 996. Ethnoentomology of The Central Kalahari San. *AM. Stud. Monograph* 22:, 29-46.

Sanderson, G.M. 1965. *A Dictionary of the Yao Language..* Goun. Print, Zomba.

Stannus, H. 1922. The Wayao of Nyasland. *Harvard Afr. Studies* 3, 229-372

Sweeney, R.C.H. 1970. *Animal Life of Malawi* Vol 1 *Invertebrates.* Inst. For Publications, Beograd.

Van Breugel, J.W. 2001. *Chewa Traditional Religion.* Claim, Blantyre.

Van Huis, A. 1996. The Traditional Uses of Arthropods in Sub-Saharan Africa Amsterdam. Proc. *Exp. & Appl. Entomology 7,* 3-20.

THE TRUTH ABOUT
LAURENS VAN DER POST (2002)

Review: J.D.F JONES Storyteller: the Many Lives of Laurens van der Post
London: J.Murray (2001) £25

In 1956, when I was nineteen years old, a year before I left my working class home and sailed to Cape Town, I watched on a small black and white television set a programme on the Bushmen of the Kalahari by Laurens van der Post. It was called: "Lost World of the Kalahari". I was absolutely entranced - by the quiet authoritative voice of Laurens van der Post and the sympathetic and informative portrait he gave of the social life of these Khoisan people. Laurens van der Post became an instant "hero" of mine. In fact he was an important influence on my life, for I eventually became an anthropologist and my doctoral thesis was on a South Indian hunter-gathering community.

After hitch-hiking up from Cape Town in October 1957, and spending some six months wandering with a rucksack around south central Africa I eventually obtained a job in Nyasaland as a tea planter - with Blantyre and East Africa, an old company founded by Hyde and Stark around the turn of the century. There I again encountered Laurens van der Post for he had recently written a book on Malawi (then Nyasaland) entitled "Venture to the Interior" (1952). It appears that the book had upset everyone in the country, and it was deeply resented by almost all the expatriot community. My tea planting friends, such as Arthur Westrop and Colin Lees regaled me on what an awful and deceitful book Laurens van der Post had written, for he had described Mulanje Mountain as an unknown and unexplored terrain (which it wasn't - John Buchanan had climbed it way back in the 1880's) and that he had misrepresented and caricatured many local people, who had in fact given him support and hospitality.

The image I had of my hero was further shattered in 1959 when I attended a scout jamboree in Harare (then Salisbury) and there became friends with a scouter from Botswana. I began talking to him about Laurens van der Post and the Bushmen - when he veritably exploded exclaiming that van der Post was a impostor who knew little about the Bushman, and that his BBC film was made not in the "wilderness" but in my friend's own back garden, where van der Post had set up camp and brought in local hunter-gatherers to be filmed.

A few years later (1964) I began studying for my O levels, and it just so happened that the book "Venture to the Interior", which had by then become a best-seller and made van der Post world famous, was a "set text" for the English paper. I had therefore to study the book in depth. It also so happened that I was working on Limbuli Estate at the time, and spending most of the week-ends with my wife Jacqui botanizing on the mountain (1), I had got to know Mulanje Mountain quite well. I must say that I found "Venture to the Interior" a great disappointment -both as to its literary quality and as an account of Mulanje. It was full of exaggeration. Crossing the saddle between Chambe and Litchenya plateau is described in the book as "easy walking but it was barely a yard wide; a razor back, with five-thousand-foot drops on either side of it, connecting gigantic peaks" (118). This is certainly literary licence taken to extreme. For a man who was later to be lauded as a prophet of the green movement, van der Post makes no mention at all of Mulanje's rich fauna and flora - apart from the prehistoric and awe-inspiring cedars, from which he imagined a pterodactyl might fly out (109). He does mention a "mountain gazelle" - by which he may have meant a klipspringer, for gazelles have never been recorded from Malawi -but this is about the limit of his natural history. I found his racial mysticism equally off-putting - in that he describes Africa as unconscious, feminine and dark, and Europe as conscious, masculine and light - and thus comes to decribe African people as belonging to the night. "He is a child of darkness" he writes (227). Such musings indicate what little understanding he had of real African cultures. Europeans in Blantyre are described as having "set, sallow, lifeless, disillusioned faces" (79) , while with regard to individual people the book is full of misleading and exaggerated caricatures. For example, we have the European ex-Army officer (Ronaldson) who lived with "a black wife and a large brood of chocolate children" and who disliked European women (131) and the eccentric owner of a small tea estate at

Likhabula (Mrs Pereira) whose house was seemingly full of cats and sex books (153). The names of the key figures on the Mulanje trip are barely disguised; Peter Quillan was R.G.M. Willan, and Dicky Vance was Fred France, the forestry officer at Likhabula. France was tragically drowned while attempting to swim across the River Ruo in spate. Given the "forebodings" that van der Post continually alludes to, it is strange that he ever allowed France to ford the stream. Van der Post's account gives you the impression that the tragic accident occurred at the top of the Ruo Gorge - but people in Mulanje always suggested to me that it happened on the small tributary "stream" above Lujeri power station. Finally, van der Post had an extremely romantic idea of Africa as a "wilderness", a pristine environment devoid of humans. He thus expresses a nostalgia for a past that never existed, for the notion that Africa is a pristine wilderness is a myth. It has long been inhabited by humans. Legend has it that Mulanje was inhabited by the Abatwa hunter-gatherers, and ancient rock paintings are to be found on Machemba Hill.

In the bookshops now is a well-researched and very readable biography of Laurens van der Post, appropriately titled "Storyteller". Written by J.D.F. Jones it gives a rich account of the many lives of van der Post - as writer, explorer, war-hero, mystic and environmentalist, and as the guru of Prince Charles and Margaret Thatcher. As an international figure and best-selling writer - his book on his experiences as a prisoner-of-war in Java "The Seed and the Sower" (1963) was made into the film "Merry Christmas Mr.Lawrence" - Laurens van der Post became an inspiration to many people. He was, as Jones remarked, a "storyteller of genius" and *I* have certainly enjoyed his writings. He had too an important influence on such conservationists as Robin Page and Ian Player. But as Jones records, van der Post was full of paradox. A radical Afrikaaner he became a staunch member of the British conservative establishment; with a genius for friendship he treated many people abominably; a great moralist and spiritual guru he seduced a fourteen year old girl under his care, and later repudiated both the young woman and his own daughter Cari, born of the union.

What the book certainly confirms is all the misgivings that people in Malawi had about Laurens van der Post, for he appears to have been something of a con-man (always out to promote himself) and that much of what he wrote about himself and his experiences was embellished, fabricated, exaggerated, distorted, inaccurate, or just plain lies or invention. He had. Jones

BRIAN MORRIS

writes, an "instinctive predilection" for the truths of the imagination, and was thus a "master fabricator", often weaving a complex web of truth and false-hood. Jones even suggests that van der Post, though a wonderful storyteller, was a "compulsive liar"(359). Thus he wrote that his first memories of life was of a shining necklace worn by his Bushman nanny Klara, but there is no evidence at all that he ever had a Bushman nurse. He writes, too, as if from first-hand experience, of the social life of the Kalahari Bushmen, but there is no real evidence that he ever "lived" with the Bushmen. He only appears to have met a few Bushmen, and then but briefly, and his writings on Bushman folklore was largely appropriated from earlier scholars. A colleague of mine Alan Barnard, who is an authority on the Khoisan people, suggested that van der Post largely lived in a fantasy world, knew little about real Bushmen cul-ture, and that much of what he wrote about these people came from his own imagination. Jones seems to confirm this.

Laurens van der Post wrote an excellent introduction to the analytical psychology of Carl Jung "Jung and the Story of our Time"(1976). He appears to have first met Jung in Zurich in 1949 - the psychologist was then 74 years old -and in the book van der Post gives the impression that he was a close and intimate friend of Jung. Jones indicates that this was also largely a figment of van der Post's vivid imagination (or deceit).

With regard to the Mulanje Mt. expedition of 1949 we learn from Jones' biography that van der Post's rather secret "mission" was to assess the livestock ca-pacity of Nyika and Mulanje for the Commonwealth Development Corporation - even though he had very little knowledge of either botany or livestock manage-ment - and that he only spent ten days on the mountain. We also learn that the France family bitterly resented the use that van der Post had made of their tragedy for his own self-promotion and profit. Jones also confirms the resentment that was expressed in Nyasaland over the book - that van der Post had absurdly inflated the "mystique of menace" surrounding Mulanje Mt. and the fact that he had publicly psychoanalysed many people whom he had met only briefly and from whom he had accepted hospitality (183). These thoughts simply echo those Arthur Westrop and Colin Lees expressed to me over forty years ago.

[1.] see my articles Epiphytic Orchids of the Limbuli Stream, Mlanje Soc.Ma-lawi Journ. 18 (1965) 59-70, Wild Flowers of Mlanje Mountain African Wild-life 21 (1967) 71-77, 152-57

Printed in the United States
By Bookmasters